青少年成长励志名著精选
The Chosen Inspirational Classics on Youth's Growth
· 中英对照 ·

[美] 简·韦伯斯特 著　张莉 胡晓鸥 聂晓黎 译

长腿叔叔

中国国际广播出版社

总序

成长是一个美好而动人的话题。因为成长,我们从天真烂漫的孩童变成至情至性的青年;从不谙世事到看透世间百态;从懵懂无知到肩负起家庭和社会的重任。在成长中,我们一点点长大,心智慢慢成熟,我们的理想和抱负也逐渐成形。而成长中的少年和青年,如朝阳,如晨露,如春前之草,充满了活力与生机。少年和青年时期是人生中最宝贵、最关键的阶段,也是进步最快的阶段,在这个阶段里,我们有迷茫,有困惑,有失落,也有梦想,有憧憬,有抱负。在得到与失去中,在成功与失败中,在欢喜与哀愁中,我们一天天地长大,一天天地读懂什么是"成长"。

列夫·托尔斯泰说过,人类被赋予了一种工作,那就是精神的成长。在成长过程中,我们渴望知识,渴望精神的充实,渴望灵魂的完善。为此,我们特地选编了世界文学宝库中八本不朽的名著,《小王子》、《长腿叔叔》、《秘密花园》、《彼得·潘》、《水孩子》、《绿野仙踪》、《丛林故事》和《成长》。它们都是有关成长、有关爱的著作,并深深地影响和感染了一代代读者。《小王子》是一部脍炙人口的儿童文学作品,被称为是仅次于《圣经》的经典读物。同时它也是一部写给成年人的,关于生命、热诚和爱的哲理童话。作品表现出来的想象力、智慧和情感，使各个年龄的读者都能从中找到乐趣，并且随时能够发现新的精神财富；《长腿叔叔》是简·韦伯斯特最负盛名的代表作，已成为世界少女的成长必读书。它讲述了孤女朱蒂受到一个理事的资助完成学业，并与之相恋的美好故事。作品中流露出来的温馨、亲切和真爱让我们感知到世间的真善美；《秘密花园》是弗朗西丝·伯内特最著名、最成功的作品，被公认为是一部无年龄界限的佳作。自私专横的小姑娘玛莉在姑父家发现了秘密花园，她不仅使荒芜的花园重现生机，自己也变成一个礼貌善良、有爱心的小姑娘；《彼得·潘》是詹姆斯·巴里影响最大的作品，也是迈克尔·杰克逊生前最喜欢的童话。彼得·潘是生活在永无岛上的永远也长不大的男孩，在海岛上他和别的小伙伴经历了许多有趣的事情；《水孩子》查尔斯·金斯利的代表作，讲述了一个扫烟囱的孩子汤姆如何变成水孩子的故事；《丛林故事》是1907年诺贝尔文学奖得主拉迪亚德·吉卜林的作品，讲述了印度少年莫格里狼群中成长为一个勇武聪慧的少年的故事。作者超凡的语言和杰出的叙事才能描绘了大自然的美妙画面，动物之间温暖的友谊和他们充满生趣的冒险；《绿野仙踪》是美国著名作家及剧作家莱曼·弗兰克·鲍姆最受读者欢迎的一部作品。小姑娘多萝西和没有脑子的稻草人、没有心脏的铁皮人和胆小的狮子齐心协力，完成了各自的心愿；《成长》是美国知名作家詹妮·M·德林克沃特的作品。爱讲故事的孤女小朱迪在失去双亲后顽强、倔强地成长，并最终收获美满的爱情。作品内容时而欢快，时而忧伤，将朱迪不平凡的成长经历展现在我们眼前。

　　塞缪尔·斯麦尔曾经说过，"最优秀的书是一种由高贵的语言和闪光的思想构成的财富，为人类所铭记、所珍惜，是我们永恒的伴侣和慰藉……书籍把我们介绍给良师益友，是我们认识迄今为止人类最伟大的灵魂。"该套丛书精选名家名作，阅读该套丛书，我们可以通过主人公的经历感受其中的真爱与温馨，鼓舞与感动,不仅可以滋养我们的心灵,提高我们的文学修养,还可以给我们人生的启迪。相信本套丛书必定会给您别样的体验,如同一泓清泉,滋润您的心田。

编者

译者序

《长腿叔叔》乍一看像是儿童读物，一部童话。细细品味，感觉它更是一部写给成人的小说，一部成人童话，因为它不但让书中的女主人公更让这个物欲社会的成年人懂得什么是爱，如何去爱，以及什么是幸福，如何看待幸福。

儿时阅读这本书，印象中讲述的是一个孤儿给资助她念大学的先生每周一封信讲述她日常生活的故事；青春懵懂的时候再读，感觉是一部感伤的爱情小说；如今将近而立之年，接到出版社编辑的邀请，要翻译再版这本书，于是一气呵成读了三遍，才真正体味到这部成人童话不仅仅是在讲述一个孤儿感伤的爱情故事，而是向世俗的成年人阐明幸福快乐的真谛——品味历程，活在当下。

《长腿叔叔》讲述的是一个在孤儿院长到十七岁的孤儿，一个穿着别人施舍的衣服一直担心被衣服的主人揭发的女孩，一个每天除了学习、吃饭和睡觉，其余时间都得为孤儿院工作的大小孩，幸运地得到不愿意透露身份的富有理事的资助，送她去上女子大学的故事。从此，她开始了全新的生活和学习，条件就是每月给那位赞助理事写一封永远不会有回信的信。这位可怜、孤独、聪明而又幸运的女孩就是朱蒂。"长腿叔叔"是朱蒂对那位神秘理事的称呼，因为她只瞥见过那位理事被车灯投射在墙上长长的身影。本书是朱蒂写给长腿叔叔的书信，主要是讲述朱蒂在大学学习生活的点点滴滴。这一封封信件，向读者展示了一位善良、独立、追求精神自由、懂得感恩的少女形象。

虽然《长腿叔叔》的作者简·韦伯斯特用简单的书信作为这本书的写作形式，但是用那位神秘理事的话讲，要培养她成为伟大的作家，写信是练习写作的最好方式。的确，越简单越琐碎的故事越贴近生活，点点滴滴才是生活，生活的点点滴滴才是人间大道。朱蒂写给"长腿叔叔"的每一字每一句都是她敏感而丰富情感的宣泄，也是她心灵成长的见证。故事中有这样两段：

"其实，最有意思的不是谈惊天动地的大事，而是生活琐事。我觉得自己发现了快乐的真谛——品味历程，活在当下。不要总是懊悔过去或者展望未来，而是要充分享受今天。比如种田，可以分为粗放耕作和精耕细作。今后，我要过精细的生活，享受人生的每一刻，而且在享受的同时能清醒地意识到自己是在享受。现实生活中，许多人不是在生活，而是在跟时间赛跑。他们一直努力攀登生命地平线上的最高峰，拼命地奔跑着，可他们却忘记了欣赏一路上美轮美奂的旖旎风光。有一天，自己老了，倦了，猛然发现原来实不实现目标结果都一样。不过，我是打算漫步人生的，一路走一路游，累积人生，享受生活中的点点滴滴，就算永远当不了伟大的作家也无所谓。您见过像我这样的哲学家吗？"

……

"回首四年的大学生活，再想起以前在孤儿院的日子，心中的暖意油然而生。刚上大学时，我为自己被剥夺了的美好童年而满腹不平，因为别的女孩子都有幸福的童年。而今，我再也不这么想了。我只是觉得那是一段不同寻常的人生经历，让我能从不同的角度去审视生命，好像是逐渐成熟了，而我对世界的独特认识正是那些正常家庭出身的孩子所缺乏的。"

记得光良的《童话》里面唱道"你哭着对我说，童话里都是骗人的，我不可能是你的王子……"可二十多年来，我对童话的阅读却乐此不疲,因为我坚信童话是播种幸福的种子,美丽的童话能净化人的心灵。从朱蒂的故事我们可以看到,一颗美丽的心灵能铸就一段美好的人生!

《长腿叔叔》就是这样一部美丽的成人童话!

CONTENTS

Blue Wednesday / 002

The Letters of Miss Jerusha Abbott

to Mr.Daddy-Long-Legs Smith / 016

目录

黑色星期三 / 003

乔茹莎·阿伯特小姐给长腿

史密斯先生的信 / 017

Daddy-Long-Legs

长腿叔叔

承载温馨的信笺

充满惊喜的爱情

Blue Wednesday

The first Wednesday in every month was a Perfectly Awful Day—a day to be awaited with dread, endured with courage, and forgotten with haste. Every floor must be **spotless**, every chair dustless, and every bed without a **wrinkle**. Ninety-seven **squirming** little orphans must be scrubbed and combed and buttoned into freshly **starched ginghams**; and all ninety-seven reminded of their manners, and told to say "Yes, sir," "No, sir," whenever a trustee spoke.

It was a distressing time; and poor Jerusha Abbott, being the oldest orphan, had to bear the brunt of it. But this particular first Wednesday, like its **predecessors**, finally dragged itself to a close. Jerusha escaped from the **pantry** where she had been making sandwiches for the asylum's guests, and turned upstairs to accomplish her regular work. Her special care was room F, where eleven little tots, from four to seven, occupied eleven little cots set in a row. Jerusha assembled her charges, straightened their rumpled frocks, wiped their noses, and started them in an orderly and willing line toward the dining room to engage themselves for a blessed half hour with bread and milk and prune pudding.

Then she dropped down on the window seat and leaned throbbing temples against the cool glass. She had been on her feet since five that morning doing everybody's bidding, scolded and hurried by a nervous **matron**. Mrs. Lippett, behind the scenes, did not always maintain that calm and pompous dignity with which she faced an audience of **trustees** and lady visitors. Jerusha gazed out across a broad stretch of frozen lawn, beyond the tall iron paling

黑色星期三

spotless
['spɒtlis]
adj. 没有污点的；极其清洁的，一尘不染的

wrinkle
['riŋkl]
n. 皱褶，皱纹

squirm
[skwə:m]
v. 蠕动；蠢动

starched
[stɑ:tʃt]
adj. 僵硬的，硬挺的，拘泥刻板的

gingham
['giŋəm]
n. 条格平布，方格花布

predecessor
['pridisesə]
n. 前任[辈]；[古]祖先

pantry
['pæntri]
n. 餐具室；食品室

matron
['meitrən]
n. 年长的已婚妇女（尤指品格高尚的）

trustee
[trʌs'ti:]
n. 受托管理人；董事；理事

每个月第一个星期三真是糟糕透顶——总是忧虑地等待着，勇敢地忍耐着，忙着忙着就又忘记了的日子。每层地板都不能有一点儿污迹，每张椅子都要一尘不染，而且每条床单都不能有半条皱痕。九十七个好动的小孤儿收拾整理完毕后，穿上刚烫好的硬挺格子衫，而且出门之前一再受嘱咐要注意自己的礼貌，告知他们只要董事们一问话，就立刻回答"是的，先生"或者"不是，先生。"

这一天可真难熬。可怜的乔茹莎·阿伯特，年龄最大，理所应该首当其冲。不过跟平常一样，这个郁闷的星期三终于要结束了。乔茹莎迅速逃离了为来访者做三明治的厨房，跑到楼上去完成她的日常工作。她特别关照F号房，F号房里住着年龄从四岁到七岁不等的十一名小孩，十一张小床整齐地排成一排。乔茹莎把他们都叫来，帮他们整理好衣服，擦干净鼻涕，让他们排列整齐，然后领着他们快快乐乐地走进餐厅享用牛奶面包和布丁，享受那半小时的感恩时光。

乔茹莎独自坐在窗台上，然后将阵阵作痛的太阳穴侧靠着冷冰冰的玻璃。从早晨五点钟起来，她一直手脚不停，听从每个人的命令，时不时还遭到神经兮兮的女监事责骂，还不时听她催命似的叫喊，利皮特太太在背地里可不是像她在董事们或者女士来访时表现得那样冷静和严肃。掠过孤儿院的

that marked the confines of the **asylum**, down **undulating** ridges **sprinkled** with country estates, to the spires of the village rising from the midst of bare trees.

The day was ended—quite successfully, so far as she knew. The trustees and the visiting committee had made their rounds, and read their reports, and drunk their tea, and now were hurrying home to their own cheerful firesides, to forget their bothersome little charges for another month. Jerusha leaned forward watching with curiosity—and a touch of **wistfulness**—the stream of carriages and automobiles that rolled out of the asylum gates. In imagination she followed first one **equipage** then another to the big houses dotted along the hillside. She pictured herself In a fur coat and a velvet hat trimmed with feathers leaning back in the seat and **nonchalantly** murmuring "Home" to the driver. But on the **doorsill** of her home the picture grew blurred.

Jerusha had an imagination—an imagination, Mrs. Lippett told her, that would get her into trouble if she didn't take care—but keen as it was, it could not carry her beyond the front porch of the houses she would enter. Poor, eager, adventurous little Jerusha, in all her seventeen years, had never stepped inside an ordinary house; she could not picture the daily routine of those other human beings who carried on their lives undiscommoded by orphans.

> Je-ru-sha Ab-bott
> You are wan-ted
> In the of-fice,
> And I think you'd
> Better hurry up!

Tommy Dillon, who had joined the choir, came singing up the stairs and down the corridor, his chant growing louder as he approached room F. Jerusha **wrenched** herself from the window and **refaced** the troubles of life.

"Who wants me?" she cut into Tommy's chant with a note of sharp anxiety.

词汇	
asylum	[əˈsailəm] n. 避难所;庇护所
undulate	[ˈʌndjuleit] v.(水面、风中的麦田等)波动,(土地等)起伏;(音量、音调或节拍上)起伏变化
sprinkle	[ˈspriŋkl] v. 洒,喷,淋
wistful	[ˈwistful] adj. 渴望的,不满足的
equipage	[ˈekwipidʒ] n. 马车及仆从
nonchalantly	[ˈnɔnʃələntli] adv. 漠不关心地,冷淡地
doorsill	[ˈdɔːsil] n. 门槛
wrench	[rentʃ] v. 猛扭,扭伤,曲解
reface	[ˈriːˈfeis] v. 重修表面

铁栅栏,乔茹莎望着远处那一大片冻枯的草地,凝视着远方的山峦叠嶂,盯着小山上若隐若现的村庄在光秃秃的树林中露出的屋顶。

就她所知,这一天应该算是圆满结束了。董事们与参访团已经走过了一圈儿,汇报也听了,茶也喝了,现在正该赶回他们温暖的炉火边了呢,正好忘记他们每个月要例行的过场。乔茹莎倾身向前,好奇地看着,马车、汽车穿过孤儿院的大门,不禁一阵幻想。幻想着她跟着一辆辆车子,回到山边的大房子,她穿着一件貂皮大衣,外面罩着天鹅绒,背靠在椅子上,淡淡地对司机说"回家",可她刚到家门口,一切却模糊不清了。

乔茹莎有个幻想——可利皮特太太说要是不小心,这幻想会给她惹上麻烦。尽管她那样深深地渴望,却仍然无法引她走进那扇幻想的大门。乔茹莎是个贫穷,爱幻想可又富于冒险精神的女孩儿。十七年以来,她从未踏入过一个正常的家庭,所以她无法想象没有孤儿干扰的正常家庭生活会是怎样的。

乔—茹—莎 阿—伯—特
叫你
去办公室,
我想啊
你最好跑快点儿!

刚加入唱诗班的汤米·迪伦一边唱一边上楼梯,一直唱下走廊去,他越靠近F号房,就越唱得带劲儿。乔茹莎努力挣脱幻想的思绪,回到现实中应付那堆恼人的琐事。

"谁叫我?"她焦虑的应答打断了汤米的歌声。

Mrs. Lippett in the office,
And I think she's mad.
Ah-a-men!

Tommy piously **intoned**, but his accent was not entirely **malicious**. Even the most hardened little orphan felt sympathy for an erring sister who was summoned to the office to face an annoyed matron; and Tommy liked Jerusha even if she did sometimes jerk him by the arm and nearly scrub his nose off.

Jerusha went without comment, but with two parallel lines on her brow. What could have gone wrong? she wondered. Were the sandwiches not thin enough? Were there shells in the nut cakes? Had a lady visitor seen the hole in Susie Hawthorn's stocking? Had—oh, horrors! —one of the **cherubic** little babes in her own room F "sassed" a trustee?

The long lower hall had not been lighted, and as she came downstairs, a last trustee stood, on the point of departure, in the open door that led to the **porte-cochère**. Jerusha caught only a fleeting impression of the man—and the impression consisted entirely of tallness. He was waving his arm toward an automobile waiting in the curved drive. As it sprang into motion and approached, head on for an instant, the glaring headlights threw his shadow sharply against the wall inside. The shadow pictured **grotesquely elongated** legs and arms that ran along the floor and up the wall of the corridor. It looked, for all the world, like a huge, wavering daddy-long-legs.

Jerusha's anxious frown gave place to quick laughter. She was by nature a sunny soul, and had always snatched the tiniest excuse to be amused. If one could derive any sort of entertainment out of the oppressive fact of a trustee, it was something unexpected to the good. She advanced to the of-fice quite cheered by the tiny **episode**, and presented a smiling face to Mrs. Lippett. To her surprise the matron was also, if not exactly smiling, at least appreciably **affable**; she wore an expression almost as pleasant as the one she **donned** for visitors.

intone
[in'təun]
v.（以拖长的单调音）吟咏，唱或吟咏（圣歌）

malicious
[mə'liʃəs]
adj. 怀恶意的，恶毒的

cherubic
[tʃe'ru:bik]
adj. 天使的，无邪的，可爱的

porte-cochère
[,pɔ:tkɔ'ʃeə(r)]
n. 可让车辆出入庭院的通道，供马车出入之门廊

grotesque
[grəu'tesk]
adj. 奇怪的，可笑的

elongate
['i:lɔŋgeit]
v. 延长，伸长

episode
['episəud]
n. 插曲，插话，(作品的一段)情节，有趣的事件

affable
['æfəbl]
adj. 和蔼可亲的，友善的，殷勤的

don
[dɔn]
v. 穿；戴

> 利皮特太太在办公室，
> 好像很生气
>
> 阿——门

汤米一副虔诚的样子，不过他那腔调儿也不完全是幸灾乐祸。即便是心肠最硬的小孤儿，对于一个做错事的姐姐被叫去见恼人的女监事，还是会同情她的。虽然她有时候会猛力揪他，有时候甚至快把鼻子给他拧掉了！可总的来说，汤米还是喜欢乔茹莎的。

乔茹莎一声不吭便去了，可她脑子里一串问号，哪儿又出问题了？她琢磨着，是三明治切得不够薄？还是蛋壳掉进杏仁蛋糕里了？还是哪位来访的女士看到苏茜·霍桑袜子上有破洞了啊？还是——哎，糟糕！——F号房里的不懂事儿的小宝贝儿对董事又无礼了？

又长又低的大厅已经关了灯，她下楼时，看见只剩下一个董事站在那儿，办公室的门开着，他好像正要离开的样子。乔茹莎迅速瞥了一眼，只觉得那个人个子好高好高。他正向外面等待的汽车挥着手，车子靠近时，他的影子被车灯投射在院内的墙上，手脚都被拉得老长老长，影子在墙上晃来晃去，真像个巨大的长腿蜘蛛。

乔茹莎紧锁的眉头终于放松下来，咯咯地笑了起来。她生性乐观，从不放过每一次开心的机会。说真的，要是人能从压迫中寻点乐趣，也算是挺好的吧。因为这段小插曲，她进办公室去见利皮特太太时脸上还挂着一丝微笑。让她吃惊的是，讨厌的女监事也冲她笑，就算不是发自内心的，至少也算友善，就像她接待访客一样令人愉悦。

"Sit down, Jerusha, I have something to say to you."

Jerusha dropped into the nearest chair and waited with a touch of breathlessness. An automobile flashed past the window; Mrs. Lippett glanced after it.

"Did you notice the gentleman who has just gone?"

"I saw his back."

"He is one of our most affluential trustees, and has given large sums of money toward the asylum's support. I am not at liberty to mention his name; he expressly **stipulated** that he was to remain unknown."

Jerusha's eyes widened slightly; she was not accustomed to being summoned to the office to discuss the **eccentricities** of trustees with the matron.

"This gentleman has taken an interest in several of our boys. You remember Charles Benton and Henry Freize? They were both sent through college by Mr. —er—this trustee, and both have repaid with hard work and success the money that was so generously expended. Other payment the gentleman does not wish. Heretofore his **philanthropies** have been directed solely toward the boys; I have never been able to interest him in the slightest degree in any of the girls in the institution, no matter how **deserving**. He does not, I may tell you, care for girls."

"No, ma'am," Jerusha murmured, since some reply seemed to be expected at this point.

"Today at the regular meeting, the question of your future was brought up."

Mrs. Lippett allowed a moment of silence to fall, then resumed in a slow, **placid** manner extremely trying to her hearer's suddenly tightened nerves.

"Usually, as you know, the children are not kept after they are sixteen, but an exception was made in your case. You had finished our school at fourteen, and having done so well in your studies—not always, I must say, in your conduct—it was determined to let you

"来，乔茹莎，坐下，我有话跟你说。"

乔茹莎迅速拣了就近的椅子坐了下来，屏息以待。汽车灯光照过窗户，利皮特太太盯了半天说道：

"你看到刚走的那位先生了吗？"

"只看到了背影。"

"他是最富有的董事之一，给我们捐了很多钱，不过我不能说他的名字，他要求不要透露他的身份。"

乔茹莎微微张大了双眼，她不喜欢跟女监事在办公室讨论董事们的怪癖。

"这位先生已经资助好几个男孩儿了。你还记得查理·班顿跟亨利·傅理兹吧？他们都是被这位——呃——先生——这位董事——送去上大学的，而且现在已经工作，正努力赚钱来回报这位先生呢。可他从不要求回报，到目前为止，他只资助过男孩子，我也从未能让他对本机构的女孩子感点儿兴趣，不管多么优秀的。这么说吧，他根本不在乎女孩儿。"

"是的，女士。"乔茹莎低声答道，不过这好像是讨厌的女监事期望的答案。

"今天在例会上，说到你的问题了。"

利皮特太太说到这儿停顿了一会儿，然后再慢条斯理地说下去，好像是故意让听者神经紧张起来。

"你也知道，一般说来，孩子们过了十六岁就不能再留下来了，你已经是个特例。十四岁就中学毕业，成绩还不错——不过，也不是一直都很好，

---

stipulate
['stɪpjuleɪt]
v. 规定，明定

eccentricity
[ˌeksen'trɪsɪti]
n. 古怪，古怪的行为，怪癖

philanthropy
[fɪ'lænθrəpi]
n. 博爱主义，慈善事业，善心

deserving
[dɪ'zɜːvɪŋ]
adj. 应得的，值得的

placid
['plæsɪd]
adj. 安静的，平和的

go on in the village high school. Now you are finishing that, and of course the asylum cannot be responsible any longer for your support. As it is, you have had two years more than most."

Mrs. Lippett overlooked the fact that Jerusha had worked hard for her board during those two years; that the convenience of the asylum had come first and her education second; that on days like the present she was kept at home to scrub.

"As I say, the question of your future was brought up and your record was discussed—thoroughly discussed."

Mrs. Lippett brought accusing eyes to bear upon the prisoner in the dock, and the prisoner looked guilty because it seemed to be expected—not because she could remember any strikingly black pages in her record.

"Of course the usual **disposition** of one in your place would be to put you in a position where you could begin to work, but you have done well in school in certain branches; it seems that your work in English has even been brilliant. Miss Pritchard, who is on our visiting committee, is also on the school board; she has been talking with your **rhetoric** teacher, and made a speech in your favor. She also read aloud an essay that you had written entitled 'Blue Wednesday'."

Jerusha's guilty expression this time was not assumed.

"It seemed to me that you showed little gratitude in holding up to **ridicule** the institution that has done so much for you. Had you not managed to be funny I doubt if you would have been forgiven. But fortunately for you, Mr. —that is, the gentleman who has just gone—appears to have an **immoderate** sense of humor. On the strength of that **impertinent** paper, he has offered to send you to college."

"To college?" Jerusha's eyes grew big.

Mrs. Lippett nodded.

"He waited to discuss the terms with me. They are unusual. The

根据你的表现,可以继续上村里的高中,现在高中也毕业了,我们不能再负担你的生活了。就这样,你已经比其他人多住了两年。"

利皮特太太完全忽视乔茹莎这两年为了她的食宿辛苦地工作,永远都把孤儿院的工作放在第一位,学习放在第二位,像今天这种日子她就得留在家干活。

"刚才说了,你的问题已经提了出来,当然,你的记录也被拿出来讨论了——彻彻底底讨论了一番。"

利皮特太太一副指责的眼光盯着她的囚犯说道。而这囚犯一副罪孽的样子,也不是因为她真的犯过什么错,而是她就该这个表现。

"当然,是讨论你该去哪工作了。不过你在学校某些科目表现突出,好像你的英文写作不错。你们校董——普里查德小姐,这次正好随团参访,她找你的作文老师谈过,很为你说了一些好话,而且她还朗读了你的作文——名叫'黑色星期三'。"

此时此刻,乔茹莎无辜的表情绝不是装出来的。

"我听出来了,你在讽刺给你吃给你穿还送你上学的孤儿院,几乎没有怀有感激之情。不知道你是不是故意讽刺,会不会得到上帝的宽恕。不过,你还真走运——那位先生,就是刚走那位,真是好笑,还就因为你那篇可恶的文章,他还想送你去念大学。"

"念大学?"乔茹莎瞪大了双眼问道。

利皮特太太只点了点头。

"他会找我谈具体时间的,这些人都很怪异。

---

disposition
[ˌdɪspəˈzɪʃən]
n. 处置;性情

rhetoric
[ˈretərɪk]
n. 修辞,华丽虚饰的语言,修辞学

ridicule
[ˈrɪdɪkjuːl]
v. 嘲笑,嘲弄,愚弄

immoderate
[ɪˈmɒdərɪt]
adj. 无节制的,过度的

impertinent
[ɪmˈpɜːtɪnənt]
adj. 鲁莽的,无礼的,粗鲁的

gentleman, I may say, is **erratic**. He believes that you have originality, and he is planning to educate you to become a writer."

"A writer?" Jerusha's mind was **numbed**. She could only repeat Mrs. Lippett's words.

"That is his wish. Whether anything will come of it, the future will show. He is giving you a very liberal **allowance**, almost, for a girl who has never had any experience in taking care of money, too liberal. But he planned the matter in detail, and I did not feel free to make any suggestions. You are to remain here through the summer, and Miss Pritchard has kindly offered to **superintend** your outfit. Your board and tuition will be paid directly to the college, and you will receive in addition during the four years you are there, an allowance of thirty-five dollars a month. This will enable you to enter on the same standing as the other students. The money will be sent to you by the gentleman's private secretary once a month, and in return, you will write a letter of **acknowledgment** once a month. That is—you are not to thank him for the money; he doesn't care to have that mentioned, but you are to write a letter telling of the progress in your studies and the details of your daily life. Just such a letter as you would write to your parents if they were living.

"These letters will be addressed to Mr. John Smith and will be sent in care of the secretary. The gentleman's name is not John Smith, but he prefers to remain unknown. To you he will never be anything but John Smith. His reason in requiring the letters is that he thinks nothing so **fosters** facility in literary expression as letter writing. Since you have no family with whom to correspond, he desires you to write in this way; also, he wishes to keep track of your progress. He will never answer your letters, nor in the slightest particular take any notice of them. He **detests** letter writing, and does not wish you to become a burden. If any point should ever arise where an answer would seem to be **imperative**—such as in the event of your being expelled, which I trust will not occur—you may

erratic
[i'rætik]
adj. 漂泊的,反复无常的,漂游的

numb
[nʌm]
v. 使…麻木,使…昏迷

allowance
[ə'lauəns]
n. 津贴,零用钱

superintend
[ˌsjuːpərin'tend]
v. 指挥,管理,监督

acknowledgement
[ək'nɔlidʒmənt]
n. 感谢,感激

foster
['fɔstə]
v. 养育,抚育,培养

detest
[di'test]
v. 厌恶

imperative
[im'perətiv]
adj. 命令式的,急需的

这位先生,相当怪僻。他相信你有天分创作,他想把你培养成一个作家。"

"作家?"乔茹莎脑子一片空白,只能呆呆地重复着利皮特太太的话。

"那只是他的希望而已。不管怎样,以后自然会有定论。他会给你足够的零用钱,对一个从没理过财的女孩子来说,是太多了。不过他都安排好了一切,不需要我的意见。你这个夏天还是住在这儿,普查德小姐会替你打点所有行李。你的食宿与学费都会直接付给学校,四年大学期间,你每个月会得到三十五块的零用钱,这样你就跟别的学生一样了。每个月的零用钱由那位先生的私人秘书寄给你,你呢,需要做的是每个月给那位先生写信表示感谢。当然,并不是要你感谢他给你零用钱,他也不在乎那点儿,你得写信告诉他你的学习和日常生活情况。就像给你父母写信一样,如果他们还活着的话。"

"这些信写给约翰·史密斯先生,他的秘书会转交给他。当然,这位先生不是叫约翰·史密斯,他希望一直替他保密。所以,对你来说,他只是约翰·史密斯先生。之所以要你给他写信是因为他觉得写信是练习写作的最好方式。因为你是孤儿,所以他希望你写信给他;另外,他也希望了解你的情况。他不会给你回信,也不会特别关注这些信。他很讨厌写信,不想因为你让他有心理负担。如果有任何紧急事件发生需要他回信——比如,你要被退学了,——不过我相信应该不会发生——你可以跟

correspond with Mr. Griggs, his secretary. These monthly letters are absolutely **obligatory** on your part; they are the only payment that Mr. Smith requires, so you must be as **punctilious** in sending them as though it were a bill that you were paying. I hope that they will always be respectful in tone and will reflect credit on your training. You must remember that you are writing to a trustee of the John Grier Home."

Jerusha's eyes longingly sought the door. Her head was in a whirl of excitement, and she wished only to escape from Mrs. Lippett's platitudes, and think. She rose and took a tentative step backward. Mrs. Lippett **detained** her with a gesture; it was an oratorical opportunity not to be slighted.

"I trust that you are properly grateful for this very rare good fortune that has befallen you? Not many girls in your position ever have such an opportunity to rise in the world. You must always remember—"

"I—yes, ma'am, thank you. I think, if that's all, I must go and sew a **patch** on Freddie Perkins's trousers."

The door closed behind her, and Mrs. Lippett watched it with dropped jaw, her **peroration** in **midair**.

obligatory
[ɔ'bligətəri]
adj. 义不容辞的,义务的,必须的
punctilious
[pʌŋk'tiliəs]
adj. 精密细心的,一丝不苟的,拘泥形式的

detain
[di'tein]
v. 扣留,扣押
patch
[pætʃ]
n. 片,补丁,碎片
peroration
[perə'reiʃ(ə)n]
n. 结语,结论,作结
midair
[mid'ɛə]
n. 半空中

他的秘书格利兹先生联系。每个月写信是你的义务,这也是史密斯先生唯一的要求,所以你一定要认真写,就当你在还债。希望你对史密斯先生尊重些,并且好好发挥你的写作水平。一定要记住,你是在给约翰·格里尔孤儿院的董事写信。"

乔茹莎渴望的眼神搜寻着办公室的门。她脑子一片混乱,兴奋不已。她只想快点逃离利皮特太太的眼皮,然后好好整理一下思维。于是她站了起来,试着向后退了一步。利皮特太太示意她留下,这可是她口若悬河发表演讲的良机。

"我相信你一定很感激这个天赐的好运,是吧?说实话,这世界上真没几个像你这样出身的女孩子能交上这样的好运。你一定要记住——"

"我会的,女士。谢谢您。要是没别的事儿,我得去替弗雷迪·帕金补裤子。"

于是乔茹莎关门离开了,利皮特太太目瞪口呆,两眼盯着大门,她的演讲不得不中断了。

The Letters of Miss Jerusha Abbott to Mr. Daddy-Long-Legs Smith

215 Fergussen Hall,
September 24th

Dear Kind-Trustee-Who-Sends-Orphans-to-College,

Here I am! I traveled yesterday for four hours in a train. It's a funny **sensation** isn't it? I never rode in one before.

College is the biggest, most **bewildering** place—I get lost whenever I leave my room. I will write you a description later when I'm feeling less **muddled**; also I will tell you about my lessons. Classes don't begin until Monday morning, and this is Saturday night. But I wanted to write a letter first just to get **acquainted**.

It seems queer to be writing letters to somebody you don't know. It seems queer for me to be writing letters at all—I've never written more than three or four in my life, so please overlook it if these are not a model kind.

Before leaving yesterday morning, I had a very serious talk with Mrs. Lippett. She told me how to behave all the rest of my life, and especially how to behave toward the kind gentleman who is doing so much for me. I must take care to be Very Respectful.

But how can one be very respectful to a person who wishes to be called John Smith? Why couldn't you have picked out a name with a little **personality**? I might as well write letters to Dear Hitching-Post or Dear Clothes-Pole.

I have been thinking about you a great deal this summer; having somebody take an interest in me after all these years, makes me feel as though I had found a sort of family. It seems as though I

乔茹莎·阿伯特小姐
给长腿史密斯先生的信

亲爱的送孤儿上大学的好心董事先生：

终于到了！昨天我坐了四个小时的火车，真的很激动呀，不是吗？我以前从来没坐过火车。

大学可真大啊，简直让人摸不着头脑——我只要一出宿舍就会迷路，等我熟悉熟悉状况，再给您写信，到时我会跟您谈谈我的学习的。现在是星期六晚上，星期一早上才开始上课。不过我想还是先写封信给您，咱们也好彼此认识一下。

给陌生人写信感觉怪怪的，而且写信对我来说本来就够稀奇的——长这么大总共就写过三封信，要是写得不好，请您见谅吧。

昨天早上出发前，利皮特太太很严肃地跟我谈话了。她嘱咐我今后要怎么怎么恭敬做人，特别是对有恩于我的好心先生更要注意自己的言行。我一定记得要非常地"尊敬"。

不过，对一个叫约翰·史密斯的人，怎么尊敬得起来呢？您为什么不挑个稍微有点个性的名字呢？我倒是很乐意给亲爱的拉杆先生、晒衣杆先生或者别的什么先生写信的。

这个夏天，我想了很多关于您的事儿。这么多年来终于有人对我感兴趣，让我有家的感觉，让我有归属感，让我感觉很温暖。我得承认，一想到

---

sensation
[sen'seiʃən]
n. 感觉,感情,感动

bewilder
[bi'wildə]
v. 使…不知所措

muddle
['mʌdl]
v. 使困惑

acquaint
[ə'kweint]
v. 使…熟知

personality
[ˌpəːsə'næliti]
n. 个性

belonged to somebody now, and it's a very comfortable sensation. I must say, however, that when I think about you, my imagination has very little to work upon. There are just three things that I know:

I. You are tall.

II. You are rich.

III. You hate girls.

I suppose I might call you Dear Mr. Girl-Hater. Only that's sort of insulting to me. Or Dear Mr. Rich-Man, but that's insulting to you, as though money were the only important thing about you. Besides, being rich is such a very external quality. Maybe you won't stay rich all your life; lots of very clever men get **smashed up** in Wall Street. But at least you will stay tall all your life! So I've decided to call you Dear Daddy-Long-Legs. I hope you won't mind. It's just a private pet name—we won't tell Mrs. Lippett.

The ten o'clock bell is going to ring in two minutes. Our day is divided into sections by bells. We eat and sleep and study by bells. It's very **enlivening**; I feel like a **firehorse** all of the time. There it goes! Lights out. Good night.

Observe with what **precision** I obey rules—due to my training in the John Grier Home.

Yours most respectfully,
Jerusha Abbott

To Mr. Daddy-Long-Legs Smith

October 1st

Dear Daddy-Long-Legs,

I love college and I love you for sending me—I'm very, very happy, and so excited every moment of the time that I can scarcely sleep. You can't imagine how different it is from the John Grier Home. I never dreamed there was such a place in the world. I'm feeling sorry for everybody who isn't a girl and who can't come

您，我对您几乎什么也不了解。关于您，我就知道三点：

1. 您个子很高；
2. 您很富有；
3. 您讨厌女孩子。

我想我可以称您为"亲爱的讨厌女孩儿先生"。不过，这也太侮辱我自己了。或者，我可以称您为"亲爱的富翁"，不过这样对您又太不敬了，好像您唯一值得一提的就是钱。而且仅仅"有钱"又太肤浅了，也许您不会一辈子都很有钱，很多聪明人都曾在华尔街惨遭失败。不过您应该永远都是那么高吧！所以我决定称您为亲爱的长腿叔叔，希望您别介意。当然，这只是私下的昵称，千万不要让利皮特太太知道。

过两分钟就要十点了，一天要打好几次钟。我们吃饭、睡觉还有上课都打钟的。我简直像匹野马，随时保持旺盛的精力。好了，熄灯了！晚安！

您看我多守规矩，多亏在约翰·格里尔孤儿院接受的训练。

最尊敬您的
乔茹莎·阿伯特
弗格森大厦215号
九月二十四日

smash up
撞毁，击毁

enliven
[inˈlaivən]
v. 使活跃

firehorse
[ˈfaiəˈhɔːs]
n. 拉救火车的马

precision
[priˈsiʒən]
n. 精确，精密度

致长腿叔叔·史密斯先生
亲爱的长腿叔叔：

我喜欢大学，也喜欢送我来这里的您——我真的非常非常非常高兴，常常兴奋地快睡不着觉。您无法想象这里跟约翰·格里尔孤儿院有多么不同！我做梦也没想到世界上还有如此一个地方！我深深地为所有不是女孩和不能来上大学的人感到遗憾！

here; I am sure the college you attended when you were a boy couldn't have been so nice.

My room is up in a tower that used to be the **contagious** ward before they built the new **infirmary**. There are three other girls on the same floor of the tower—a senior, who wears **spectacles** and is always asking us please to be a little more quiet, and two freshmen named Sallie McBride and Julia Rutledge Pendleton. Sallie has red hair and a **turn-up** nose and is quite friendly; Julia comes from one of the first families in New York and hasn't noticed me yet. They room together and the senior and I have singles. Usually freshmen can't get singles; they are very scarce, but I got one without even asking. I suppose the **registrar** didn't think it would be right to ask a properly brought-up girl to room with a **foundling**. You see there are advantages!

My room is on the northwest corner with two windows and a view. After you've lived in a ward for eighteen years with twenty roommates, it is restful to be alone. This is the first chance I've ever had to get acquainted with Jerusha Abbott. I think I'm going to like her.

Do you think you are?

Tuesday

They are organizing the freshman basketball team and there's just a chance that I shall make it. I'm little of course, but terribly quick and wiry and tough. While the others are **hopping** about in the air, I can **dodge** under their feet and grab the ball. It's loads of fun practicing—out in the athletic field in the afternoon with the trees all red and yellow and the air full of the smell of burning leaves, and everybody laughing and shouting. These are the happiest girls I ever saw—and I am the happiest of all!

I meant to write a long letter and tell you all the things I'm learning (Mrs. Lippett said you wanted to know) but 7th hour has

我相信您读的大学一定没有这么好!

在新的医务室盖好前,我被安排住在原来的传染病房大楼里。我们这层楼还有另外三个女孩儿——一个戴眼镜的高年级女生——她总让别人安静点;还有两个新生,莎莉·麦克白和朱莉娅·彭莱顿。莎莉一头红发,鼻子微翘,人很友好。朱莉娅出身纽约上流社会,她还没注意到我。她们住同一间房,那高年级女生跟我住单人间。我猜是管理处的老师觉得让正常家庭长大的孩子跟孤儿住在一起不太妥当。所以您看,还是有好处的。

我的房间在西北角,有两扇窗,外面景色不错。在跟二十个孩子同屋十八年后,一个人住终于可以好好清静一下。我想这正好可以让我好好认识一下乔茹莎·阿伯特。我想我会喜欢她的。

您呢?

十月一日

学校在招募新生篮球队,我报名了,我想这对我来说是个好机会。没错,我是个子矮小,不过我身体灵活,而且结实,别人跳起来时,我可以从她们身下钻过抢到球。秋日午后,我们总在一片红黄相间的树林边的运动场上练球,还时常闻到一股烧落叶的味道,大家笑着、叫着,开心极了。这是我所见的最开心的女孩们了,而我是其中最开心的一个。

我本来打算写封长信跟您谈谈我的功课(利皮特太太说过您想了解的)。不过这刚第七节课结束,

---

contagious
[kənˈteidʒəs]
adj. 传染性的,会蔓延的,会传播的

infirmary
[inˈfə:məri]
n. 治疗室

spectacles
[ˈspektəkls]
n. 眼镜

turn-up
完全出人意料的结果

registrar
[ˌredʒisˈtrɑ:]
n. 记录者,登记者,登记官员

foundling
[ˈfaundliŋ]
n. 弃儿

hop
[hɔp]
v. 单脚跳,跳跃,跃过

dodge
[dɔdʒ]
v. 避开,躲避

just rung, and in ten minutes I'm due at the athletic field in gymnasium clothes. Don't you hope I'll make the team?

Yours always,
Jerusha Abbott

PS. (9 o'clock)
Sallie McBride just **poked** her head in at my door. This is what she said:

"I'm so homesick that I simply can't stand it. Do you feel that way?"

I smiled a little and said no, I thought I could pull through. At least homesickness is one disease that I've escaped! I never heard of anybody being asylumsick, did you?

October 10th

Dear Daddy-Long-Legs,

Did you ever hear of Michael Angelo?

He was a famous artist who lived in Italy in the Middle Ages. Everybody in English Literature seemed to know about him and the whole class laughed because I thought he was an **archangel**. He sounds like an archangel, doesn't he? The trouble with college is that you are expected to know such a lot of things you've never learned. It's very embarrassing at times. But now, when the girls talk about things that I never heard of, I just keep still and look them up in the encyclopedia.

I made an awful mistake the first day. Somebody mentioned Maurice Maeterlinck, and I asked if she was a freshman. That joke has gone all over college. But anyway, I'm just as bright in class as any of the others—and brighter than some of them!

Do you care to know how I've furnished my room? It's a symphony in brown and yellow. The wall was tinted **buff**, and I've bought yellow **denim** curtains and **cushions** and a mahogany desk

过十分钟我又得换上运动服去运动场上集合了。您希望我参加篮球队吧?

您永远的
乔茹莎·阿伯特
星期二

poke
[pəuk]
v. 拨开,刺;探索

顺便告诉您:莎莉·麦可白刚探头进来问道:"我想家想得不行了,你会不会呢?"我笑着回答道:"不会。"我还行吧,至少我是绝对不会患上"思乡病"的,我也从没问过有没有人会得"思院病",是吧?

(晚九时)

亲爱的长腿叔叔:

您知道麦克·安吉罗吗?

archangel
['ɑːkeindʒəl]
n. 天使长,大天使

他是意大利中世纪著名的艺术家,英文系的同学好像都知道。我闹了个笑话,老师提到他,我回答说他是个天使长。听起来挺像天使长,不是吗?念大学可真麻烦,得学很多不知道的东西,有时候还真挺恼人的,不过现在只要女孩们提到我不知道的,我就保持沉默,然后回去查查百科全书。

buff
[bʌf]
n. 浅黄色
denim
['denim]
n. 粗斜纹布
cushion
['kuʃən]
n. 垫子

第一天上课我就犯了个错误,很尴尬。有人提到莫里斯·梅特林克(译者注:比利时作家,因《青鸟》而声名大噪),我就问她是不是个新生,这个笑话后来传遍了整个大学。不管怎么说,我在课堂上表现还不错,至少不比别人差,甚至比一些同学还要好。

您想知道我的屋子是什么样的吗?主色调是褐色和黄色。墙是浅黄色的,我买的斜纹布窗帘和靠垫都是黄色的,添了一张红木书桌,二手的,花了

(secondhand for three dollars) and a **rattan** chair and a brown rug with an ink spot in the middle. I stand the chair over the spot.

The windows are up high; you can't look out from an ordinary seat. But I **unscrewed** the looking glass from the back of the **bureau**, **upholstered** the top, and moved it up against the window. It's just the right height for a window seat. You pull out the drawers like steps and walk up. Very comfortable!

Sallie McBride helped me choose the things at the senior **auction**. She has lived in a house all her life and knows about furnishing. You can't imagine what fun it is to shop and pay with a real five-dollar bill and get some change—when you've never had more than a **nickel** in your life. I assure you, Daddy dear, I do appreciate that allowance.

Sallie is the most entertaining person in the world—and Julia Rutledge Pendleton the least so. It's queer what a mixture the registrar can make in the matter of roommates. Sallie thinks everything is funny—even **flunking**—and Julia is bored at everything. She never makes the slightest effort to be amiable. She believes that if you are a Pendleton, that fact alone admits you to heaven without any further examination. Julia and I were born to be enemies.

And now I suppose you've been waiting very impatiently to hear what I am learning?

Ⅰ. Latin: Second Punic War. **Hannibal** and his forces pitched camp at Lake Trasimenus last night. They prepared an ambuscade for the Romans, and a battle took place at the fourth watch this morning. Romans in retreat.

Ⅱ. French: 24 pages of the Three Musketeers and third conjugation, irregular verbs.

Ⅲ. Geometry: Finished cylinders; now doing cones.

Ⅳ. English: Studying exposition. My style improves daily in clearness and brevity.

rattan
[rə'tæn]
n. 藤,藤茎,藤杖

unscrew
['ʌn'skru:]
v. 拧开

bureau
[bjuə'rəu]
n. 局,办公处

upholster
[ʌp'həulstə]
v. 以帘幕,地毯,家具装饰

auction
['ɔ:kʃən]
n. 拍卖

nickel
['nikl]
n. 镍,镍币

flunk
[flʌŋk]
v. 失败,考试不及格

Hannibal
['hænibəl]
n. 汉尼拔（公元前247~前183,迦太基统帅）

三块钱；还买了一把藤椅，一张地毯，不过地毯中间有一点墨迹，不过我觉得还行。

屋子窗户很高，坐普通的椅子看不到外面。不过我把屋子后部上方的镜子拧下来靠着窗户了，靠窗坐着高度正好。抽屉一格一格的，像楼梯一样，一直往上的。

莎莉·麦克白帮我在高年级学生的跳蚤市场上挑了几件家具。她从小到大都在家住，对于家居装饰很在行。您这辈子也没机会体会连五毛钱都没有的时候，所以您是很难体会购物的乐趣的。用一张五块的去买东西，还能找回些零钱来！亲爱的叔叔，我向您保证，我对您给的零用钱真的是心存感激的。

莎莉最好了，而朱莉娅·彭莱顿跟她恰恰相反。管理处安排的室友组合真是怪异到了极点。莎莉觉得什么都好玩儿，连"挂科"她也觉得有趣；可朱莉娅觉得什么都很无聊，她从未试着对别人友好一些。她相信只要是彭莱顿家族的人，毋庸置疑，都是可以上天堂的。所以朱莉娅跟我天生就是对头。

您现在一定想听听我的功课吧。

1. 拉丁文：昨晚讲的，迦太基人第二次战争。汉尼拔人的统帅带领部队在特拉西梅洛湖（译者注：Trasimenus，拉丁语，意大利半岛的最大湖泊）安营扎寨，正准备伏击诺曼人。今天上午接着讲第四部分，诺曼人撤退。

2. 法文：《三个火枪手》第24页，第三个连词，不规则动词。

3. 几何学：圆柱体讲完了；现在讲圆锥体。

4. 英文：写阐述性文章。我写的文章比以前更清晰、简洁了。

V. Physiology: Reached the digestive system. Bile and the **pancreas** next time. Yours, on the way to being educated.

Jerusha Abbott

PS. I hope you never touch alcohol, Daddy?
It does dreadful things to your liver.

Wednesday

Dear Daddy-Long-Legs,

I've changed my name.

I'm still "Jerusha" in the catalog, but I'm "Judy" everyplace else. It's sort of too bad, isn't it, to have to give yourself the only pet name you ever had? I didn't quite make up the Judy though. That's what Freddie Perkins used to call me before he could talk plain.

I wish Mrs. Lippett would use a little more **ingenuity** about choosing babies' names. She gets the last names out of the telephone book—you'll find Abbott on the first page—and she picks the Christian names up anywhere; she got Jerusha from a **tombstone**. I've always hated it; but I rather like Judy. It's such a silly name. It belongs to the kind of girl I'm not—a sweet little blue-eyed thing, petted and spoiled by all the family, who **romps** her way through life without any cares. Wouldn't it be nice to be like that? Whatever faults I may have, no one can ever accuse me of having been spoiled by my family! But it's sort of fun to pretend I've been. In the future please always address me as Judy.

Do you want to know something? I have three pairs of kid gloves. I've had kid **mittens** before from the Christmas tree, but never real kid gloves with five fingers. I take them out and try them

pancreas
['pænkriəs]
n. 胰脏

5. 生物：讲到消化系统了，下次课讲胆汁和胰脏。

您正在念大学的
乔茹莎·阿伯特
十月十日

补充一下：叔叔，希望您别喝酒，好吗？对您的肝脏不好。

亲爱的长腿叔叔：

我改名字了。

我现在叫朱蒂，不过学校名单上我还是叫乔茹莎。自己为自己取个小名实在很糟糕，不是吗？不过朱蒂也不是我随便想的名儿。弗蕾迪·帕金讲话还不流利的时候，他一直那么叫我的。

ingenuity
[,indʒi'nju:iti]
n. 智巧，创造力，精巧的设计

我希望以后利皮特太太在给小宝贝儿们取名字时能多动动脑筋。她照着电话本替我们取姓氏——您要是翻开第一页就会看到阿伯特，名字呢，想到哪儿就是哪儿了，乔茹莎是她从一块墓碑上看到的，我一直都很讨厌这名字，不过我挺喜欢朱蒂的，这名字简单，而且这名字一看就像是长着一双蓝蓝的眼睛、甜甜的、被家人宠坏了的、一辈子什么也不用愁的、跟我完全不同的女孩子。那样不是很好吗?! 而我呢，不管犯了什么错，都没人说是我的家人把我宠坏的，不过假装一下也挺好玩的。以后请您也管我叫朱蒂吧。

tombstone
['tu:mstəun]
n. 墓碑

romp
[rɔmp]
v. 嬉闹玩耍

mitten
['mitn]
n. 连指手套

您还想知道什么呢？我有三双小手套，从圣诞树上摘下来的小连指手套，可不是那种真的带五个手指的连指手套哦。我戴着出门，经常试着戴上，

on every little while. It's all I can do not to wear them to classes.

(Dinner bell. Good-bye.)

Friday

What do you think, Daddy? The English instructor said that my last paper shows an unusual amount of originality. She did, truly. Those were her words. It doesn't seem possible, does it, considering the eighteen years of training that I've had? The aim of the John Grier Home (as you doubtless know and heartily approve of) is to turn the ninety-seven orphans into ninety-seven twins.

The unusual artistic ability which I exhibit was developed at an early age through drawing chalk pictures of Mrs. Lippett on the **woodshed** door.

I hope that I don't hurt your feelings when I criticize the home of my youth? But you have the upper hand, you know, for if I become too **impertinent** you can always stop payment on your

不过没有带去上过课。

(晚餐铃响了,再见。)

星期三

英文老师说我上次写的文章表现出了非凡的创造力。她真的是这么说的!这都是她的原话!叔叔,您觉得呢?想想我这十八年来接受的训练,这似乎不太可能。不是吗?约翰·格里尔孤儿院的目标就是要把九十七个小孤儿变成九十七个样貌举止都一模一样的人。

不寻常的艺术天分倒可能是小时候在门板上画利皮特太太培养出来的。

woodshed
['wudʃed]
n. 贮放柴薪的木棚

某 孤 儿

背面　　正面

impertinent
[im'pə:tinənt]
adj. 鲁莽的,无礼的,粗鲁的

希望我说养我长大的孤儿院坏话的时候,不会惹您不高兴。不过我要是态度愈加恶劣,您有权利

checks. That isn't a very polite thing to say—but you can't expect me to have any manners; a foundling asylum isn't a young ladies' finishing school.

You know, Daddy, it isn't the work that is going to be hard in college. It's the play. Half the time I don't know what the girls are talking about; their jokes seem to relate to a past that everyone but me has shared. I'm a foreigner in the world and I don't understand the language. It's a **miserable** feeling. I've had it all my life. At the high school the girls would stand in groups and just look at me. I was queer and different and everybody knew it. I could feel "John Grier Home" written on my face. And then a few **charitable** ones would make a point of coming up and saying something polite. I hated every one of them—the charitable ones most of all.

Nobody here knows that I was brought up in an asylum. I told Sallie McBride that my mother and father were dead, and that a kind old gentleman was sending me to college—which is entirely true so far as it goes. I don't want you to think I am a coward, but I do want to be like the other girls, and that Dreadful Home **looming** over my childhood is the one great big difference. If I can turn my back on that and shut out the **remembrance**, I think I might be just as desirable as any other girl. I don't believe there's any real, underneath difference, do you?

Anyway, Sallie McBride likes me!

Yours ever,
Judy Abbott
(Née Jerusha)

Saturday morning

I've just been reading this letter over and it sounds pretty uncheerful. But can't you guess that I have a special topic due Monday

随时停止您的资助。这样说是不太尊敬您,可孤儿院不是淑女培训学校,所以您别指望我那么有礼貌。

叔叔,您知道吗,大学里最难的不是功课,而是娱乐。我常常听不懂女孩子们都在谈些什么,她们讲的笑话似乎都跟她们的过去有关,而我的过去却跟她们有很大不同,我在她们中间就像是个外国人,我听不懂她们的话,这让我感觉很郁闷,长这么大一直都有这种感觉。高中时,女孩们常常会站在一起,看着我。我跟她们不同,这每个人都知道,我总感觉"约翰·格里尔孤儿院"几个字就写在我脸上,之后就会有一些好心人来安慰我。我恨她们每一个人——尤其是那些好心人。

这里没有人知道我是在孤儿院长大的。我告诉莎莉·麦克白我的父母都去世了,是一位好心的先生送我上大学的——目前为止,这都是事实。我希望您不要认为我很懦弱,不过我真的希望跟其他女孩子一样,可我童年那可怕的"家"就是和她们最大的不同。如果我能不去想这点,不去想过去,我想我应该可以变得跟其他女孩儿一样可爱的。我相信人本来是没有差别的。

不管怎样,莎莉·麦克白喜欢我!

您永远的
朱蒂·阿伯特
(正式的名儿乔茹莎)
星期五

我刚又把这封信读了一遍,语气好像不是很高兴。不过您可能不知道,我星期一早上要交一篇特

---

miserable
['mizərəbl]
adj. 悲惨的,痛苦的

charitable
['tʃæritəbl]
adj. 仁慈的

loom
[lu:m]
v. 朦胧地出现,隐约可见

rememberance
[ri'membə,ræns]
n. 记忆力

morning and a review in **geometry** and a very **sneezy** cold?

Sunday

I forgot to mail this yesterday so I will add an **indignant** postscript. We had a **bishop** this morning, and what do you think he said?

"The most **beneficent** promise made us in the *Bible* is this, 'The poor ye have always with you.' They were put here in order to keep us charitable."

The poor, please observe, being a sort of useful domestic animal. If I hadn't grown into such a perfect lady, I should have gone up after service and told him what I thought.

October 25th

Dear Daddy-Long-Legs,

I've made the basketball team and you ought to see the bruise on my left shoulder. It's blue and mahogany with little **streaks** of orange. Julia Pendleton tried for the team, but she didn't make it. Hooray!

You see what a mean disposition I have.

geometry
[dʒi'ɔmitri]
n. 几何(学)

sneezy
['sni:zi]
adj. 打喷嚏的

indignant
[in'dignənt]
adj. 愤慨的,愤愤不平的

bishop
['biʃəp]
n. 主教

beneficent
[bi'nefisənt]
adj. 仁慈的,慈善的

streak
[stri:k]
n. 条理,斑纹

殊的报告,还要复习几何学,而且感冒还很严重。

星期六早晨

昨天我忘了寄信,今天我要补充一点。今天早上我们听主教讲道了,您瞧瞧他讲得怎么样?

"《圣经》向我们做出过最仁慈的承诺,'世界上总是有弱者',他们的存在是让我们去爱他们。"

弱者,请注意,是指有用的家养动物,我要不是个大姑娘,我就想冲上去告诉他我想的想法。

星期日

亲爱的长腿叔叔:

我成功入选篮球队了,您真该看看我的左肩,又青又紫的,周围还是橘色的。朱莉娅·彭莱顿也想加入,不过她没入选。太好了!

您看,我天生就是个坏心眼儿。

朱蒂打篮球

College gets nicer and nicer. I like the girls and the teachers and the classes and the campus and the things to eat. We have ice cream twice a week and we never have cornmeal **mush**.

You only wanted to hear from me once a month, didn't you? And I've been **peppering** you with letters every few days! But I've been so excited about all these new adventures that I must talk to somebody; and you're the only one I know. Please excuse my **exuberance**; I'll settle pretty soon. If my letters bore you, you can always toss them into the wastebasket. I promise not to write another till the middle of November.

Yours most loquaciously,
Judy Abbott

November 15th

Dear Daddy-Long-Legs,

Listen to what I've learned today:

The area of the **convex surface** of the **frustum** of a regular pyramid is half the product of the sum of the perimeters of its bases by the **altitude** of either of its **trapezoids**.

It doesn't sound true, but it is—I can prove it!

You've never heard about my clothes, have you, Daddy? Six dresses, all new and beautiful and bought for me—not handed down from somebody bigger. Perhaps you don't realize what a **climax** that marks in the career of an orphan? You gave them to me, and I am very, very, very much obliged. It's a fine thing to be educated—but nothing compared to the **dizzying** experience of owning six new dresses. Miss Pritchard, who is on the visiting committee, picked them out—not Mrs. Lippett, thank goodness. I have an evening dress, pink **mull** over silk (I'm perfectly beautiful in that), and a blue church dress, and a dinner dress of red veiling

大学越来越有意思了。我喜欢女同学们，喜欢老师，喜欢上课，喜欢这所大学还喜欢这里的饭菜。我们一周吃两次冰淇淋，再也不用吃孤儿院的玉米糊了。

您只要我一月写一封信，对吧？可我每隔几天就给您写了一封，主要是我对这些新鲜经历是如此的兴奋，需要找个人分享，而您是我唯一认识的人。请原谅我的激动吧，我会很快静下心来的。如果我的信打扰了您，您可以随便扔进垃圾桶里，我保证十一月中旬以前不再写信就是了。

您太长舌的朋友
朱蒂·阿伯特
十月二十五日

亲爱的长腿叔叔：

看看我今天都学了什么吧：

一个正棱台的凸面面积等于锥体上下底部周长和乘以梯形的高再乘以二分之一。

看起来好像不对，不过确实是这样的——我可以证明！

叔叔，我还没给您讲过我的衣服，对吧？我有六身儿衣服，全都是新的，非常漂亮，而且是专为我买的——不是大孩子穿不了留下来的。您也许无法理解这对一个孤儿来说是一生中多么重要的一个转折点，可这些是您送给我的，我真的非常非常非常感谢。能继续念大学很开心，不过真的，没比拥有六件新衣服让我更快乐的了。参访委员会的普查德小姐替我挑的，庆幸没让利皮特太太来。我的衣服有这些：一件晚礼服，粉色的棉布加丝的（我穿上非常漂亮）；还有一身儿去教堂穿的，蓝色的；一套正装，红色镶边的，很有东方韵味儿，我穿上

---

mush
[mʌʃ]
n. 浓粥

pepper
['pepə]
v. 打扰,烦扰

exuberance
[ig'zju:bərəns]
n. 茂盛,健康,丰富

convex surface
凸面

frustum
['frʌstəm]
n. 截头锥体

altitude
['æltitju:d]
n. 高度,海拔

trapezoid
['træpizɔid]
n. 歪方形,梯形,不等边四边形

climax
['klaimæks]
n. 高潮,极点,层进法

dizzying
['diziŋ]
adj. 极快的,极高的

mull
[mʌl]
n. 软布(岬,失败,黑泥土)

with Oriental trimming (makes me look like a **Gypsy**) and another of rose-colored **challis**, and a gray street suit, and an everyday dress for classes. That wouldn't be an awfully big wardrobe for Julia Rutledge Pendleton, perhaps, but for Jerusha Abbott—oh, my!

I suppose you're thinking now what a **frivolous**, shallow, little beast she is, and what a waste of money to educate a girl?

But, Daddy, if you'd been dressed in checked ginghams all your life, you'd appreciate how I feel. And when I started to the high school, I entered upon another period even worse than the checked ginghams.

The poor box.

You can't know how I dreaded appearing in school in those miserable poor-box dresses. I was perfectly sure to be put down in class next to the girl who first owned my dress, and she would whisper and **giggle** and point it out to the others. The bitterness of wearing your enemies' cast-off clothes eats into your soul. If I wore silk stockings for the rest of my life, I don't believe I could **obliterate** the scar.

LATEST WAR BULLETIN!
News from the Scene of Action

At the fourth watch on Thursday the 13th of November, Hannibal routed the advance guard of the Romans and led the **Carthaginian** forces over the mountains into the plains of Casilinum. A **cohort** of light armed Numidians engaged the **infantry** of Quintus Fabius Maximus. Two battles and light **skirmishing**. Romans **repulsed** with heavy losses.

I have the honor of being,
Your special correspondent from the front

J. Abbott

PS. I know I'm not to expect any letters in return, and I've

Gypsy
['dʒipsi]
n. 吉卜赛人,吉卜赛语,像吉卜赛的人

challis
['ʃælis]
n. [纺]有印花之轻质毛料,印花丝毛料

frivolous
['frivələs]
adj. 轻佻的,妄动的,琐碎的

giggle
['gigl]
v. 傻笑

obliterate
[ə'blitəreit]
v. 擦掉…的痕迹;抹去

Carthaginian
[,kɑ:θə'dʒiniən]
adj. 迦太基的;迦太基人的

cohort
['kəuhɔ:t]
n. (罗马)步兵大队;一队人

infantry
['infəntri]
n. 步兵(部队);步兵团

skirmishing
['skə:miʃiŋ]
n. (小)冲突

repulse
[ri'pʌls]
v. 击退;驱逐

像个吉卜赛人;还有一套正装是玫红色印花丝毛料的衣服;还有一身儿灰色的便装以及一身儿上课穿的衣服。这或许对朱莉娅·彭莱顿来说并不算什么,但对乔茹莎·阿伯特来说就——噢!我的天!

我猜您现在一定想——这女孩儿不知羞耻,真是肤浅!让这样一个女孩儿念大学真浪费钱!

不过叔叔,您要是这辈子一直都穿别人不要的破破旧旧的衣服,您会明白我的感受的。我上高中的时候,我进入了另外一个阶段,比原来更糟糕,非常尴尬的阶段。

救济箱!

您无法想象我多么痛恨穿那些讨厌的救济服走进学校!而且还就是那么凑巧,注定还要被安排坐在衣服原主人的旁边,衣服的主人则偷偷地跟别的同学又讲又笑还对我指指点点。身上穿着讨厌的人那些不要的衣服,这种痛深深地啃蚀着我的灵魂。即使我以后穿一辈子的丝袜,也无法抹去他们对我心灵的伤害。

最新战报!
来自前线的报道

十一月十三日星期四四点,汉尼拔彻底击败罗马人的先锋部队,率领迦太基人翻山越岭最后到达了卡西利努平原。一队轻武装的努米底亚(译者注:北非古国)军队和昆塔斯·费边·马克西马斯(译者注:古罗马将军)的部队发生了小规模的冲突。两场战争加上小规模的冲突,罗马人溃败。

您很荣幸的特别通讯员
从前线发回的报道

您虚荣的
J. 阿伯特
十一月十五日

附言:我知道我不该奢望收到您的回信,而且

been warned not to bother you with questions, but tell me, Daddy, just this once—are you awfully old or just a little old? And are you perfectly bald or just a little bald? It is very difficult thinking about you in the abstract like a theorem in geometry.

Given a tall rich man who hates girls, but is very generous to one quite impertinent girl, what does he look like?

RSVP.

December 19th

Dear Daddy-Long-Legs,

You never answered my question and it was very important. ARE YOU BALD?

I have it planned exactly what you look like—very satisfactorily—until I reach the top of your head, and then I am stuck. I can't decide whether you have white hair or black hair or sort of **sprinkle** gray hair or maybe none at all.

Here is your portrait:

But the problem is, shall I add some hair?

Would you like to know what color your eyes are? They're gray and your eyebrows stick out like a porch roof (**beetling,** they're called in novels) and your mouth is a straight line with a tendency to turn down at the corners. Oh, you see, I know! You're a **snappy** old thing with a **temper**.

(Chapel bell.)

9:45 P. M.

I have a new unbreakable rule: never, never to study at night no matter how many written reviews are coming in the morning. Instead, I read just plain books—I have to, you know, because

我也被告诫过不要问您问题。可是叔叔，就问您一个问题，就一个——您是很老呢还是只有一点点老？您头上还有些头发还是都秃头了？从没见过您而又要想象您的样子，真的像几何定理，太抽象了，太难了。

一位个子高高的、讨厌女孩子的、很有钱的、而且对一个不知羞耻的女孩子却非常宽容的先生，他到底是长得什么样子呢？

请您告诉我。

亲爱的长腿叔叔：

您还没有回答我的问题呢，可这对我来说真的很重要。

您有头发吗？

我画了一张您的像——画得一直都很顺利，可画到头顶，就不知道该怎么画了。不知道您是白发？黑发？还是灰发？或是根本没有头发？

旁边是您的画像。

不过问题是，我该不该画头发上去？

您想知道我把您的眼睛画成什么颜色了吗？灰色。我把您的眉毛画得突出（小说里面都这样说的，突出），我把您的嘴巴画成了一条直线，画到嘴角就朝下弯了。哦，没错！您是一个很有个性，充满活力的人！（敲钟了！）

晚上9:45

我给自己订了一条严格的规定：不管第二天是不是有作业要交，绝不，绝不在晚上做功课。不过，我是读一些基础类书籍——没办法，您知道

sprinkle
['spriŋkl]
v. 使星星点点地分布于；点缀

beetle
['bi:tl]
v. 突出；伸出；凸出

snappy
['snæpi]
adj. 暴躁的；厉声说话的

temper
['tempə]
n. 暴躁；怒气

there are eighteen blank years behind me. You wouldn't believe, Daddy, what an **abyss** of ignorance my mind is; I am just realizing the depths myself. The things that most girls with a properly **assorted** family and a home and friends and a library know by **absorption**, I have never heard of. For example:

I never read *Mother Goose* or *David Copperfield* or *Ivanhoe* or *Cinderella* or *Bluebeard* or *Robinson Crusoe* or *Jane Eyre* or *Alice in Wonderland* or a word of Rudyard Kipling. I didn't know that Henry the Eighth was married more than once or that Shelley was a poet. I didn't know that people used to be monkeys and that the Garden of Eden was a beautiful myth. I didn't know that R. L. S. stood for Robert Louis Stevenson or that George Eliot was a lady. I had never seen a picture of the "Mona Lisa" and (it's true but you won't believe it) I had never heard of Sherlock Holmes.

Now, I know all of these things and a lot of others besides, but you can see how much I need to **catch up**. And oh, but it's fun! I look forward all day to evening, and then I put an "engaged" on the door and get into my nice red bathrobe and **furry** slippers and pile all the cushions behind me on the couch and light the **brass** student lamp at my elbow, and read and read and read. One book isn't enough. I have four going at once. Just now, they're Tennyson's poems and *Vanity Fair* and Kipling's *Plain Tales* and—don't laugh—*Little Women*. I find that I am the only girl in college who wasn't brought up on *Little Women*. I haven't told anybody though (that *would* stamp me as queer) . I just quietly went and bought it with $1.12 of my last month's allowance; and the next time somebody mentions pickled limes, I'll know what she is talking about!

(Ten o'clock bell. This is a very interrupted letter.)

Saturday

Sir,

I have the honor to report fresh explorations in the field of

abyss
[ə'bis]
n. 任何深不可测的事物,深邃

assort
[ə'sɔːt]
v. 把…分类;把…分级

absorption
[əb'sɔːpʃən]
n. 全神贯注;专心致志

catch up
赶上

furry
['fəːri]
adj. 毛皮的;覆有毛皮的;毛皮制的

brass
[brɑːs]
adj. 黄铜制的,黄铜色的

的,十八年来我错过的太多。您无法相信,叔叔,我脑子里有多少需要填补的地方,我逐渐意识到我自己还有很多很多需要充实。一个拥有正常家庭,拥有朋友,拥有图书馆相伴的女孩子本来应该知道的东西,我却从没听说过。比如:

我从没听过《鹅妈妈》、《大卫·科波菲尔》、《劫后英雄传》、《灰姑娘》、《蓝胡子》、《鲁宾逊漂流记》、《简·爱》还有《爱丽丝梦游仙境记》等等;我也从没听说过鲁德亚德·吉卜林(译者注:英国作家,1865~1936,1907年获诺贝尔文学奖);也不知道亨利八世居然结过两次婚,雪莱是个诗人;不知道人是从猿进化来的,还有"伊甸园"的故事原来是个美丽的神话;从来不知道R.L.S.是罗伯特·路易斯·斯蒂文森的缩写,还有乔治·艾略特是个女作家;也从没看过一幅叫"蒙娜丽莎"的画,(也许你不相信,但它是真的)我也没听说过什么福尔摩斯的。

如今,这些我都知道了,还知道好多其他的呢。不过,您瞧我多么需要赶上别的同学。噢!不过读书很开心!上一整天的课终于等到黄昏,终于可以在门口挂上"读书中"的标语,穿上我舒适的红睡袍,用枕头当靠背,打开手边的台灯,然后一直读啊读。一本不够,还有四本呢,分别是丁尼森的诗集,《名利场》,吉卜林的《山中故事》——别笑啊——还有《小妇人》,我发现我是大学里唯一没有读过《小妇人》的女孩。不过我谁也没告诉(别人会觉得我另类的),这是我偷偷溜出去,用上个月的零花钱花了一块一毛二买的。下次有人提起腌酸橙,我就知道她在说什么了!

(十点的钟声响了,这封信被打断了好几次。)

十一月十九日

先生:
很荣幸向您报告刚学的几何。上周五我们结束

geometry. On Friday last we abandoned our former works in **parallelepipeds** and proceeded to **truncated prisms**. We are finding the road rough and very uphill.

Sunday

The Christmas holidays begin next week and the trunks are up. The corridors are so **cluttered** that you can hardly get through, and everybody is so **bubbling** over with excitement that studying is getting left out. I'm going to have a beautiful time on vacation; there's another freshman who lives in Texas staying behind, and we are planning to take long walks and—if there's any ice—learn to skate. Then there is still the whole library to be read—and three empty weeks to do it in!

Good-bye, Daddy, I hope that you are feeling as happy as I am.

Yours ever,
Judy

PS. Don't forget to answer my question. If you don't want the trouble of writing, have your secretary telegraph. He can just say:

Mr. Smith is quite bald,
or
Mr. Smith is not bald,
or
Mr. Smith has white hair.

And you can deduct the twenty-five cents out of my allowance.
Good-bye till January—and a merry Christmas!
Toward the end of the Christmas vacation.
Exact date unknown.

Dear Daddy-Long-Legs,

Is it snowing where you are? All the world that I see from my tower is **draped** in white and the **flakes** are coming down as big as

parallelepiped
[pærəle'lepiped]
n. 平行六面体

truncated
['trʌŋkeitid]
adj. 截形的

prism
['prizəm]
n. 棱柱

clutter
['klʌtə]
v. 嘈杂的声音；吵闹声

bubble
['bʌbl]
v. 充满生气，情绪高涨

先前的平行六面体开始学习截棱柱。我们学得很吃力，感觉像爬坡。

星期六

下周就开始过圣诞假期了。大厅里全是行李箱，都准备出行，堵得厅都很难通过，假期一来同学们都兴奋不已。我要好好享受这个假期，另一个德州的新生也要留下来，我们打算长距离散步，结冰的话，我们还要学溜冰。还有一整幢图书馆要读——整整三个星期都可以泡图书馆！

晚安，叔叔，希望您跟我一样高兴。

您永远的
朱蒂
星期日

补充一下：别忘了回答我的问题哦。如果你不想劳神费力回信，您可以叫秘书给我发电报。他可以这样来回答：

> 史密斯先生头秃秃的，
> 或者
> 史密斯先生不是秃头，
> 或者
> 史密斯先生有白发。

您可以从我的零用钱里面扣二十五分来发电报。一月再见啦——祝您圣诞快乐！

drape
[dreip]
v. 装饰

flake
[fleik]
n. 雪片

亲爱的长腿叔叔：

您住的地方下雪了吗？从窗户一眼望去，外面的世界全白了，覆盖着一层厚厚的积雪，天空依然飘着雪花，像爆米花那么大一粒儿。此刻是傍晚时

popcorn. It's late afternoon—the sun is just setting (a cold yellow color) behind some colder violet hills, and I am up in my window seat using the last light to write to you.

Your five gold pieces were a surprise! I'm not used to receiving Christmas presents. You have already given me such lots of things—everything I have, you know—that I don't quite feel that I deserve **extras**. But I like them just the same. Do you want to know what I bought with my money?

Ⅰ. A silver watch in a leather case to wear on my **wrist** and get me to recitations on time.

Ⅱ. Matthew Arnold's poems.

Ⅲ. A hot water bottle.

Ⅳ. A steamer rug. (My tower is cold.)

Ⅴ. Five hundred sheets of yellow manuscript paper. (I'm going to commence being an author pretty soon.)

Ⅵ. A dictionary of **synonyms**. (To enlarge the author's vocabulary.)

Ⅶ. (I don't much like to confess this last item, but I will.) A pair of silk stockings.

And now, Daddy, never say I don't tell all!

It was a very low motive, if you must know it, that **prompted** the silk stockings. Julia Pendleton comes into my room to do geometry, and she sits **cross-legged** on the couch and wears silk stockings every night. But just wait—as soon as she gets back from vacation I shall go in and sit on her couch in my silk stockings. You see, Daddy, the miserable creature that I am—but at least I'm honest; and you knew already, from my asylum record, that I wasn't perfect, didn't you?

To **recapitulate** (that's the way the English instructor begins every other sentence), I am very much obliged for my seven presents. I'm pretending to myself that they came in a box from my family in California. The watch is from father, the **lap rug** from mother, the hot water bottle from grandmother—who is always

分，冰冷的太阳刚刚落到远处冷冷的紫色山。此刻，我坐在窗台上，趁着黄昏的一点余光给您写信。

收到您的五个金币真是太让我吃惊了！我不太习惯收到圣诞礼物。您已经给了我这么多了——我拥有的一切都是您给的——我觉得我拥有的太多了。不过我还是非常喜欢您的礼物的，您想知道我用您给的钱买了些什么吗？

1. 一只银色的手表，装在一只皮盒子里，戴在手腕上能提醒我时间。

2. 马修·阿罗德的诗集。

3. 一个热水壶。

4. 一张小毯子。（我的小屋很冷）

5. 五百张黄色稿纸。（我要开始写作了）

6. 一本同义词典。（可以增加我的词汇量）

7. （虽然我不太想告诉您最后一件，可是我会的）一双丝袜。

叔叔，现在您不会说我没说完了吧！

如果您一定想知道的话，我只好这样说：朱莉娅·彭莱顿每晚都要穿着丝袜到我房间来做几何题，而且总跷着腿坐在我的椅子上。不过等着瞧，等她放假回来，我就要穿着丝袜坐到她的屋子里。您瞧，叔叔，我真坏！可是，至少我很诚实，而且我在约翰·格里尔孤儿院的记录您也知道，我本来就不是完美的人，是吧？

扼要重述一下（英文老师课堂上每隔几句话总这么说）——再次感谢您送的上面七个礼物！我假装它们就是装在大箱子里，家人从加州寄来的。手表是爸爸送的，毯子是妈妈送的，热水壶是奶奶送

---

extra
['ekstrə]
n. 额外费用
wrist
[rist]
n. 腕；腕关节

synonym
['sinənim]
n. 同义字

prompt
[prɔmpt]
v. 提示；引起，激起
cross-legged
盘着腿的；翘着腿的

recapitulate
[,ri:kə'pitjuleit]
v. 扼要重述；概括
lap rug
（主英）围膝盖的小毯

worrying for fear I shall catch cold in this climate—and the yellow paper from my little brother Harry. My sister Isobel gave me the silk stockings, and Aunt Susan the Matthew Arnold poems; Uncle Harry (little Harry is named for him) gave me the dictionary. He wanted to send chocolates, but I insisted on synonyms.

You don't object, do you, to playing the part of a composite family?

And now, shall I tell you about my vacation, or are you only interested in my education as such? I hope you appreciate the **delicate** shade of meaning in "as such". It is the latest addition to my vocabulary.

The girl from Texas is named Leonora Fenton. (Almost as funny as Jerusha, isn't it?) I like her, but not so much as Sallie McBride; I shall never like anyone so much as Sallie—except you. I must always like you the best of all, because you're my whole family rolled into one. Leonora and I and two sophomores have walked 'cross country every pleasant day and explored the whole neighborhood, dressed in short skirts and **knit** jackets and caps, and carrying **hockey** sticks to **whack** things with. Once we walked into town—four miles—and stopped at a restaurant where the college girls go for dinner. Broiled lobster (35 cents) and for dessert, **buckwheat** cakes and maple syrup (15 cents). Nourishing and cheap.

It was such a lark! Especially for me, because it was so awfully different from the asylum—I feel like an escaped **convict** every time I leave the campus. Before I thought, I started to tell the others what an experience I was having. The cat was almost out of the bag when I grabbed it by its tail and pulled it back. It's awfully hard for me not to tell everything I know. I'm a very **confiding** soul by nature; if I didn't have you to tell things to, I'd burst.

We had a **molasses** candy pull last Friday evening, given by the house matron of Fergussen to the left-behinds in the other halls. There were twenty-two of us altogether, freshmen and sophomores

的——奶奶总担心我冬天感冒——黄色稿纸是哈里哥哥送的，丝袜是姐姐伊莎贝尔送的，苏珊姑姑送的马修的诗集；哈里叔叔（哈里哥哥的爸爸）送的是词典，他本来要送巧克力的，可我坚持要词典。

假装您就是我的家人，您不会反对吧？

您想听听我的假期安排呢还是仍旧只是关心我的教育情况？希望您能理解我说的"仍旧"二字背后隐藏的意义，这是我最近才深刻领会到其中意义的一个词。

德州女孩儿名叫里奥诺娜·芬顿。（名字跟乔茹莎差不多好玩，是吧？）我挺喜欢她的，不过，除了您，我最喜欢的就是莎莉·麦克白了。您永远是我最喜欢的人，因为您是我家人的化身。只要天气好，我和里奥诺娜以及两个二年级的女孩儿穿着短裙，套着针织短上衣，手里还拿着曲棍球的竿子一路走到乡间散步，看看周围的景色。有一次，我们还步行到镇上，大约走了四英里，然后走进一家餐馆，大学里的女孩子经常在那儿吃晚餐。点的龙虾（35美分），吃完后又点了个煎饼（15美分）。天啊，真是便宜啊！

简直太高兴了！对我来说，这简直跟在孤儿院的时候太不一样了——每当我离开学校，我总觉得好像个逃犯似的。根本没经过思考，我就开始跟别人分享我的感受了。话到嘴边，本来我不想说的，可我已经说了。我真的没办法不去说我的感受，我生来诚实，要不是对您倾诉，我肯定会憋死的。

我们上星期五做了蜜糖吃，场地是由我们大楼的管理人员提供的，在另一大厅的左角处。新生、二年级的还有三年级和四年级的师兄师姐们总共有

---

delicate
['delikit]
adj. 需要小心处理的；微妙的；棘手的

knit
[nit]
n. 编织衣物；编织衣料

hockey
['hɔki]
n. 曲棍球

whack
[(h)wæk]
v.【口】（用棍棒等）重打；猛击

buckwheat
['bʌkwi:t]
n.【植】荞麦

convict
['kɔnvikt]
n.【律】（服刑的）囚犯，已决犯

confiding
[kən'faidiŋ]
adj. 易信任别人的

molasses
[mə'læsiz]
n.【美】糖蜜；糖浆

and juniors and seniors all united in amicable accord. The kitchen is huge, with copper pots and kettles hanging in rows on the stone wall—the littlest **casserole** among them about the size of a washboiler. Four hundred girls live in Fergussen. The chef, in a white cap and **apron**, fetched out twenty-two other white caps and aprons—I can't imagine where he got so many—and we all turned ourselves into cooks.

It was great fun, though I have seen better candy. When it was finally finished, and ourselves and the kitchen and the **doorknobs** all thoroughly sticky, we organized a procession and still in our caps and aprons, each carrying a big fork or spoon or frying pan, we marched through the empty corridors to the officers' parlor where half a dozen professors and instructors were passing a **tranquil** evening. We **serenaded** them with college songs and offered refreshments. They accepted politely but dubiously. We left them sucking chunks of molasses candy, sticky and speechless.

So you see, Daddy, my education progresses!

Don't you really think that I ought to be an artist instead of an author?

Vacation will be over in two days and I shall be glad to see the girls again. My tower is just a **trifle** lonely; when nine people occupy a house that was built for four hundred, they do **rattle** around a bit.

Eleven pages—poor Daddy, you must be tired! I meant this to be just a short little thank-you note—but when I get started I seem to have a ready pen.

二十二人齐聚一堂，厨房特别大，铜锅、水壶等挂在墙上，其中最小的焙锅都跟煮衣锅差不多大——弗格森总共住着四百来个女孩儿。戴着白色帽子，穿着白围裙的"主厨"拿出另外二十二顶白帽和二十二条围裙——真不知道他从哪儿弄来的——于是我们二十二个女孩儿全成了厨师。

虽然我吃过比这更好吃的蜜糖，可这真的太有意思了！结束时，我们手上、厨房还有门把手上全都黏糊糊的。我们头戴白帽，身穿围裙，每人手里要么捏着一把大汤匙要么一口平底锅，列队站着。随后，我们走过宽敞的大厅到了教师休息室，那儿有六七个教授和老师们正在休息。我们为他们唱校歌，然后送上蜜糖，他们礼貌地接受下来，但是一脸迷惑的样子。他们大口大口地吃着黏糊糊的蜜糖，一句话也没说。

所以，叔叔，您瞧，这就是我的大学！
难道您真觉得我该成为作家而不是艺术家？

再过两天假期就要结束了，我又可以高兴地见到女同学们了。我在小屋有点寂寞了。想想四百个女孩儿住那幢楼，每个屋子里住九个人呢，的确有点吵。

写了十一页了！可怜的叔叔，您一定看累了吧！我本来只打算写一封简短的感谢信的，谁知道一提笔就没办法停下来。

Good-bye, and thank you for thinking of me—I should be perfectly happy except for one little threatening cloud on the horizon. Examinations come in February.

Yours with love,
Judy

PS. Maybe it isn't proper to send love? If it isn't, please excuse. But I must love somebody and there's only you and Mrs. Lippett to choose between, so you see—you'll have to put up with it, Daddy dear, because I can't love her.

On the Eve

Dear Daddy-Long-Legs,

You should see the way this college is studying! We've forgotten we ever had a vacation. Fifty-seven irregular verbs have I introduced to my brain in the past four days—I'm only hoping they'll stay till after examinations.

Some of the girls sell their textbooks when they're through with them, but I intend to keep mine. Then after I've graduated I shall have my whole education in a row in the bookcase, and when I need to use any detail, I can turn to it without the slightest hesitation. So much easier and more accurate than trying to keep it in your head.

Julia Pendleton dropped in this evening to pay a social call, and stayed a solid hour. She got started on the subject of family, and I couldn't switch her off. She wanted to know what my mother's **maiden name** was—did you ever hear such an impertinent question to ask of a person from a foundling asylum? I didn't have the courage to say I didn't know, so I just miserably **plumped** on the first name I could think of, and that was Montgomery. Then she wanted to know whether I belonged to the Massachusetts Montgomerys or the Virginia Montgomerys.

再见！谢谢您的圣诞礼物——我真的非常非常高兴。不过，心里面还是忐忑不安的，二月份就要考试了。

爱您的
朱蒂
接近圣诞假期的尾声
确切日期记不清

补充一下：致爱可能不合适吧？如果不妥，请您原谅。我总得有个爱的人，不过，对我而言，只有您跟利皮特太太可二选一，您看，亲爱的叔叔，您就忍忍吧，因为我实在没办法爱她。

亲爱的长腿叔叔：

您瞧瞧我们这大学读得！几乎忘了还有一个假期！前面四天，我记了五十七个不规则动词，只希望考试完了之后一直都还记得。

有些同学学完之后就开始卖课本，可我一直都保留着。等我毕业的时候，我书架上一排排的课本将是我整个大学生活的见证，而且我需要查什么细节的时候也很方便，比记在脑袋里要容易得多，而且更准确。

朱莉娅·彭莱顿今晚上又来我屋了，整整呆了一个小时，真难受。她开始谈家庭，我没办法避开不谈。她想知道我妈妈娘家姓什么——您见过谁如此无礼去问一个孤儿院长大的人这个问题吗？我没勇气说我不知道，所以我很不高兴地随便说了一个，说的是蒙哥玛利。可她还接着问是不是麻省的蒙哥玛利家族或者弗吉尼亚的蒙哥玛利家族。

---

maiden name
n. （女子）婚前姓，娘家姓
plump
[plʌmp]
v. （沉重或突然）倒下,坠下

Her mother was a Rutherford. The family came over in the ark, and were connected by marriage with Henry the Eighth. On her father's side they date back further than Adam. On the topmost branches of her family tree there's a superior breed of monkeys, with very fine silky hair and extra long tails.

I meant to write you a nice, cheerful, entertaining letter tonight, but I'm too sleepy—and scared. The freshman's lot is not a happy one.

Yours, about to be examined,
Judy Abbott

Sunday

Dearest Daddy-Long-Legs,

I have some awful, awful, awful news to tell you, but I won't begin with it; I'll try to get you in a good humor first.

Jerusha Abbott has commenced to be an author. A poem entitled "From My Tower" appears in the February *Monthly*—on the first page, which is a very great honor for a freshman. My English instructor stopped me on the way out from **chapel** last night, and said it was a charming piece of work except for the sixth line, which had too many feet. I will send you a copy in case you care to read it.

Let me see if I can't think of something else pleasant—oh, yes! I'm learning to skate, and can **glide** about quite respectably all by myself. Also I've learned how to slide down a rope from the roof of the gymnasium, and I can **vault** a bar three feet and six inches high—I hope shortly to pull up to four feet.

We had a very inspiring sermon this morning preached by the Bishop of Alabama. His text was: "Judge not that ye be not judged." It was about the necessity of overlooking mistakes in others, and not discouraging people by harsh judgments. I wish you might have heard it.

她妈妈是鲁斯福德家的,说起这个家族的起源,得追溯到亨利八世,这个家族曾经是亨利八世的姻亲。她爸爸那边则追溯到亚当之前,还到更久远,她家的祖先都是猴子变来的,头上长金毛,尾巴还特长。

今晚写这些是希望您度过一个欢乐美好而开心的一晚,可是我现在太困了,而且有点怕,学校对新生宿舍管理很严格的。

您要考试的
朱蒂·阿伯特
圣诞前夕

最亲爱的长腿叔叔:

我有个很坏很坏很坏的消息要告诉您,不过我不会以此开头的。我得先让您高兴高兴。

乔茹莎·阿伯特开始写作了。一首名叫"凭窗远眺"的诗已经刊登在二月的《月刊》上了——就在首页。对一名新生来说,太光荣了。昨晚,我的英文老师在做晚礼拜回家的路上遇上我说我的那首诗除了第六行韵脚太多,其他都很棒。我会寄一份给您,您好好看看。

看看还能不能想点其他让您高兴的事呢?噢,有了!我正偷偷地学溜冰,而且水平还很不错呢。而且,我还学会了如何从体育馆的屋顶用绳索爬下来,我还能跨越三尺六高的栏杆呢,希望很快能跨过四尺。

---

chapel
['tʃæpəl]
n. (学校、医院、王宫等的)附属礼拜堂

glide
[glaid]
v. 悄悄地走;(事情)渐变

vault
[vɔ:lt]
v. 撑竿跳过

This is the sunniest, most blinding winter afternoon, with **icicles** dripping from the fir trees and all the world bending under a weight of snow—except me, and I'm bending under a weight of sorrow.

Now for the news—courage, Judy!—you must tell.

Are you surely in a good humor? I **flunked** mathematics and Latin prose. I am **tutoring** in them, and will take another examination next month. I'm sorry if you're disappointed, but otherwise I don't care a bit because I've learned such a lot of things not mentioned in the catalog. I've read seventeen novels and bushels of poetry—really necessary novels like *Vanity Fair* and *Richard Feverel* and *Alice in Wonderland*. Also Emerson's *Essays* and Lockhart's *Life of Scott* and the first volume of Gibbon's *Roman Empire* and half of Benvenuto Cellini's *Life*—wasn't he entertaining? He used to **saunter** out and casually kill a man before breakfast.

icicle
['aisikl]
n. 冰柱;垂冰

今天上午,阿拉巴马主教给我们讲了一堂振奋人心课。他说:"勿要论断别人,否则会被别人论断。"人很有必要忽略别人身上的一些缺点,而且不要用刻薄的语言来打击别人。希望您听过这句话。

好了,现在要告诉您坏消息了——勇敢点,朱蒂!你一定要讲出来。

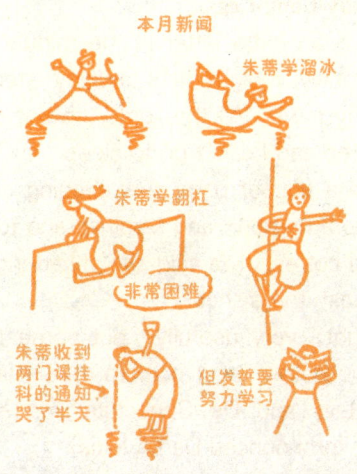

您"确定"您开心吗?我的几何和拉丁文被挂了。现在在重修,下个月补考。如果这让您生气了,我很抱歉。不过,我不是很在意,因为我学了很多课本上没有的知识。我读了十七本小说了,还有很多诗。小说有《名利场》,还有《理查德·法弗尔》,《爱丽丝梦游仙境记》等;还有爱默生的散文选,洛克哈特的《斯科特的自传》,还有吉本的《罗马帝国衰亡史》的第一卷,还读了半本本威努托·切利尼(译者注:约1500~1571,意大利雕塑家、金银工艺师、作家)的《自传》——他是不是很有意思?他曾经喜欢闲游,而且在某天早饭前杀了一个人。

flunk
[flʌnk]
v.(在考试等中)失败,不及格

tutor
['tju:tə]
v. 当…的教师;辅导;指导

saunter
['sɔ:ntə]
v. 闲逛;漫步

So you see, Daddy, I'm much more intelligent than if I'd just stuck to Latin. Will you forgive me this once if I promise never to flunk again?

Yours in **sackcloth**,
Judy

Dear Daddy-Long-Legs,

This is an extra letter in the middle of the month because I'm sort of lonely tonight. It's awfully stormy; the snow is beating against my tower. All the lights are out on the campus, but I drank black coffee and I can't go to sleep.

I had a supper party this evening consisting of Sallie and Julia and Leonora Fenton—and sardines and toasted **muffins** and salad and **fudge** and coffee. Julia said she'd had a good time, but Sallie stayed to help wash the dishes.

I might, very usefully, put some time on Latin tonight—but, there's no doubt about it, I'm a very **languid** Latin scholar. We've finished **Livy** and **De Senectute** and are now engaged with De Amicitia (pronounced Damn Icitia).

Should you mind, just for a little while, pretending you are my grandmother? Sallie has one and Julia and Leonora each two, and they were all comparing them tonight. I can't think of anything I'd rather have, it's such a respectable relationship. So, if you really don't object—when I went into town yesterday, I saw the sweetest cap of Cluny lace **trimmed** with **lavender** ribbon. I am going to make you a present of it on your eighty-third birthday.

!!!!!!!!!!!!!

That's the clock in the chapel tower striking twelve. I believe I am sleepy after all.

Good night, Granny.
I love you dearly.
Judy

所以您瞧，叔叔，我比死读拉丁文学到的更多呢。要是我保证以后绝不再考试不及格，您能原谅我吗？

您伤心的
朱蒂
星期日

亲爱的长腿叔叔：

这是本月中旬额外写的一封信，因为今晚我觉得有点寂寞。外面狂风暴雨，啪嗒啪嗒敲打着我的小屋。校园里的灯都灭了，我喝了点儿黑咖啡，睡不着。

今晚我参加了一个晚餐派对，参加的人有莎莉、朱莉娅和里奥诺娜·芬顿——我们准备了沙丁鱼、小松糕、沙拉、糖果还有咖啡等。茱莉娅说她玩得很开心，不过是莎莉留下来帮着刷盘子的。

我本来今晚该多花点时间学拉丁文的——毫无疑问，我的拉丁文学得不怎么样。我们已经学完李维的作品以及西塞罗的《论老年》，现在正在学他的《论友谊》（讨厌的拉丁文）。

您介不介意假装一下我的祖母吧？莎莉有一个，茱莉娅和里奥诺娜都有两个，她们今晚都会拿出来比了。而我希望拥有的，我却无法想象他们的样子，他们是多么值得尊敬啊。所以，您要是真的不介意——昨天我进城时，我看到镶紫色缎带的蕾丝无边帽，十分可爱，我要送给您作83岁的生日礼物。

！！！！！！！！！！！！

教堂的钟声敲了十二下了，我有点困了。

晚安，祖母
爱您的，
朱蒂

---

sackcloth
['sækklɔθ]
n. 粗布衣

muffin
['mʌfin]
n. 松饼

fudge
[fʌdʒ]
n. 乳脂软糖

languid
['læŋgwid]
adj. 不感兴趣的，没精打采的

Livy
全名 Titus Liv,提图斯·李维,公元前59年~公元17年,古罗马历史学家

De Senectute
《论老年》,马库斯·图留斯·西塞罗的作品,西塞罗是古罗马著名政治家、演说家、雄辩家、法学家和哲学家

trim
[trim]
v. 装点,布置

lavender
['lævində]
adj. 淡紫色的;干薰衣草的

The Ides of March

Dear D. L. L.,

I am studying Latin prose composition. I have been studying it. I shall be studying it. I shall be about to have been studying it. My reexamination comes the 7th hour next Tuesday, and I am going to pass or BUST. So you may expect to hear from me next, whole and happy and free from conditions, or in fragments.

I will write a respectable letter when it's over. Tonight I have a pressing engagement with the **Ablative Absolute**.

Yours—in evident haste,
J. A.

March 26th

Mr. D. L. L. Smith,

Sir: You never answer any questions; you never show the slightest interest in anything I do. You are probably the horridest one of all those horrid trustees, and the reason you are educating me is, not because you care a bit about me, but from a sense of duty.

I don't know a single thing about you. I don't even know your name. It is very **uninspiring** writing to a thing. I haven't a doubt but that you throw my letters into the wastebasket without reading them. Hereafter I shall write only about work.

My reexaminations in Latin and geometry came last week. I passed them both and am now free from conditions.

Yours truly,
Jerusha Abbott

亲爱的长腿叔叔：

我最近在学拉丁散文写作，我一直在学习，我会一直学的。我正打算要学习呢。下周二第七节课就要考试了，我得考过啊，要不得挂科了。下次我要说的是一个完整的、快乐的和独立于任何客观因素的故事。

事情结束之后，我会写一封很恭敬的信。今晚我得好好学拉丁文的独立夺格（译者注：这是拉丁语中一个极为重要的用法，相当于英语中的独立主格）。

Ablative Absolute
（拉丁语法）离格词

您匆忙的
J.A.
三月悠闲的一天

长腿叔叔史密斯先生：

先生：您从没回答过任何问题，而且您也从未对我所做的事情表现出一点儿兴趣。您可能是孤儿院那些董事中最讨厌的一个，您资助我上大学不是因为您关心我，而是出于义务。

uninspiring
[ʌnin'spaiəriŋ]
adj. 不鼓舞人的；引不起兴趣的

我对您一点儿也不了解，甚至连您叫什么也不知道。写信给"一件事物"是很没意思的事情。我一点也不怀疑您可能根本没看我的信就丢进了垃圾桶。我以后只写与功课相关的事情。

上周，我的几何学和拉丁文补考都通过了，很容易就过关了，现在我终于解脱了。

您最真实的
乔茹莎·阿伯特
三月二十六日

April 2d

Dear Daddy-Long-Legs,

I am a BEAST.

Please forget about that dreadful letter I sent you last week—I was feeling terribly lonely and miserable and **sore-throaty** the night I wrote. I didn't know it, but I was just coming down with **tonsillitis** and **grippe** and lots of things mixed. I'm in the **infirmary** now, and have been here for six days; this is the first time they would let me sit up and have a pen and paper. The head nurse is very **bossy**. But I've been thinking about it all the time and I shan't get well until you forgive me.

Here is a picture of the way I look, with a **bandage** tied around my head in rabbit's ears.

Doesn't that arouse your sympathy? I am having **sublingual gland** swelling. And I've been studying physiology all the year without ever hearing of sublingual glands. How futile a thing is education!

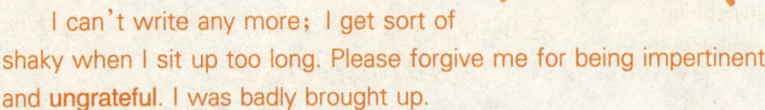

I can't write any more; I get sort of shaky when I sit up too long. Please forgive me for being impertinent and **ungrateful**. I was badly brought up.

Yours with love,
Judy Abbott
The Infirmary

April 4th

Dearest Daddy-Long-Legs,

Yesterday evening just toward dark, when I was sitting up in bed looking out at the rain and feeling awfully bored with life in a great institution, the nurse appeared with a long white box

亲爱的长腿叔叔：

我是个坏孩子！

请您忘记我上周给您那封胡乱说一气的信吧——写信那天晚上，我觉得非常孤独，心情极度糟糕，嗓子还隐隐作痛，我自己并不知道扁桃体发炎，染了流感什么的。我现在躺在学校医院病房里，已经住六天了。今天是医生说我可以起来了，而且他们还给了我纸笔。护士长很凶。我一直忐忑不安，要是得不到您的原谅，我恐怕很难再好起来了。

下面画的是我现在的模样，一条绷带绕过我的头，绑个大结，上面像兔子的两只耳朵。

这样会得到您同情吗？我的舌下腺肿了。这一年来，我一直在学生理学，可我从来没听过舌下腺。念大学有什么用呢！

我不能再写了，坐久了感觉有点头晕。请原谅我的不尊不敬，不知道感恩，主要是缺乏家教。

爱您的
朱蒂·阿伯特
四月二日

最亲爱的长腿叔叔：

昨天，傍晚黄昏时分，我坐了起来，望着窗外的雨，当时心里有一种强烈的感觉，感觉人生真是太没意思了。突然，一名护士带给了我一个长长的

---

sore-throaty
嗓子发炎的
tonsillitis
[tɔnsi'laitis]
n.【医】扁桃腺炎
grippe
[grip]
n.【法】流行性感冒
infirmary
[in'fə:məri]
n. 医院；医务室
bossy
['bɔsi]
adj. 爱指挥他人的，跋扈的
bandage
['bændidʒ]
n. 绷带
sublingual gland
舌下腺
ungrateful
[ʌn'greitful]
adj. 讨厌的，令人不快的

addressed to me, and filled with the loveliest pink **rosebuds**. And much nicer still, it contained a card with a very polite message written in a funny little **uphill** backhand (but one which shows a great deal of character). Thank you, Daddy, a thousand times. Your flowers make the first real, true present I ever received in my life. If you want to know what a baby I am, I lay down and cried because I was so happy.

Now that I am sure you read my letters, I'll make them much more interesting, so they'll be worth keeping in a safe with red tape around them—only please take out that dreadful one and burn it up. I'd hate to think that you ever read it over.

Thank you for making a very sick, cross, miserable freshman cheerful. Probably you have lots of loving family and friends, and you don't know what it feels like to be alone. But I do.

Good-bye—I'll promise never to be horrid again, because now I know you're a real person; also I'll promise never to bother you with any more questions.

Do you still hate girls?

Yours forever,
Judy

8th hour, Monday

Dear Daddy-Long-Legs,

I hope you aren't the trustee who sat on the toad? It went off—I was told—with quite a pop, so probably he was a fatter trustee.

Do you remember the little **dugout** places with gratings over them by the laundry windows in the John Grier Home? Every spring when the hoptoad season opened we used to form a collection of toads and keep them in those window holes; and occasionally they would spill over into the laundry, causing a very pleasurable

rosebud
['rəuzbʌd]
n. 玫瑰花蕾
uphill
['ʌp'hil]
adj. 上坡的

白色盒子，里面装着最美丽的玫瑰花。更高兴的是里面还附有一张制作精巧措辞考究的问候卡，而且是颇有个性的反手斜体字（感觉挺有个性的）。叔叔，谢谢您，万分感谢！您的花让我第一次感觉如此真实，第一次如此清晰地呈现在我的生命中。您要知道我是多么的孩子气，我高兴地躺在床上号啕大哭。

现在，我确定您读了我的信。我以后会写得有意思一点，这样才值得您用红丝带捆起来好好收藏——不过，只请您找出前面那封可恶的信烧掉它。一想到您看那封信，就很痛恨自己。

谢谢您让一个生病的、神经兮兮而且郁闷的新生重新快乐起来。也许，您有很多至爱的家人和朋友，所以您无法明白孤独的滋味儿。可我明白。

晚安！我保证以后决不再胡说了，因为我现在知道您是活生生的人，而且我也保证以后再也不问您问题了。

您还讨厌女孩子吗？

您永远的

朱蒂

医院病房中

四月四日

亲爱的长腿叔叔：

但愿您不是坐在癞蛤蟆上的那位理事。听说当时"嘭"的一声巨响，所以可能是一位比您胖的理事。

您记得约翰·格里尔孤儿院洗衣房窗外那些覆盖着栅栏的空洞吗？每逢春季，蛤蟆鼓噪时，我们常常捉许多蛤蟆藏在窗外的那些洞里。有时蛤蟆跳

dugout
['dʌgaut]
n. 挖在山坡（或地下）的洞；防空洞

commotion on wash days. We were severely punished for our activities in this direction, but in spite of all discouragement the toads would collect.

And one day—well, I won't bore you with particulars—but somehow, one of the fattest, biggest, juiciest **toads** got into one of those big leather armchairs in the trustees' room, and that afternoon at the trustees' meeting... But I dare say you were there and recall the rest?

Looking back **dispassionately** after a period of time, I will say that punishment was merited, and—if I remember rightly—adequate.

I don't know why I am in such a **reminiscent** mood except that spring and the reappearance of toads always awakens the old **acquisitive** instinct. The only thing that keeps me from starting a collection is the fact that no rule exists against it.

After chapel, Thursday

What do you think is my favorite book? Just now, I mean; I change every three days. *Wuthering Heights*. Emily Brontë was quite young when she wrote it, and had never been outside of Haworth churchyard. She had never known any men in her life; how could she imagine a man like Heathcliffe?

I couldn't do it, and I'm quite young and never outside the John Brier asylum—I've had every chance in the world. Sometimes a dreadful fear comes over me that I'm not a genius. Will you be awfully disappointed, Daddy, if I don't turn out to be a great author? In the spring when everything is so beautiful and green and budding, I feel like turning my back on lessons, and running away to play with the weather. There are such lots of adventures out in the fields! It's much more entertaining to live books than to write them.

Ow!!!!!!

commotion
[kəˈməuʃən]
n. 骚动,喧闹

toad
[təud]
n. 蟾蜍,癞蛤蟆

dispassionately
[disˈpæʃənitli]
adv. 不动感情地

reminiscent
[remiˈnis(ə)nt]
adj. 回忆往事的;怀旧的

acquisitive
[əˈkwizitiv]
adj. 想获得的;贪得无厌的;可学得的

进洗衣房,引起一阵快活的骚动。虽然我们会为此受到严厉的惩罚,可我们还是要捕捉蛤蟆。

有一天——我就不详细啰嗦了——一只又大又肥身上黏黏糊糊的蛤蟆不知怎的,蹿进了理事休息室,爬到了一张大的皮手扶椅上。结果,下午开会的时候……您还记得当时的情景吧?

现在静静地回想起来,我受到惩罚是罪有应得的。要是没记错的话,当时的惩罚也不算过分。

不知道我为什么如此怀旧,难道春天蛤蟆的出现触动了我好玩的天性?大学里没有禁止捕蛙,而我捕捉蛤蟆的愿望却没了。

星期一第八节课

您知道我最喜欢哪本书吗?我是说现在。我的爱好三天一变,我最喜欢《呼啸山庄》。艾米莉·勃朗特写了这本书的时候还很年轻,而且从未离开过哈沃兹教区,她一生也从未接触过男性,她是怎么创造出希斯·克利夫这样一个人来的呢?

我也是很年轻啊,也没走出过孤儿院——具备了成功的种种条件,可我却不能。有时候我很气馁,觉得自己不是天才。长腿叔叔,我要是成不了大作家,您会失望吗?春天来了,四处都是绿油油的青草,花团锦簇,一派生机勃勃的景象,一切都那么美好,我真想丢下功课,跑到大自然中去尽情地玩耍。野外有各式各样的新鲜事物!享受书中的故事要比写书有趣多了。

啊呀呀!!!!!!

That was a shriek which brought Sallie and Julia and (for a disgusted moment) the senior from across the hall. It was caused by a **centipede** like this:

Only worse. Just as I had finished the last sentence and was thinking what to say next—plump!—it fell off the ceiling and landed at my side. I tipped two cups off the tea table in trying to get away. Sallie whacked it with the back of my **hairbrush**—which I shall never be able to use again—and killed the front end, but the rear fifty feet ran under the bureau and escaped.

This dormitory, owing to its age and ivy-covered walls, is full of centipedes. They are dreadful crea-tures. I'd rather find a tiger under the bed.

Friday, 9:30 P. M.

Such a lot of troubles! I didn't hear the rising bell this morning, then I broke my **shoestring** while I was hurrying to dress and dropped my collar button down my neck. I was late for breakfast and also for first-hour **recitation**. I forgot to take any blotting paper and my fountain pen **leaked**. In **trigonometry** the professor and I had a disagreement touching a little matter of **logarithms**. On looking it up, I find that she was right. We had mutton **stew** and pie-plant for lunch—hate 'em both; they taste like the asylum. Nothing but bills in my mail (though I must say that I never do get anything else; my family are not the kind that write). In English class this afternoon we had an unexpected written lesson. This was it:

> I asked no other thing,
> No other was denied.
> I offered Being for it;

centipede
['sentipi:d]
n.【昆】蜈蚣

我这一声叫喊把莎莉、朱莉娅还有（真倒霉！）楼道一端的大四毕业生都招来了。原来是我看到了一条蜈蚣，长得大概是这样子的：

真的比画的还可怕。我刚写完上句正在思考下句，啪嗒！一只蜈蚣从天而降，落到了我桌上。我跃身而起，桌上两只杯子被打翻了。莎莉用我的梳子，弄断了蜈蚣前半身儿——这把梳子我没法再用了，可蜈蚣后半身儿五十只脚却爬下镜台不见了。

hairbrush
['heəbrʌʃ]
n. 毛刷,发刷

因为宿舍楼很古旧，墙上长满了常春藤，蜈蚣活动频繁，简直比老虎藏在床下还可怕。

星期四做礼拜后

shoestring
['ʃu:striŋ]
n.【美】鞋带

recitation
[resi'teiʃ(ə)n]
n. 背诵,朗诵,当众吟诵

leak
[li:k]
v.（水,瓦斯等的）漏出

trigonometry
[trigə'nɔmitri]
n.【数】三角

logarithm
['lɔgəriθm]
n.【数】对数

stew
[stju:]
n. 炖肉,焖菜

倒霉的事总是接二连三！早上我没听见闹铃，慌忙穿了衣服，不但拉断了鞋带，领口的扣子被扯掉沿着脖子掉了下去。早饭也晚了，第一节背诵课也迟到了，钢笔还漏水，而且没带吸墨纸。上三角几何课讲到对数的时候，我和教授在一个小问题上出现分歧。查了下书，还是她对了。中午吃的炖羊肉和大黄茎，我都不爱吃，跟孤儿院的饭一样难吃。没有任何信件，只收到了账单（说实话，除了账单我也没有收到过别的什么，我的家人从来就不写信）。意外的是，下午的英语课改成了写作课。内容是这样的：

我别无他求，
也不会遭到拒绝。
为此我献上了生命，

> The mighty merchant smiled.
> Brazil? He twirled a button
> Without a glance my way:
> But, madam, is there nothing else
> That we can show today?

That is a poem. I don't know who wrote it or what it means. It was simply printed out on the blackboard when we arrived and we were ordered to comment upon it. When I read the first verse I thought I had an idea—the mighty merchant was a **divinity** who distributes blessings in return for virtuous deeds—but when I got to the second verse and found him twirling a button, it seemed a **blasphemous** supposition, and I hastily changed my mind. The rest of the class was in the same **predicament**; and there we sat for three-quarters of an hour with blank paper and equally blank minds. Getting an education is an awfully wearing process!

But this didn't end the day. There's worse to come.

It rained so we couldn't play golf, but had to go to gymnasium instead. The girl next to me **banged** my elbow with an Indian club. I got home to find that the box with my new blue spring dress had come, and the skirt was so tight that I couldn't sit down. Friday is sweeping day, and the maid had mixed all the papers on my desk. We had tombstone for dessert (milk and **gelatin** flavored with **vanilla**) . We were kept in chapel twenty minutes later than usual to listen to a speech about womanly women. And then—just as I was settling down with a sigh of well-earned relief to *The Portrait of a Lady*, a girl named Ackerly, a doughfaced, deadly, unintermittently stupid girl, who sits next to me in Latin because her name begins with A (I wish Mrs. Lippett had named me Zabriski), came to ask if Monday's lesson **commenced** at paragraph 69 or 70, and stayed one hour. She has just gone.

Did you ever hear of such a discouraging series of events? It isn't the big troubles in life that require character. Anybody can rise

万能的商人微笑着说：
巴西？他捻着纽扣，
根本不瞅我一眼，
女士，难道我们今天
就没有别的可以奉献？

这是一首诗，我不知道作者是谁，也不知道什么意思。到教室的时候，黑板上工整地写着这首诗，要我们评论。读完第一段，似懂非懂的感觉。万能的商人可能是指赐福给行善者的神灵，可是到第二段，他捻着纽扣，这似乎又有些亵渎神明，顿时又觉得我的理解有问题。其他同学和我差不多，我们坐了整整三刻钟，盯着一张白纸，脑子里一片空白。读书真的很折磨人。

这还没完呢，更倒霉的在后面。

雨天不能打高尔夫，所以只好到健身房去。我的胳膊肘还撞到了旁边那个姑娘的体操棒上。回到宿舍，我的蓝色新春装送来了，可裙子穿上又太紧太小，连坐下都很困难。星期五是打扫宿舍的日子，可清洁女工把我的桌子弄得乱七八糟。饭后甜食又吃"墓石"（一种香草牛奶冻）。礼拜还拖延了二十分钟，为的是讲妇人之道。而且，我好不容易缓了口气坐下来看《贵妇人的画像》，结果笨手笨脚、死气沉沉而且脸像面团的阿克尔莉跑来问我，星期一的课是从第六十九段还是从第七十段开始讲。上拉丁文课她坐我旁边，因为她和我的姓一样，都是A字打头（真希望利皮特太太给我起了个Z字母开头的姓，比如扎布里斯基之类的）。她在我屋里整整坐了一个小时，刚走。

还有谁像我这么祸不单行呢？可英雄并不总是在危急时刻才出现啊。任何人都能站出来应对危

---

divinity
[di'viniti]
n. 神性；神威

blasphemous
['blæsfiməs]
adj. 亵渎的

predicament
[pri'dikəmənt]
n. 尴尬的处境，困境；危境

bang
[bæŋ]
v. 猛击，猛撞

gelatin
['dʒelətin]
n. 凝胶；明胶；动物胶

vanilla
[və'nilə]
n. 【植】香子兰；香草

commence
[kə'mens]
v. 开始

to a crisis and face a crushing tragedy with courage, but to meet the petty **hazards** of the day with a laugh—I really think that requires spirit.

It's the kind of character that I am going to develop. I am going to pretend that all life is just a game which I must play as skillfully and fairly as I can. If I lose, I am going to shrug my shoulders and laugh—also if I win.

Anyway, I am going to be a sport. You will never hear me complain again, Daddy dear, because Julia wears silk stockings and centipedes drop off the wall.

Yours ever,
Judy

Answer soon.

May 27th

Daddy-Long-Legs, Esq.
Dear Sir: I am in receipt of a letter from Mrs. Lippett. She hopes that I am doing well in deportment and studies. Since I probably have no place to go this summer, she will let me come back to the asylum and work for my board until college opens.

I HATE THE JOHN GRIER HOME.
I'd rather die than go back.

Yours most truthfully,
Jerusha Abbott

Cher Daddy-Jambes-Longes,
Vous etes un brick!
Je suis tres heureuse about the farm, *parsque je n'ai jamais* been on a farm *dans ma vie* and I'd hate to *retourner chez* John Grier, *et* wash dishes *tout l'été*. There would be danger of *quelque chose affreuse* happening, *parsque j'ai perdue ma humilité d'autre fois et j'ai peur* that I would just break out *quelque jour et* smash every cup and

hazard
['hæzəd]
n. 危险；危害物；危险之源

机，勇敢面对人间一切悲剧。可要对日常生活中的纷纷扰扰付诸一笑，真得有点性格才行。

以后我要培养这种个性，要把生活当成一个竞技场，尽可能提高竞技水平，跟别人公平竞争。胜也好，败也好，最后耸耸肩膀，一笑了之。

不管怎样，今后我要好好做人，认真做事。亲爱的长腿叔叔，以后您再也不会听我抱怨朱莉娅穿长筒丝袜了，也不会抱怨蜈蚣从天而降了。

请速回信。

您永远的朱蒂
星期五，上午九点半

长腿叔叔：

亲爱的先生，今天收到利皮特太太的来信。她希望我在学校表现良好，做个品学兼优的学生。如果我这个夏天没地方去，她愿意让我假期回孤儿院去工作，解决假期的食宿问题，直到大学开学。

我讨厌回约翰·格里尔孤儿院！！

宁死也不愿回去！

您最诚实的
乔茹莎·阿伯特

亲爱的长腿叔叔：

您太好了！

能去农庄，我实在是太高兴了！我这辈子还没去过农庄，最关键的是我讨厌回约翰·格里尔孤儿

saucer *dans la maison.*

Pardon *brièveté et* paper. *Je ne peux pas* send *des mes nouvelles parseque je suis dans* French class *et j'ai peur que Monsieur le Professeur* is going to call on me *tout de suite.*

He did!

Au revoir,

Je vous aime beaucoup.
Judy

May 30th

Dear Daddy-Long-Legs,

Did you ever see this campus? (That is merely a rhetorical question. Don't let it annoy you.) It is a heavenly spot in May. All the shrubs are in blossom and the trees are the loveliest young green—even the old pines look fresh and new. The grass is dotted with yellow **dandelions** and hundreds of girls in blue and white and pink dresses. Everybody is joyous and **carefree,** for vacation's coming, and with that to look forward to, examinations don't count.

Isn't that a happy frame of mind to be in? And oh, Daddy! I'm the happiest of all! Because I'm not in the asylum any more; and I'm not anybody's **nursemaid** or typewriter or bookkeeper (I should have been, you know, except for you).

I'm sorry now for all my past badnesses.

I'm sorry I was ever impertinent to Mrs. Lippett.

I'm sorry I ever slapped Freddie Perkins.

I'm sorry I ever filled the sugar bowl with salt.

I'm sorry I ever made faces behind the trustees' backs.

I'm going to be good and sweet and kind to everybody because I'm so happy. And this summer I'm going to write and write and write and begin to be a great author. Isn't that an **exalted** stand to

院去刷一个夏天的碗。

请原谅我就写到这儿，我在上法文课，估计老师很快就会叫我了。

果然叫我了！

再见！

爱您的
朱蒂
五月二十七日

亲爱的长腿叔叔：

您没见过我们学校吧？（这只是一个反问句，请别在意。）五月份的时候，学校里景色美极了。灌木丛中有各色小花，树上一片翠绿——连最苍老的松树也换新装。绿草地上星星点点点缀着黄色蒲公英和几百个身着各色衣裙的女孩儿，蓝色的，白色的，还有粉色的。她们无忧无虑、快快乐乐地在草地上玩耍。伴随着令人期待的假期，考试的忧虑早就抛到九霄云外了。

这种感觉真是太棒了！叔叔，而我是里面最快乐的一个！因为我不用呆在约翰·格里尔孤儿院了，不再替谁当保姆、打字员、或者会计（可您知道，要不是您，我本应该是其中一个的）。

请原谅我所做的一切坏事；

请原谅我过去对利皮特太太态度很不好；

请原谅我打过弗雷迪·帕金；

请原谅我还把盐倒到糖罐里；

请原谅我还在理事们身后做过鬼脸。

在学校太快乐了！我以后要好好做人，要善待身边的一切。从今年夏天起，我要开始写作了，努力成为一名伟大的作家。这还不算崇高的理想吗？

---

dandelion
['dændilaiən]
n. 【植】蒲公英

carefree
['kɛəfri:]
adj. 无忧无虑的；轻松愉快的

nursemaid
['nə:meid]
n. 育婴女佣；保姆

exalt
[ig'zɔ:lt]
v. 使喜悦，使得意，使激动

take? Oh, I'm developing a beautiful character! It droops a bit under cold and frost, but it does grow fast when the sun shines.

That's the way with everybody. I don't agree with the theory that **adversity** and sorrow and disappointment develop moral strength. The happy people are the ones who are bubbling over with kindliness. I have no faith in **misanthropes**. (Fine word! Just learned it.) You are not a misanthrope, are you, Daddy?

I started to tell you about the campus. I wish you'd come for a little visit and let me walk you about and say:

"That is the library. This is the gas plant, Daddy dear. The **Gothic** building on your left is the gymnasium, and the Tudor Romanesque beside it is the new infirmary."

Oh, I'm fine at showing people about. I've done it all my life at the asylum, and I've been doing it all day here. I have honestly.

And a man, too!

That's a great experience. I never talked to a man before (except occasional trustees, and they don't count). Pardon, Daddy. I don't mean to hurt your feelings when I **abuse** trustees. I don't consider that you really belong among them. You just tumbled onto the Board by chance. The trustee, as such, is fat and **pompous** and **benevolent**. He pats one on the head and wears a gold watch chain.

That looks like a June bug, but is meant to be a portrait of any trustee except you.

However—to **resume**:

I have been walking and talking and having tea with a man. And with a very superior man—with Mr. Jervis Pendleton of the House of Julia; her uncle, in short (in long, perhaps I ought to say; he's as tall as you).

我在逐步培养美好的人格！虽然时而遭受寒霜打击，可灿烂的阳光总会使我的情绪迅速高涨起来。

这是众生之路。我不相信所谓逆境、忧伤或失意会造就道德力量，只有幸福快乐的人才会使人热情洋溢！我也不相信所谓厌世者（很好的词儿，刚学的）。长腿叔叔，您不是一个厌世者，对吧？

我一上来就告诉您学校的美景，是我希望您能来参观一下，我可以陪您到处走走，由我来告诉您：

"亲爱的叔叔，那儿是图书馆，这儿是煤气厂。您左手边的哥特式建筑是体育馆，它旁边都铎时期的罗马式建筑是新盖的医院。"

噢！我是个很好的导游哦。以前在约翰·格里尔孤儿院，我常常带人参观的。今天还领人走了一整天。真的，不骗您。

而且是一位男士！

这次经历真是异乎寻常！除了个别理事，我从没跟男人说过话，但他们不算。对不起，叔叔，我不是故意要冒犯您。我并没有把您当成是那些理事之一。我印象中的理事通常是长得肥头大耳、傲慢、装着一副慈善模样、喜欢摸人脑袋，而且身上还挂着个金怀表。

那样子看起来像一只金甲虫，可您除外。下面是我画的他们的样子：

不过——继续讲：

我陪一位男士散步、聊天、喝茶。他是一个很了不起的人物——朱莉娅家族的杰维·彭莱顿先生。简单地说，是她叔叔（详细说来，我应

adversity
[əd'və:siti]
n. 逆境；厄运；(经济方面的)窘境

misanthrope
['misənθrəup]
n. 不愿与人来往者；厌世者

Gothic
['gɔθik]
adj.【建】哥特式的

abuse
[ə'bju:z]
v. 辱骂；毁谤

pompous
['pɔmpəs]
adj. 爱炫耀的；浮夸的；自负的

benevolent
[bi'nevələnt]
adj. 行善的，慈善的

resume
[ri'zju:m]
v. 重新开始，继续

Being in town on business, he decided to run out to the college and call on his niece. He's her father's youngest brother, but she doesn't know him very intimately. It seems he glanced at her when she was a baby, decided he didn't like her, and has never noticed her since.

Anyway, there he was, sitting in the reception room very proper with his hat and stick and gloves beside him; and Julia and Sallie with seventh-hour recitations that they couldn't cut. So Julia **dashed** into my room and begged me to walk him about the campus and then deliver him to her when the seventh hour was over. I said I would, obligingly but **unenthusiastically,** because I don't care much for Pendletons.

But he turned out to be a sweet lamb. He's a real human being—not a Pendleton at all. We had a beautiful time; I've longed for an uncle ever since. Do you mind pretending you're my uncle? I believe they're superior to grandmothers.

Mr. Pendleton reminded me a little of you, Daddy, as you were twenty years ago. You see I know you intimately, even if we haven't ever met!

He's tall and **thinnish** with a dark face all over lines, and the funniest underneath smile that never quite comes through but just **wrinkles** up the corners of his mouth. And he has a way of making you feel right off as though you'd known him a long time. He's very **companionable**.

We walked all over the campus from the **quadrangle** to the athletic grounds; then he said he felt weak and must have some tea. He proposed that we go to College Inn—it's just off the campus by the pine walk. I said we ought to go back for Julia and Sallie, but he said he didn't like to have his nieces drink too much tea; it made them nervous. So we just ran away and had tea and muffins and **marmalade** and ice cream and cake at a nice little table out on the **balcony**. The inn was quite conveniently empty, this being the end of the month and allowances low.

该跟您说,他和您差不多高)。他到城里办事,顺便来学校看看侄女。他是朱莉娅爸爸最小的弟弟,但朱莉娅和他关系很一般。似乎在她的童年时代,他看了她一眼,不是很喜欢她,就再也没怎么关注她了。

不管怎么说,他来了,端端正正地坐在接待室里,帽子、手杖、手套放在旁边。莎莉和朱莉娅第七节是朗诵课,不能翘课,所以朱莉娅冲进我房间,求我陪她叔叔转转校园,等下第七节课再领他去找她。出于礼貌,我只好答应了。说实话,我对彭莱顿家族没多少好感。

不过他是一个温文尔雅的人——很有风度,一点也不像彭莱顿家族出身的人。我们愉快地度过了一段时间。从那时起,我就渴望有个叔叔。您来作我的叔叔,好吗?我觉得叔叔比祖母要好。

彭莱顿先生让我想起了您,叔叔,像二十年前的您。您瞧,我对您多么熟悉,尽管我们从没见过面。

彭莱顿先生瘦高瘦高的,皮肤黝黑,轮廓分明,他一咧嘴角就能让您觉得很舒服。虽然认识他不久,可是感觉一见如故。

我们从广场逛到体育场,走过了每一个角落。他说他累了,想喝杯茶,提议我们去学院的茶餐厅。餐厅不远,就在校门外的小路旁。我说我们该回去叫朱莉娅和莎莉一起去,可他说他不喜欢自己的侄女喝太多茶,喝多了茶会让她变得神经紧张。所以就我俩去了,找了张靠窗的小桌子坐了下来,点了茶、小松糕、冰淇淋还有饼干。因为到月底了,大家的零用钱也都花得差不多了,所以餐厅里几乎没别人。

---

dash
[dæʃ]
v. 猛冲,急奔

unenthusiastically
[ˌʌnɪnˌθjuːziˈæstɪklɪ]
adv. 不热心地;没有热情地

thinnish
[ˈθɪnɪʃ]
adj. 有点细的;有点瘦的;有点软弱的

wrinkle
[ˈrɪŋkl]
v. 使起皱纹

companionable
[kəmˈpænjənəb(ə)l]
adj. 好交往的;友善的

quadrangle
[kwɔˈdræŋgl]
n. 四边形

marmalade
[ˈmɑːməleɪd]
n. (带碎果皮的)橘子(或柠檬)果酱

balcony
[ˈbælkənɪ]
n. 阳台,露台

We had the jolliest time! But he had to run for his train the minute he got back and he barely saw Julia at all. She was **furious** with me for taking him off; it seems he's an unusually rich and desirable uncle. It **relieved** my mind to find he was rich, for the tea and things cost sixty cents **apiece**.

This morning (it's Monday now) three boxes of chocolates came by express for Julia and Sallie and me. What do you think of that? To be getting candy from a man!

I begin to feel like a girl instead of a foundling.

I wish you'd come and take tea some day and let me see if I like you. But wouldn't it be dreadful if I didn't? However, I know I should.

Bien! I make you my **compliments**.

"*Jamais je ne t'oublierai.*"

Judy

PS. I looked in the glass this morning and found a perfectly new dimple that I'd never seen before. It's very curious. Where do you suppose it came from?

June 9th

Dear Daddy-Long-Legs,

Happy day! I've just finished my last examination—**physiology**. And now:

Three months on a farm!

I don't know what kind of a thing a farm is. I've never been on one in my life. I've never even looked at one (except from the car window), but I know I'm going to love it, and I'm going to love being free.

I am not used even yet to being outside the John Grier Home. Whenever I think of it excited little thrills chase up and down my back. I feel as though I must run faster and faster and keep looking

furious
['fjuəriəs]
adj. 狂怒的

relieve
[ri'li:v]
v. 使宽慰,使放心

apiece
[ə'pi:s]
adv. 各个;每个;每人;每样

我们聊得很开心!可刚回到学校,火车就快到点了,所以只匆匆见了朱莉娅一面。朱莉娅对我把她叔叔带出去喝茶很不高兴。看来他是一位超级富有而且是让人羡慕的叔叔。知道他很富有,我还好受点,因为茶和点心很贵,每样要六毛钱呢。

今天早上(今天是星期一)快递送来了三盒巧克力,给朱莉娅、莎莉还有我每人一盒。您觉得怎么样?一位男士送来了巧克力!

我开始感到自己像个女孩子,而不是个孤儿。

我希望您什么时候也来吃茶点,让我看看喜不喜欢您。可是,如果我不喜欢您,那不是太糟糕

compliment
['kɔmplimənt]
n. 赞美的话;恭维;敬意

了?不过,我应该会喜欢您的。

好了,向您致敬!

永远不会忘记您的

朱蒂

五月三十日

补充一下:今天早晨照镜子,发现脸上长了个酒窝,以前从没注意到过。奇怪,从哪儿长出来的呢?

physiology
[,fizi'ɔlədʒi]
n. 生理学

亲爱的长腿叔叔:

今天真高兴!考完了最后一科——生物。

然后呢,我要到农庄去呆三个月!

我从来没去过农庄,一点概念也没有。(除了坐车的时候朝窗外看到过)我从来没见过。不过,我想我会喜欢的。我逐渐爱上自由了。

除了约翰·格里尔孤儿院,别的地方我都不熟悉。每次一想到这一点,就感到异常兴奋。感觉好像应该跑快点,再快点,一边跑一边回头看,看看

over my shoulder to make sure that Mrs. Lippett isn't after me with her arm **stretched** out to grab me back.

I don't have to mind anyone this summer do I?

Your nominal authority doesn't annoy me in the least; you are too far away to do any harm. Mrs. Lippett is dead forever, so far as I am concerned, and the Semples aren't expected to overlook my moral welfare, are they? No, I am sure not. I am entirely grown up. Hurrah!

I leave you now to pack a trunk, and three boxes of **teakettles** and dishes and sofa cushions and books.

Yours ever,
Judy

PS. Here is my physiology exam. Do you think you could have passed?

Lock Willow Farm,
Saturday night

Dearest Daddy-Long-Legs,

I've only just come and I'm not unpacked, but I can't wait to tell you how much I like farms. This is a heavenly, heavenly, heavenly spot! The house is square like this:

And old. A hundred years or so. It has a **veranda** on the side which I can't draw and a sweet porch in front. The picture really doesn't do it justice—those things that look like feather **dusters** are maple trees, and the prickly ones that border the drive are **murmuring** pines and **hemlocks**. It stands on the top of a hill and looks way off over miles of green meadows to another line of hills.

stretch
[stretʃ]
v. 伸直；伸出；伸长

利皮特太太是不是在我身后伸手要抓我回去。

这个夏天我不用顾忌什么了，对吗？

您的权威吓唬不了我，您离我太远了，对我不会造成伤害。对我来说，利皮特太太已经永远离去了。森普尔斯夫妇不会监督我的言行举止了吧？不，再也不会了。我已经长大了！万岁！

teakettle
['tiːˌketl]
n. 茶壶

就写到这里吧，现在我要去收拾行李了，还得装三个大箱子，带上茶壶、盘子、枕头还有书等等。

您永远的

朱蒂

六月九日

补充一下：这是我的生物试卷，看看您能考过吗？

最亲爱的长腿叔叔：

我已经到了，还没整理好行李，可我迫切地想跟您分享我是多么喜欢农庄。这里真是很好很好很好的地方！房子整体是方形的，如下图：

veranda
[vəˈrændə]
n. 阳台；游廊；走廊

duster
[ˈdʌstə]
n. 除尘器

murmur
[ˈməːmə]
v. 轻柔持续地发出声音

hemlock
[ˈhemlɔk]
n.【美】铁杉；铁杉木

房子很古旧，大约有一百年的历史。我没画出的那部分有一个可爱的门廊。我画得不好，跟真实的房屋有一定差距——那些像鸡毛掸子似的东西是枫树，车道旁带刺儿的是松树和铁杉。房屋坐落在一座小山顶上，放眼望去是大片大片的绿草地。

That is the way Connecticut goes, in a series of **marcel** waves; and Lock Willow Farm is just on the **crest** of one wave. The barns used to be across the road where they **obstructed** the view, but a kind flash of lightning came from heaven and burnt them down.

The people are Mr. and Mrs. Semple and a hired girl and two hired men. The hired people eat in the kitchen, and the Semples and Judy in the dining room. We had ham and eggs and biscuits and honey and jelly-cake and pie and pickles and cheese and tea for supper—and a great deal of conversation. I have never been so entertaining in my life; everything I say appears to be funny. I suppose it is because I've never been in the country before, and my questions are backed by an all-inclusive ignorance.

The room marked with a cross is not where the murder was committed, but the one that I occupy. It's big and square and empty, with **adorable** old-fashioned furniture and windows that have to be propped up on sticks and green shades trimmed with gold that fall down if you touch them. And a big square mahogany table—I'm going to spend the summer with my elbows spread out on it, writing a novel.

Oh, Daddy, I'm so excited! I can't wait till daylight to explore. It's 8:30 now, and I am about to blow out my candle and try to go to sleep. We rise at five. Did you ever know such fun? I can't believe this is really Judy. You and the Good Lord give me more than I deserve. I must be a very, very, very good person to pay. I'm going to be. You'll see.

Good night,
Judy

marcel
[mɑ:'sel]
n.（头发上烫的）波形

crest
[krest]
n. 顶饰

obstruct
[əb'strʌkt]
v. 妨碍, 阻扰, 阻止

adorable
[ə'dɔ:rəbl]
adj.【口】可爱的

　　康涅狄格州的地貌就像波浪卷发，洛克威洛农场就坐落在浪尖上。谷仓原先在道路的一边，正好挡住了视线，幸好上天一阵雷电把它夷为平地。

　　农庄里住着申普夫妇，一名女工和两名男工。工人都在厨房用餐，而申普夫妇和朱蒂在饭厅用餐。晚饭吃的火腿、蛋、饼干、蜂蜜、果冻蛋糕、馅饼、泡菜、奶酪，晚饭后一边喝茶，一遍聊天，聊了很久。我从来没讲过这么多的话，我说什么都似乎很搞笑。我想是因为我从没到过农庄，对很多东西不了解的原因吧。

　　那个打了叉的房间，不是指发生过谋杀案什么的，而是我住的房间。我住的屋子又大又宽敞。屋里的旧式家具非常可爱，窗户是用棍子撑开的，窗帘是绿色镶金边的，轻轻一接触就会自动放下来。屋里还有一张方形大红木桌子——我准备整个夏天都趴在这张桌上写小说。

　　噢！叔叔，我实在太兴奋了！我盼望着快点天亮，好去四处瞧瞧。现在是晚上八点半，我得灭了蜡烛，想办法睡着。我们五点起床。您有过这么好玩的经历吗？我不敢相信我真的是朱蒂。您和仁慈的上帝给予我的太多了，我一定要做一个非常非常非常非常好的人来报答您。我会的，您等着瞧吧。

　　晚安！

朱蒂
洛克威洛农庄
星期六晚上

PS. You should hear the frogs sing and the little pigs squeal—and you should see the new moon! I saw it over my right shoulder.

Lock Willow,
July 12th

Dear Daddy-Long-Legs,

How did your secretary come to know about Lock Willow? (That isn't a rhetorical question. I am awfully curious to know.) For listen to this: Mr. Jervis Pendleton used to own this farm, but now he has given it to Mrs. Semple who was his old nurse. Did you ever hear of such a funny coincidence? She still calls him "Master Jervie" and talks about what a sweet little boy he used to be. She has one of his baby curls put away in a box, and it's red—or at least reddish!

Since she discovered that I know him, I have risen very much in her opinion. Knowing a member of the Pendleton family is the best introduction one can have at Lock Willow. And the cream of the whole family is Master Jervie—I am pleased to say that Julia belongs to an inferior branch.

The farm gets more and more entertaining. I rode on a hay **wagon** yesterday. We have three big pigs and nine little **piglets**, and you should see them eat. They are pigs! We've oceans of little baby chickens and ducks and turkeys and **guinea** fowls. You must be mad to live in a city when you might live on a farm.

It is my daily business to hunt the eggs. I fell off a beam in the barn loft yesterday, while I was trying to crawl over to a nest that the black hen has stolen. And when I came in with a **scratched** knee, Mrs. Semple **bound** it up with witch hazel, murmuring all the time, "Dear! Dear! It seems only yesterday that Master Jervie fell off that very same beam and scratched this very same knee."

The scenery around here is perfectly beautiful. There's a valley and a river and a lot of wooded hills, and way in the distance, a tall

补充：屋外一片蛙声和小猪仔的叫声，您要是能听到该多好呀，还有那一轮新月！我往右抬头就能看到那轮弯弯的月亮！

亲爱的长腿叔叔：

您的秘书怎么会知道洛克威洛农庄呢？（这不是反问，我确实想知道。）这家农庄的主人曾经是杰维·彭莱顿先生。后来，他把农场送给了他的奶妈——申普太太了。您有没见过这么凑巧的事情呢？申普太太到现在还叫他"杰维少爷"，还讲他小时候是多么多么可爱。而且申普太太还将他小时候的一撮卷发珍藏起来，头发是红色的——至少是淡红色的！

自从申普太太知道我认识他，就对我另眼相看了。认识彭莱顿家族的一员可以说是在洛克威洛农庄最好的见面礼。杰维少爷是彭莱顿家族的骄傲——不过我很庆幸朱莉娅是最下层的一员。

农庄越来越好玩了。昨天我坐了运草的马车。我们有三只大猪和九只小猪崽，您应该看看它们怎么吃的。猪就是猪啊！我们有很多小鸡、小鸭、火鸡，还有珍珠鸡。您要是在农场住过，您会受不了城市的喧嚣的。

我每天的事情就是拣鸡蛋。昨天在谷仓里，我想爬过去摸一个鸡窝（黑鸡有时偷偷在那儿下蛋），一不小心摔了一跤。回去后，申普太太一边替我包扎刮破的膝盖，一边还自言自语道："我的天啦！杰维少爷也从那儿摔过，就好像昨天发生的事情，他也是刮破了这边膝盖！"

这里的景色真是美不胜收啊。山谷，河流，蓊蓊郁郁的山林，无边无际的小路，还有一座高高的

---

wagon
['wægən]
n. (四轮)运货马车

piglet
['piglit]
n. 小猪(尤指乳猪)

guinea
['gini]
n.【鸟】珠鸡

scratch
[skrætʃ]
v. 抓；搔

bound
[baund]
v. bind 的过去式，绑，镶边，装订，约束

blue mountain that simply melts in your mouth.

We **churn** twice a week; and we keep the cream in the spring house which is made of stone with the brook running underneath. Some of the farmers around here have a separator, but we don't care for these new-fashioned ideas. It may be a little harder to take care of cream raised in pans, but it's enough better to pay. We have six calves; and I've chosen the names for all of them.

1. Sylvia, because she was born in the woods.
2. Lesbia, after the Lesbia in Catullus.
3. Sallie.
4. Julia—a spotted, nondescript animal.
5. Judy, after me.
6. Daddy-Long-Legs. You don't mind, do you, Daddy? He's pure Jersey and has a sweet disposition. He looks like this—you can see how appropriate the name is.

churn
[tʃə:n]
v. 用搅乳器搅制（奶油）

青山美得让人说不出话。

我们每周打两次奶油，打好之后把奶油搁置在石头砌成的冷藏室里，冷藏室下面有一条小河潺潺流淌着。邻家的农民有分离器，我们不喜欢这种新鲜玩意儿。我们还是用锅来搅拌，虽然麻烦些，但质量更好，是值得的。我们有六头小牛，而且我给它们都——取了名字：

1. 西尔维亚，因为她出生在林中。

2. 莱斯比亚，根据卡图鲁斯作品中的人物命名的。

3. 莎莉。

4. 朱莉娅，一只花斑的很无聊的动物。

5. 朱蒂，以我的名字命名的。

6. 长腿叔叔。您不会介意我叫它这个名儿吧？这头小牛是纯泽西血统，而且非常可爱。下面是我画的它的样子——您瞧给它取这个名儿是很恰当的：

I haven't had time yet to begin my immortal novel; the farm keeps me too busy.

Yours always,
Judy

PS (1). I've learned to make doughnuts.

PS (2). If you are thinking of raising chickens, let me recommend Buff Orpingtons. They haven't any pinfeathers.

PS (3). I wish I could send you a pat of the nice, fresh butter I churned yesterday. I'm a fine dairymaid!

PS (4). This is a picture of Miss Jerusha Abbott, the future great author, driving home the cows.

Sunday

Dear Daddy-Long-Legs,

Isn't it funny? I started to write to you yesterday afternoon, but as far as I got was the heading, "Dear Daddy-Long-Legs," and then I remembered I'd promised to pick some blackberries for supper, so I went off and left the sheet lying on the table, and when I came back today, what do you think I found sitting in the middle of the page? A real true Daddy-Long-Legs!

I picked him up very gently by one leg, and dropped him out of the window. I wouldn't hurt one of them for the world. They always remind me of you.

immortal
[i'mɔ:tl]
adj. 不朽的,流芳百世的

我还没时间开始我的大作呢,我在农庄就没闲着。

您永远的朱蒂
于洛克威洛农庄
七月十二日

补充:

1. 我学会了做油炸圈饼。

2. 如果您想养鸡,我推荐您养奥尔平顿种,这种鸡腿上不长毛。

3. 昨天我亲自打了奶油,我真想送给您一块儿。而且,我成了一个不错的挤奶姑娘。

4. 下面是未来的大作家——乔茹莎·阿伯特赶牛回家的图。

亲爱的长腿叔叔:

很有趣吧?昨天下午我刚开始给您写信,可刚开始写"亲爱的长腿叔叔",突然想起来我答应采些黑莓当晚餐甜点,然后我便出去了。信笺留在了桌上,等我回来时,您知道发生了什么事吗?我发现一个真正的长腿蜘蛛坐在我的信笺中央!

于是我轻轻地拎起它的一只脚,放到了窗外。我不想伤它,因为我看到它便想到了您。

We hitched up the spring wagon this morning and drove to the Center to church. It's a sweet little white frame church with a spire and three **Doric** columns in front (or maybe Ionic—I always get them mixed).

A nice, sleepy sermon with everybody drowsily waving **palmleaf** fans, and the only sound aside from the minister, the **buzzing** of locusts in the trees outside. I didn't wake up till I found myself on my feet singing the hymn, and then I was awfully sorry I hadn't listened to the sermon; I should like to know more of the psychology of a man who would pick out such a **hymn**. This was it:

Come, leave your sports and earthly toys
And join me in celestial joys.
Or else, dear friend, a long farewell.
I leave you now to sink to hell.

I find that it isn't safe to discuss religion with the Semples. Their god (whom they have inherited **intact** from their remote Puritan ancestors) is a narrow, irrational, unjust, mean, **revengeful**, **bigoted** person. Thank heaven I don't inherit any god from anybody! I am free to make mine up as I wish him. He's kind and sympathetic and imaginative and forgiving and understanding—and he has a sense of humor.

I like the Semples immensely; their practice is so superior to their theory. They are better than their own god. I told them so—and they are horribly troubled. They think I am blasphemous—and I think they are! We've dropped **theology** from our conversation.

This is Sunday afternoon.

Doric
['dɔrik]
adj. 【建】多利安式的

palmleaf
['pɑ:m'li:f]
n. 棕榈叶

buzzing
['bʌziŋ]
n. 嗡嗡叫声

hymn
[him]
n. 赞美诗，圣歌

intact
[in'tækt]
adj. 完整无缺的；原封不动的

revengeful
[ri'vendʒful]
adj. 燃起复仇念头的；报复的

bigoted
['bigətid]
adj. 心胸狭窄的

theology
[θi'ɔlədʒi]
n. 宗教理论，宗教体系

今天早上，我们开着小货车来到了中心教堂。教堂很精致，十分可爱。从外面看，教堂整体是白色的，教堂塔尖也是白色的，还有三根多利安式的柱子矗立在教堂前面（也可能是爱奥尼亚的，我经常混淆这二者）。

牧师的布道声软绵绵的，让人昏昏欲睡。听众们懒洋洋地扇着芭蕉扇。除了牧师的声音，只听见窗外树林中蟋蟀唧唧作响。我一直睡到大家起立唱赞美诗。我忽然觉得没听到布道很内疚，真想知道选择这首赞美诗的人是怎么想的，诗是这样的：

来吧，扔下你世俗的娱乐消遣，
和我享受天国的欢欣快乐。
要不，别了，朋友，
任你沦入地狱受尽苦难。

我发现和申普夫妇讨论宗教很不好。他们信仰的上帝（是他们从他们的祖先清教徒那里继承来的），他们的信仰自私狭隘、不讲理、不公正、卑劣、报复心强而且顽固不化。感谢老天，我的信仰不是从谁那儿遗传下来的，所以我可以自由地创造自己信仰的上帝！他善良、有同情心、想象力丰富、宽容大度、通情达理，而且还有幽默感。

我非常喜欢申普夫妇。他们做得比他们祖先要好，他们胜过了他们的上帝。听我这么一说，他们惊呆了，认为我亵渎上帝，可我觉得是他们亵渎了上帝。所以我们不再讨论信仰了。

现在是星期日的下午。

Amasai (hired man) in a purple tie and some bright yellow buckskin gloves, very red and shaved, has just driven off with Carrie (hired girl) in a big hat trimmed with red roses and a blue muslin dress and her hair curled as tight as it will curl. Amasai spent all the morning washing the **buggy**; and Carrie stayed home from church **ostensibly** to cook the dinner, but really to iron the **muslin** dress.

In two minutes more when this letter is finished I am going to settle down to a book which I found in the attic. It's entitled *On the Trail*, and **sprawled** across the front page in a funny little-boy hand:

Jervis Pendleton
If this book should ever roam,
Box its ears and send it home.

He spent the summer here once after he had been ill, when he was about eleven years old; and he left *On the Trail* behind. It looks well read—the marks of his **grimy** little hands are frequent! Also in a corner of the attic there is a **waterwheel** and a **windmill** and some bows and arrows. Mrs. Semple talks so constantly about him that I begin to believe he really lives—not a grown man with a silk hat and walking stick, but a nice, dirty, tousleheaded boy who **clatters** up the stairs with an awful **racket**, and leaves the screen doors open, and is always asking for cookies. (And getting them, too, if I know Mrs. Semple!) He seems to have been an adventurous little soul—and brave and truthful. I'm sorry to think he is a Pendleton; he was meant for something better.

We're going to begin threshing oats tomorrow; a steam engine is coming and three extra men.

It grieves me to tell you that Buttercup (the spotted cow with one horn, mother of Lesbia) has done a **disgraceful** thing. She got into the orchard Friday evening and ate apples under the trees, and ate and ate until they went to her head. For two days she has been

buggy
['bʌgi]
n.【美】四轮单马轻便马车

ostensibly
[ɔs'tensəbli]
adv. 表面上

muslin
['mʌzlin]
n. 平纹细布,(做床单、枕头套等的)棉布

sprawl
[sprɔ:l]
v. 散乱;杂乱地扩展

grimy
['graimi]
adj. 污秽的

waterwheel
['wɔ:təwi:l]
n. 水车;吊水机

windmill
['windmil]
n. 风车

clatter
['klætə]
v. 发出哗啦声,发出当啷声

racket
['rækit]
n. 球拍

disgraceful
[dis'greisful]
adj. 不名誉的,可耻的,失体面的

阿马萨（男工）和卡莉（女工）刚刚驾马车走了。阿马萨精神抖擞的样子，胡子剃得干干净净，系着紫色领带，戴着鹅黄鹿皮手套。卡莉戴着一顶镶有红玫瑰的大帽子，穿着一身儿蓝裙子，卷得特别小的卷发。阿马萨花了整整一上午洗他那辆小马车，卡莉没去教堂，装作留下来做饭的样子，实际上是要烫她那身儿薄纱裙。

过一会儿等我写完这封信，我就要去埋头读一本书了，这本书是我在小阁楼里找到的，书名叫《在路上》，扉页看起来是一个稚嫩的小男孩的笔迹，上面写的是：

杰维·彭莱顿

如果这本书迷了路，

请揪着它的耳朵，送它回屋。

他十一岁时生了一场病，来这儿疗养了一个夏天，离开时他把这本书落在这里了。看起来他读得挺认真的——到处都是肮脏的小手留下的污迹。小阁楼的一个角落里还有一辆水车、一个风车和一些弹弓。申普太太常常说起他，总让我觉得他还没有长成一位头戴丝帽，手拿手杖的绅士，还只是个稚嫩的、头发乱乱的、浑身脏兮兮的小孩子，他还在楼梯上爬上爬下，从不记得关纱门，还嚷嚷着要小饼干吃（我知道申普太太是很宠他，他一张口准会给他）。他似乎是个喜欢冒险的孩子，勇敢而真诚。可惜他出身彭莱顿家族，他应该可以生在更好的家庭的。

明天我们要收燕麦了，雇了一架蒸汽机，还有三名工人，很快就到了。

很伤心地告诉您那头叫巴特卡普的母牛（就是莱斯比亚的妈妈，它头上只有一只角，花斑母牛）闯祸了。周五傍晚，它跑进果园偷吃苹果树下的苹

perfectly dead drunk! That is the truth I am telling. Did you ever hear anything so **scandalous**?

>Sir,
>I remain,
>Your affectionate orphan,
>Judy Abbott

PS. Indians in the first chapter and **highwaymen** in the second. I hold my breath. What *can* the third contain? "Red Hawk leapt twenty feet in the air and bit the dust." That is the subject of the frontispiece. Aren't Judy and Jervie having fun?

September 15th

Dear Daddy,

I was weighed yesterday on the flour scales in the general store at the Corners. I've gained nine pounds! Let me recommend Lock Willow as a health resort.

>Yours ever,
>Judy

scandalous
['skændələs]
adj. 可耻的，丢脸的；令人愤慨的

果，吃啊吃啊，结果给醉倒了。它烂醉如泥了整整两天！真的，不骗您！您听过这么丢脸的事情吗？

此致

敬礼！

您感情丰富的孤儿
朱蒂·阿伯特
星期日

highwayman
['haiweimən]
n. (旧时道路上)拦路抢劫的强盗，响马

补充：《在路上》这本书第一章讲印第安人，第二章讲路劫。哇喔！第三章讲什么呢？章节介绍写着"印第安人被抛了二十英尺高，然后落地身亡"。杰维和朱蒂看了怎么能不觉得好玩呢？

亲爱的长腿叔叔：

昨天，路过拐角的杂货店，我顺便在他们的面粉秤上量了下体重，胖了九磅！我郑重向您推荐，最佳健康疗养中心——洛克威洛农庄！

您永远的
朱蒂
九月十五日

September 25th

Dear Daddy-Long-Legs,

Behold me—a sophomore! I came up last Friday, sorry to leave Lock Willow, but glad to see the campus again. It is a pleasant sensation to come back to something familiar. I am beginning to feel at home in college, and in command of the situation; I am beginning, in fact, to feel at home in the world—as though I really belonged in it and had not just **crept** in on **sufferance**.

I don't suppose you understand in the least what I am trying to say. A person important enough to be a trustee can't appreciate the feelings of a person unimportant enough to be a foundling.

And now, Daddy, listen to this. Whom do you think I am rooming with? Sallie McBride and Julia Rutledge Pendleton. It's the truth. We have a study and three little bedrooms—*voilà*!

Sallie and I decided last spring that we should like to room together, and Julia made up her mind to stay with Sallie—why, I can't imagine, for they are not a bit alike; but the Pendletons are naturally conservative and **inimical** (fine word!) to change. Anyway, here we are. Think of Jerusha Abbott, late of the John Grier Home for Orphans, rooming with a Pendleton. This is a democratic country.

Sallie is running for class president, and unless all signs fail, she is going to be elected. Such an atmosphere of **intrigue**—you should see what politicians we are! Oh, I tell you, Daddy, when

亲爱的长腿叔叔：

转眼间，我已经是大二的学生了！上星期五离开洛克威洛返的校。虽然很不愿意离开，不过很高兴又开学了，回到熟悉的地方感觉真好。我逐渐习惯了大学生活，所有事情基本上能自理了，我逐渐适应这个社会了——感觉我不是被人勉强收留的，而是真正的社会成员了。

我想您可能根本不能理解我说的话，可一位当理事的大人物怎么可能理解一个没人要的孤儿的想法呢？

叔叔，您听听。您猜猜我跟谁同屋？莎莉·麦克白与朱莉娅·彭莱顿。是真的！我们宿舍有三个卧室和一间书房！请看下图：

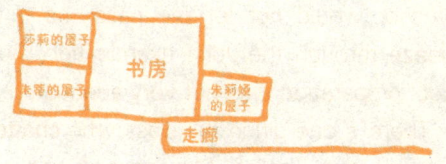

从去年春天开始，莎莉跟我就决定住一起，不知道怎么回事儿，朱莉娅又想跟莎莉住。我简直猜不出来为什么，她们俩一点共同之处都没有。也许彭莱顿家族的人生性保守，好与人为敌（好词儿！）。总之，我们仨住到了一起。想想，约翰·格里尔孤儿院的孤儿，乔茹莎·阿伯特和显赫的彭莱顿家族成员住在一起。真是个民主国家啊！

莎莉要竞选班委，除非一切信号都是假象，否则她当选是没问题的。班上的气氛就说明了这点——瞧瞧，我们简直像一个个政治家！噢！忘了

---

creep
[kri:p]
v. 蹑手蹑足地走；缓慢地行进

sufferance
[ˈsʌfərəns]
n. 忍受，忍耐；忍耐力

inimical
[iˈnimikl]
adj. 敌意的，不友好的

intrigue
[inˈtri:g]
n. 阴谋，诡计；密谋

we women get our rights, you men will have to look alive in order to keep yours. Election comes next Saturday, and we're going to have a torchlight **procession** in the evening, no matter who wins.

I am beginning chemistry, a most unusual study. I've never seen anything like it before. **Molecules** and atoms are the material employed, but I'll be in a position to discuss them more definitely next month.

I am also taking **argumentation** and logic.

Also history of the whole world.

Also plays of William Shakespeare.

Also French.

If this keeps up many years longer, I shall become quite intelligent.

I should rather have elected economics than French, but I didn't dare, because I was afraid that unless I reelected French, the professor would not let me pass—as it was, I just managed to **squeeze** through the June examination. But I will say that my high-school preparation was not very adequate.

There's one girl in the class who **chatters** away in French as fast as she does in English. She went abroad with her parents when she was a child, and spent three years in a convent school. You can imagine how bright she is compared with the rest of us—irregular verbs are mere playthings. I wish my parents had chucked me into a French convent when I was little instead of a foundling asylum. Oh, no, I don't either! Because then maybe I should never have known you. I'd rather know you than French.

Good-bye, Daddy. I must call on Harriet Martin now, and, having discussed the chemical situation, casually drop a few thoughts on the subject of our next president.

Yours in politics,
J. Abbott

procession
[prə'seʃən]
n. 游行

molecules
['mɔlikju:l]
n. 分子

argumentation
[,ɑ:gjumen'teiʃən]
n. 立论

说，叔叔，我们妇女争取到权利的时候，男人们最好加倍小心！下星期六就投票，不管谁当选，晚上都会举行火炬游行。

我开始学化学，非同寻常的科目。以前从没有听说过还有这个学科。现在已经学到分子和原子，下个月我就可以跟您谈更多的东西了。

我们也上了辩论课，逻辑课。

还有世界史。

还有莎士比亚戏剧。

还有法文。

像这样再过几年，我会越学越聪明的。

不过，我更喜欢选经济学，而不是法文。不过我不敢选经济学，因为我要是不继续学法文，到时候教授可能不会让我通过，六月份的考试我才勉强通过，主要是我高中的基础太差了。

squeeze
[skwi:z]
v. 勉强得到

chatter
['tʃætə]
v. 喋喋不休，唠叨

班上有个女孩儿法文说得跟英文一样流利。小时候她随父母出国在修道院学校学过三年。您可以想象她比其余同学多占优势，讲那些不规则动词对她来说简直就是小菜一碟，像玩儿游戏。我多么希望小时候父母把我扔到法国修道院而不是什么孤儿院。唉，不是，我不是这个意思。如果真是那样，我又怎么可能认识您呢？我不会法语没关系，我倒宁愿认识您。

晚安，叔叔，我现在要去拜访哈莉特·马丁了，跟她讨论一下化学反应的问题，顺便再谈谈我对下一届班长的看法。

您积极参政的
J·阿伯特
九月二十五日

October 17th

Dear Daddy-Long-Legs,

Supposing the swimming tank in the gymnasium were filled full of lemon jelly, could a person trying to swim manage to keep on top or would he sink?

We were having lemon jelly for dessert, when the question came up. We discussed it heatedly for half an hour and it's still unsettled. Sallie thinks that she could swim in it, but I am perfectly sure that the best swimmer in the world would sink. Wouldn't it be funny to be drowned in lemon jelly?

Two other problems are engaging the attention of our table.

1st. What shape are the rooms in an **octagon** house? Some of the girls insist that they're square; but I think they'd have to be shaped like a piece of pie. Don't you?

2d. Suppose there were a great big hollow sphere made of looking glass and you were sitting inside. Where would it stop reflecting your face and begin reflecting your back? The more one thinks about this problem, the more puzzling it becomes. You can see with what deep **philosophical** reflection we engage our leisure!

亲爱的长腿叔叔：

假如体育馆的游泳池里面都装满了柠檬果子冻，一个人是上浮还是下沉？

晚餐后我们吃柠檬果子冻的时候，有人就提出这个问题。我们争论了半个小时，很激烈，最后还是没有结论。莎莉认为她可以在里面游，我却认为即使是世界最棒的游泳好手也会沉下去的。能死在柠檬果子冻里不也很好玩吗？

我们还讨论了一系列问题：

第一，八角形房子的房间是什么形状的？有同学坚持说房间是方形的，我想那些房间一定像馅饼，您觉得呢？

第二，如果坐在一个四周全是镜子的巨大空心球里，镜子搁在哪儿才不照脸而照背？我越想越想不明白。您看我们业余时间都讨论多么深奥的哲学问题！

octagon
['ɔktəgən]
n. 八边形；八角形

philosophical
[,filə'sɔfikəl]
adj. 哲学的

Did I ever tell you about the election? It happened three weeks ago, but so fast do we live, that three weeks is ancient history. Sallie was elected, and we had a torchlight parade with transparencies saying "McBride Forever!" and a band consisting of fourteen pieces (three mouth organs and eleven combs).

We're very important persons now in "258." Julia and I come in for a great deal of reflected glory. It's quite a social **strain** to be living in the same house with a president.

Bonne nuit, *cher* Daddy.

> *Acceptez mes compliments,*
> *Très respectueux.*
> *Je suis,*
> *Votre* Judy.

November 12th

Dear Daddy-Long-Legs,

We beat the freshmen at basketball yesterday. Of course we're pleased—but, oh, if we could only beat the juniors! I'd be willing to be black and blue all over and stay in bed a week in a witch-hazel compress.

Sallie has invited me to spend the Christmas vacation with her. She lives in Worcester, Massachusetts. Wasn't it nice of her? I shall love to go. I've never been in a private family in my life, except at Lock Willow, and the Semples were grown-up and old and don't count. But the McBrides have a houseful of children (anyway two or three) and a mother and father and grandmother, and an Angora cat. It's a perfectly complete family! Packing your trunk and going away *is* more fun than staying behind. I'm terribly excited at the prospect.

Seventh hour—I must run to **rehearsal**. I'm to be in the Thanksgiving theatricals. A prince in a tower with a velvet tunic and

我跟您提过选举的事儿吗？三周前就选完了，不过时间过得真快，三个星期前发生的事情好像已经是很久远的历史了一样。莎莉当选了，我们当晚打着"麦克白万岁！"的标语展开火炬游行，随行的是由十四个人组成的乐队（三把真口琴和十一把梳子假扮口琴当乐器）。

现在，我们258室完全成了焦点，朱莉娅和我也跟着沾了不少光，不过跟领袖同住一个屋也有相当的社会压力哦。

晚安，亲爱的叔叔。

我是您的

朱蒂

十月十七日

strain
[strein]
n. 负担，沉重压力

亲爱的长腿叔叔：

昨天与大一的篮球赛我们赢了。当然，我们很开心咯。噢！要是能打赢三年级就好了，即使打得浑身青一块紫一块，扎上绷带，在医院躺上一周，我们也心甘情愿。

莎莉邀请我去她家过圣诞假。她家在麻省的沃塞斯特。她真好，不是吗？我很想去。除了洛克威洛农庄，我从没去过别人家，而且申普家只有大人和老人，那不算。然而，麦克白家有一屋子小孩儿，还有妈妈、爸爸和祖母，还有一只安哥拉猫。她家才是一个完完整整的家庭！一想起来就激动不已！

就要下第七节课了，我得赶紧去排练感恩节的演出。我演的是一位王子，身穿天鹅绒上衣，一头

rehearsal
[ri'hə:səl]
n. 排练，试演；练习

yellow curls. Isn't that a lark?

> Yours,
> J. A.

> *Saturday*

Do you want to know what I look like? Here's a photograph of all three that Leonora Fenton took.

The light one who is laughing is Sallie, and the tall one with her nose in the air is Julia, and the little one with the hair blowing across her face is Judy—she is really more beautiful than that, but the sun was in her eyes.

> "Stone Gate,"
> Worcester, Mass.,
> *December 31st*

Dear Daddy-Long-Legs,

I meant to write to you before and thank you for your Christmas check, but life in the McBride household is very absorbing, and I don't seem able to find two **consecutive** minutes to spend at a desk.

I bought a new gown—one that I didn't need, but just wanted. My Christmas present this year is from Daddy-Long-Legs; my family just sent love.

I've been having the most beautiful vacation visiting Sallie. She lives in a big old-fashioned brick house with white **trimmings** set back from the street—exactly the kind of house that I used to look at so curiously when I was in the John Grier Home, and wonder what it could be like inside. I never expected to see with my own eyes—but here I am! Everything is so comfortable and restful and homelike; I walk from room to room and drink in the **furnishings**.

It is the most perfect house for children to be brought up in; with shadowy **nooks** for hide and seek, and open fireplaces for

金黄色卷发,住在城堡里,多有趣!

您的
J.A.
十一月十二日

您想知道我长得什么样吗?这次附上我们三人的合照吧,是里奥诺拉·芬顿帮拍的。

笑容满面的是莎莉,目空一切的高个子是朱莉娅。头发被风吹到脸上的矮个子是朱蒂。实际上朱蒂比照片上要长得漂亮,主要是太阳刺得她眼睛睁不开。

星期六

亲爱的长腿叔叔:

早想给您写信了,谢谢您圣诞节给我寄的支票。我在麦克白家过得太充实了,几乎就没有闲暇时间坐下来写信。

我买了一件新衣服,不是必须要买的,是我想要。今年的圣诞礼物是长腿叔叔寄来的,家人送来了爱。

我在莎莉家度过了最快乐的一个假期。她家住在一栋宽敞的旧式砖房里,整个看是白色的,背靠着街道——那是我在约翰·格里尔孤儿院时常常远望时看到的房子,经常很好奇住在里面是什么感觉,我从来不敢奢望能亲眼见到——可我现在真的要住进去了啊!一切都那么舒适、宁静、自在。我来回逛游每个房间,醉心于她家的每一处布置。

这样的家最适合养孩子了。有阴暗角落可以捉迷藏,有壁炉可以爆爆米花,下雨的时候可以在阁

---

consecutive
[kən'sekjutiv]
adj. 连续不断的

trimming
['trimiŋ]
n. (常复数)饰物;装饰品

furnishing
['fə:niʃiŋ]
n. (常用复)家具;室内陈设

nook
[nuk]
n. 角落

popcorn, and an attic to romp in on rainy days, and slippery **banisters** with a comfortable flat knob at the bottom, and a great big sunny kitchen, and a nice, fat, sunny cook, who has lived in the family thirteen years and always saves out a piece of dough for the children to bake. Just the sight of such a house makes you want to be a child all over again.

And as for families! I never dreamed they could be so nice. Sallie has a father and mother and grandmother, and the sweetest three-year-old baby sister all over curls, and a medium-sized brother who always forgets to wipe his feet, and a big, good-looking brother named Jimmie, who is a junior at Princeton.

We have the jolliest times at the table—everybody laughs and jokes and talks at once, and we don't have to say **grace** beforehand. It's a relief not having to thank somebody for every mouthful you eat. (I dare say I'm blasphemous; but you'd be, too, if you'd offered as much **obligatory** thanks as I have.)

Such a lot of things we've done—I can't begin to tell you about them. Mr. McBride owns a factory, and Christmas eve he had a tree for the employees' children. It was in the long packing room, which was decorated with evergreens and holly. Jimmie McBride was dressed as Santa Claus, and Sallie and I helped him distribute the presents.

Dear me, Daddy, but it was a funny sensation! I felt as benevolent as a trustee of the John Grier Home. I kissed one sweet, sticky little boy—but I don't think I patted any of them on the head!

And two days after Christmas, they gave a dance at their own house for me.

It was the first really true ball I ever attended—college doesn't count where we dance with girls. I had a new white evening gown (your Christmas present—many thanks) and long white gloves and white satin slippers. The only drawback to my perfect, utter, absolute happiness was the fact that Mrs. Lippett couldn't see me

banister
['bænistə]
n.（常复数）栏杆

楼上玩耍。楼梯扶手滑滑的，下端还有个舒适平坦的扶手。厨房宽敞明亮，还有一个胖胖的、性格开朗的好厨师，他在麦克白家已经有十三年了，经常留一小块儿面包卷让孩子们烤着玩。看到这样的情景，真想回到童年啊！

我做梦都没想到他们家的人会那么友好！莎莉有爸爸、妈妈，祖母，一个三岁的小妹妹，满头卷发，可爱至极。还有一个不大不小的弟弟，进门总忘记擦脚。还有一个高大英俊的哥哥叫吉米，在普林斯顿大学念大三。

吃饭的时候是最开心的——每个人都有说有笑。饭前也不用祈祷，也不用为吃到嘴里的每口饭感恩，真是太放松了。（我的确对上帝不够恭敬，您若是像我一样总要对一切千恩万谢，想必也会受不了的。）

grace
[greis]
n. 恩惠，善意

obligatory
[ɔ'bligətəri]
adj. 义不容辞的；有义务的

我们做了很多事情，都不知道该从哪儿说起。麦克白先生有一家工厂，圣诞夜前夕，他为员工的孩子们准备了一棵圣诞树。放在了一个装饰着漂亮的常青树和冬青的包装工房里。吉米扮成圣诞老人，莎莉跟我帮他分发圣诞礼物。

叔叔啊，真是太好玩儿了！我觉得自己像约翰·格里尔孤儿院的理事一样仁慈。我亲吻了一个个可爱的小男孩——不过，我没有拍他们的脑袋！

圣诞节之后的第二天，他们在家里专门为我举行了一场舞会。

这是我第一次参加的真正的舞会——大学的舞会不算，只能和女生跳舞。我穿了一件崭新的白色晚礼服（您送的圣诞礼物——非常感谢！），戴着白色的长手套，还穿了一双可爱的白鞋，我真得太幸福了！我完全沉醉在那幸福的温暖中！唯一遗憾的只是利皮特太太没有看到我还跟吉米·麦克白领跳

leading the **cotillion** with Jimmie McBride. Tell her about it, please, the next time you visit the J. G. H.

> Yours ever,
> Judy Abbott

PS. Would you be terribly displeased, Daddy, if I didn't turn out to be a great author after all, but just a plain girl?

6:30, Saturday

Dear Daddy,

We started to walk to town today, but mercy! how it poured. I like winter to be winter with snow instead of rain.

Julia's desirable uncle called again this afternoon—and brought a five-pound box of chocolates. There are advantages you see about rooming with Julia.

Our innocent **prattle** appeared to amuse him and he waited over a train in order to take tea in the study. And an awful lot of trouble we had getting permission. It's hard enough entertaining fathers and grandfathers, but uncles are a step worse; and as for brothers and cousins, they are next to impossible. Julia had to swear that he was her uncle before a notary public and then have the county clerk's **certificate** attached. (Don't I know a lot of law?) And even then I doubt if we could have had our tea if the dean had chanced to see how youngish and good-looking Uncle Jervis is.

Anyway, we had it, with brown bread Swiss cheese sandwiches. He helped make them and then ate four. I told him that I had spent last summer at Lock Willow, and we had a beautiful gossipy time about the Semples, and the horses and cows and

了交谊舞。拜托您下次去约翰·格里尔孤儿院时，告诉她一下。

您永远的
朱蒂·阿伯特
"芝麻开门"
麻省，沃塞斯特
十二月三十日

补充：叔叔，我要是成不了大作家，而只是一个普通的女孩子，您会不会很失望呢？

亲爱的叔叔：

我们今天步行去城里，路上遇到了大雨！可怜啊！我更喜欢冬天像冬天的样子，该下雪而不是下大雨！

朱莉娅可爱的叔叔今天下午又来了——还带来了一盒五磅重的巧克力。您瞧，跟朱莉娅同屋还是有好处的。

他似乎挺喜欢跟我们闲聊，还故意错过一班火车，为的是和我们在书房喝茶聊天。为了得到许可，我们可是费了九牛二虎之力。爸爸或祖父来访就很难，更不用说叔叔了，至于兄弟表亲几乎是不可能。朱莉娅必须在公证人面前发誓他是她叔叔，然后才能给她开公证处的证明（我还是懂点法律的吧？）虽然如此，我还是怀疑要是监管看到杰维叔叔那么年轻帅气，我们喝不喝得成茶还是个问题。

不管怎么说，我们还是喝了茶，还吃了黑面包和瑞士奶酪做的三明治。是杰维叔叔帮我们做的三明治，他自己吃了四块儿。我告诉他去年夏天我是在洛克威洛农庄度过的。聊到申普夫妇、小马还有

---

cotillion
[kə'tiljən]
n. 方舞；方舞舞曲

prattle
['prætl]
n. 无聊话；咿咿呀呀声

certificate
[sə'tifikit]
n. 证明书；执照

chickens. All the horses that he used to know are dead, except Grover, who was a baby colt at the time of his last visit—and poor Grove now is so old he can just **limp** about the **pasture**.

He asked if they still kept doughnuts in a yellow crock with a blue plate over it on the bottom shelf of the pantry—and they do! He wanted to know if there was still a woodchuck's hole under the pile of rocks in the night pasture—and there is! Amasai caught a big, fat, gray one there this summer, the twenty-fifth great-grandson of the one Master Jervie caught when he was a little boy.

I called him "Master Jervie" to his face, but he didn't appear to be insulted. Julia says that she has never seen him so **amiable**: he's usually pretty unapproachable. But Julia hasn't a bit of tact; and men, I find, require a great deal. They purr if you rub them the right way and spit if you don't. (That isn't a very elegant metaphor. I mean it figuratively.)

We're reading Marie Bashkirtseff's journal. Isn't it amazing? Listen to this: "Last night I was seized by a fit of despair that found **utterance** in **moans**, and that finally drove me to throw the dining room clock into the sea."

It makes me almost hope I'm not a genius; they must be very wearing to have about—and awfully **destructive** to the furniture.

Mercy! how it keeps pouring. We shall have to swim to chapel tonight.

Yours ever,
Judy

limp
[limp]
v. 缓慢费力地前进

pasture
['pɑ:stʃə]
n. 牧草地,放牧场

amiable
['eimjəbl]
adj. 和蔼可亲的;厚道的

utterance
['ʌtərəns]
n. 说话方式;语调

moan
[məun]
n. 呻吟声;呜咽声

destructive
[dis'trʌktiv]
adj. 破坏的;毁灭性的

牛跟小鸡,开心极了。除了格洛弗,他知道的牛都已经死了。他上一次去的时候格洛弗还是只小牛呢,现在已经很老了。

他问我们有没有把油炸圈饼放在黄色的罐里,然后用蓝色的盘子盖上,最后放在橱柜底部。没错!他还问我,在夜间,是不是牧场上的一堆石头下有个土拨鼠洞——还真的有哎!今年夏天,阿马萨抓到了一只又大又肥的灰色土拨鼠,估计是杰维少爷小时候抓到那只的第二十五代孙子。

我管他叫"杰维少爷",他一点也不在乎。朱莉娅说她从没见他叔叔这么友好过,一般是很难以亲近他的。我想是朱莉娅不懂技巧。我发现跟男士相处一定要动脑筋,要顺毛摸,否则就该咬人了(我只是打个形象的比喻)。

我们正在看玛丽·巴斯格谢夫的日记,写得真棒!看看这句:"昨晚,绝望慢慢吞噬着我的心,我发出痛苦的呻吟,可我无法控制自己,冲向餐厅将挂钟扔到了大海里。"

我希望自己不要成为一个天才。天才一定很讨厌,他们只会破坏家具。

可怜啊!怎么大雨就下个不停了!今晚我们恐怕要游到教堂去了。

您永远的
朱蒂
星期六六点半

Jan. 20th

Dear Daddy-Long-Legs,

Did you ever have a sweet baby girl who was stolen from the **cradle** in infancy?

Maybe I am she! If we were in a novel, that would be the denouement, wouldn't it?

It's really awfully queer not to know what one is—sort of exciting and romantic. There are such a lot of possibilities. Maybe I'm not American; lots of people aren't. I may be straight **descended** from the ancient Romans, or I may be a **Viking's** daughter, or I may be the child of a Russian exile and belong by rights in a Siberian prison, or maybe I'm a Gypsy—I think perhaps I am. I have a very wandering spirit, though I haven't as yet had much chance to develop it.

Do you know about that one scandalous blot in my career—the time I ran away from the asylum because they punished me for stealing cookies? It's down in the books free for any trustee to read. But really, Daddy, what could you expect? When you put a hungry little nine-year-old girl in the pantry **scouring** knives, with the cookie jar at her elbow, and go off and leave her alone; and then suddenly pop in again, wouldn't you expect to find her a bit crumby? And then when you **jerk** her by the elbow and box her ears, and make her leave the table when the pudding comes, and tell all the other children that it's because she's a thief, wouldn't you expect her to run away?

I only ran four miles. They caught me and brought me back; and every day for a week I was tied, like a naughty **puppy**, to a **stake** in the backyard while the other children were out at recess.

Oh, dear! There's the chapel bell, and after chapel I have a committee meeting. I'm sorry because I meant to write you a very entertaining letter this time.

Auf Wiedersehen
Cher Daddy
Pax tibi!
Judy

亲爱的长腿叔叔：

您有过一个在襁褓中被人抱走的女儿吗？

也许我就是她！要是在小说里，那就可能是这样的结局，不是吗？

对自己的身世一无所知，真是太奇怪了——不过也让人有点激动，甚至有点浪漫，因为有各种可能性。可能我不是美国人，很多人都不是。可能我的祖先是古罗马人，或许是维京人（译者注：北欧海盗）的女儿，抑或是俄罗斯流放者的孩子，本应关在西伯利亚的监狱里，抑或是吉卜赛人——我想可能是的，因为我喜欢四处游荡，虽然至今还没有什么机会出游。

您知道我以前的记录吗？我从约翰·格里尔孤儿院逃跑过，因为我偷饼干吃，他们要处罚我。这个是有记录的，任何理事都可以自由地翻阅。不过，叔叔，你想，您把一个饥饿的小女孩放在餐室，旁边搁着一罐饼干，然后留下她一个人就离开了。后来又突然闯进来，当然会发现她嘴角有饼干屑，于是抓着她的胳膊，扇了她两个耳光。到吃饭的时候，蛋糕送上餐桌，可您命令她走开，还告诉所有孩子谁叫她偷吃东西，您想她不想要逃走吗？

可是，我只跑了几里路就被他们抓了回来。整整一个星期，其他的孩子在外面玩，而我像一只不听话的小狗一样被拴在后院的柱子上不许出去。

天啦！教堂的钟响了！一会儿我要去开会。很抱歉，本来今天打算写一封有趣的信给您的。

再见，亲爱的叔叔！

朱蒂
一月二十日

---

cradle
['kreidl]
n. 婴儿时期

descend
[di'send]
v. 下来；落下

viking
['vaikiŋ]
n.【史】北欧海盗

scour
['skauə]
v. 急速穿过；走遍（某地）搜索

jerk
[dʒə:k]
v. 把⋯猛地一拉

puppy
['pʌpi]
n. 小狗，幼犬

stake
[steik]
n. 桩,标桩;棍子,棒

PS. There's one thing I'm perfectly sure of. I'm not a Chinaman.

February 4th

Dear Daddy-Long-Legs,

Jimmie McBride has sent me a Princeton **banner** as big as one end of the room; I am very grateful to him for remembering me, but I don't know what on earth to do with it. Sallie and Julia won't let me hang it up; our room this year is furnished in red, and you can imagine what an effect we'd have if I added orange and black. But it's such a nice, warm, thick felt, I hate to waste it. Would it be very improper to have it made into a **bathrobe**? My old one **shrank** when it was washed.

I've entirely **omitted** of late telling you what I am learning, but though you might not imagine it from my letters, my time is exclusively occupied with study. It's a very bewildering matter to get educated in five branches at once.

"The test of true scholarship," says chemistry professor, "is a **painstaking** passion for detail."

另：有一点我很肯定，我不是中国人。

亲爱的长腿叔叔：

吉米送给我一面普林斯顿的校旗，有我房间的墙壁那么大。我很感谢他还记得我，可我不知道怎么处置这面旗子。莎莉和朱莉娅不同意我挂在墙上。今年我们的房间主色调是红色，如果我再挂上橙色和黑色的旗子，您可以想象效果会怎样。旗子是用暖和厚实的毯子做的，我讨厌浪费。做成浴袍不至于太难看吧，正好我的那件缩水穿不了了。

banner
[ˈbænə]
n. 旗帜

bathrobe
[ˈbɑːθrəub]
n.【美】浴衣

shrank
[ˈʃræŋk]
v. shrink 的过去式，缩水

六点

早起的鸟儿有食吃

对了，最近我基本上没谈我的功课。虽然没写在信里，其实我大部分时间都放在了功课上。同时学习五门功课，相当晕头。

化学老师会说："真正的学者重视每一个细节。"

omit
[əuˈmit]
v. 忽略不做；忘记

painstaking
[ˈpeinsteikiŋ]
adj. 十分小心的；仔细的；煞费苦心的

"Be careful not to keep your eyes **glued** to detail," says history professor. "Stand far enough away to get a perspective on the whole."

You can see with what nicety we have to trim our sails between chemistry and history. I like the historical method best. If I say that William the Conqueror came over in 1492, and Columbus discovered America in 1100 or 1066 or whenever it was, that's a mere detail that the professor overlooks. It gives a feeling of security and **restfulness** to the history recitation that is entirely lacking in chemistry.

Sixth-hour bell—I must go to the laboratory and look into a little matter of **acids** and salts and alkalies. I've burned a hole as big as a plate in the front of my chemistry apron, with **hydrochloric** acid. If the theory worked, I ought to be able to **neutralize** that hole with good strong **ammonia**, oughtn't I?

Examinations next week, but who's afraid?

Yours ever,
Judy

March 5th

Dear Daddy-Long-Legs,

There is a March wind blowing, and the sky is filled with heavy, black moving clouds. The crows in the pine trees are making such a **clamor**! It's an **intoxicating**, **exhilarating**, calling noise. You want to close your books and be off over the hills to race with the wind.

We had a paper chase last Saturday over five miles of **squashy** 'cross country. The fox (composed of three girls and a bushel or so of confetti) started half an hour before the twenty-seven hunters. I was one of the twenty-seven; eight dropped by the wayside; we ended nineteen. The trail led over a hill, through a cornfield, and into a **swamp** where we had to leap lightly from hummock to hummock. Of course half of us went in ankle deep. We kept losing the trail, and

glue
[glu:]
v. 紧附,似用胶固定

restfulness
['restfulnis]
n. 安闲,悠闲;安静,宁静

acid
['æsid]
n.【化】酸

hydrochloric
[,haidrəu'klɔ:rik]
adj.【化】氯化氢的

neutralize
['nju:trəlaiz]
v.【化】【电】使中和

ammonia
[ə'məunjə]
n.【化】氨,阿摩尼亚;氨水

clamor
['klæmə]
n. 吵闹声,喧嚣声;噪声

intoxicating
[in'tɔksikeitiŋ]
adj. 使醉的

exhilarating
[ig'ziləreitiŋ]
adj. 令人振奋的;使人高兴的

squashy
['skwɔʃi]
adj. 泥泞的

swamp
[swɔmp]
n. 沼泽;沼泽地

历史教授却说:"不要过分注重细节,高瞻远瞩才能从整体上把握事物的规律。"

您看,就化学课和历史课,需要我们多么细心认真地进行思维转换啊!比较而言,我更喜欢历史。威廉一世于1492年征服英国,哥伦布在1100或1066年或者哪年发现美洲大陆,历史教授完全不计较这些细节,所以上历史课轻松快乐,化学课可完全不同。

该上第六节课了——我得去实验室做酸、盐和碱的实验了。我的围裙在做化学实验的时候被盐酸烧了个大洞。从理论上讲,我可以加强氨中和那个洞,对吧?

下星期考试,我可不怕!

您永远的朱蒂
二月四日

亲爱的长腿叔叔:

三月,春风吹拂,天空层层乌云飘动,松树上乌鸦啼叫,多让人心醉!像是在召唤着我。真想合上书本,跑到山顶去追云逐风啊!

上周六,我们在湿乎乎的野外玩游戏,整整追跑了五英里。三个女孩扮狐狸,带着一盒彩色碎纸,二十七名猎人在半个小时后出发。我扮的是猎人,途中有八名猎人掉队了,只剩下我们十九个猎人紧追不舍。我们沿纸屑跟着翻山,越过玉米地,然后进入沼泽地。沼泽地有很多泥潭,我们只得轻轻地从一块干地跳到另一块干地。在这里,多半人都踩入了齐脚踝的泥潭。狐狸们常常失去踪迹,我

wasted twenty-five minutes over that swamp. Then up a hill through some woods and in at a **barn** window! The barn doors were all locked and the window was up high and pretty small. I don't call that fair, do you?

But we didn't go through; we **circumnavigated** the barn and picked up the trail where it issued by way of a low shed roof onto the top of a fence. The fox thought he had us there, but we fooled him. Then straight away over two miles of rolling meadow, and awfully hard to follow, for the **confetti** was getting **sparse**. The rule is that it must be at the most six feet apart, but they were the longest six feet I ever saw. Finally, after two hours of steady **trotting**, we tracked Monsieur Fox into the kitchen of Crystal Spring (that's a farm where the girls go in bobsleds and hay wagons for chicken and waffle suppers) and we found the three foxes **placidly** eating milk and honey and biscuits. They hadn't thought we would get that far; they were expecting us to stick in the barn window.

Both sides insist that they won. I think we did, don't you? Because we caught them before they got back to the campus. Anyway, all nineteen of us settled like locusts over the furniture and clamored for honey. There wasn't enough to go round, but Mrs. Crystal Spring (that's our pet name for her; she's by rights a Johnson) brought up a jar of strawberry jam and a can of maple **syrup**—just made last week—and three loaves of brown bread.

We didn't get back to college till half-past six—half an hour late for dinner—and we went straight in without dressing, and with perfectly **unimpaired** appetites! Then we all cut evening chapel, the state of our boots being enough of an excuse.

I never told you about examinations. I passed everything with the utmost ease—I know the secret now, and am never going to flunk again. I shan't be able to graduate with honors though, because of that beastly Latin prose and geometry freshman year. But I don't care. Wot's the hodds so long as you're 'appy? (That's a quotation. I've been reading the English classics.)

barn
[bɑ:n]
n. 谷仓，粮仓

circumnavigate
[,sə:kəm'nævigeit]
v. 绕一周；环航

confetti
[kən'feti(:)]
n. 五彩碎纸

sparse
[spɑ:s]
adj. 稀疏的；稀少的

trot
[trɔt]
v.（人）慢跑，急行

placidly
['plæsidli]
adv. 平静地；满足地

syrup
['sirəp]
n. 糖浆；果汁

unimpaired
['ʌnim'pɛəd]
adj. 未受损伤的；未削弱的

们费了二十五分钟才过了沼泽。然后接着翻山越岭，最后到达了一个仓库！可仓库门上了锁，窗户又高又小，她们真要赖，不是吗？

我们并没有爬窗户，而是绕着仓库，在后边找到了一些纸屑。于是我们爬过一个低矮的小棚，翻过一道篱笆。狐狸以为能在这里能骗倒我们，但是他们未能得逞。接下来，我们径直穿过绵延两英里的草地，纸屑越来越少，追踪越来越困难。原定两堆纸屑的距离不得超过六英尺，可他们的六英尺也太长了吧！我们整整追踪了两个小时，终于在水晶泉的厨房里追到了狐狸们（水晶泉是个农场，姑娘们通常是滑连橇或者坐运草车到那里去吃晚餐，一边吃鸡，一边闲聊）。到了之后，我们发现那三只狐狸正在安静地喝着牛奶，吃着蜂蜜和饼干，她们以为我们被挡在仓库了呢！

最后双方都认为自己赢了，我觉得是我们赢，您说呢？她们还没有回学校就被我们抓到了。我们十九个人全部坐下来，像蝗虫一样吵着嚷着要吃蜂蜜。蜂蜜不够了，水晶泉太太（这是我们对她的昵称，她本名叫约翰逊）拿出上星期刚做的一罐草莓酱和一罐糖浆，还有三块黑面包。

我们一直玩到六点半才回学校。晚饭已过了半小时，我们没换衣服就直奔餐厅，胃口丝毫没减！晚上的礼拜大家都请假了，理由很充分，我们的靴子都沾满了泥。

我从没跟您提过考试的事，其实我每科都轻松通过了——因为我现在知道了窍门，再也不会挂科了。虽然如此，我也不能以优异的成绩毕业了，因为大一可恶的拉丁文和几何学挂过。不过我也不在乎。"只要心情好，不会不开心。"（这句是从书上摘的，我正在读英国文学的经典。）

Speaking of classics, have you ever read *Hamlet*? If you haven't, do it right off. It's perfectly **corking**. I've been hearing about Shakespeare all my life, but I had no idea he really wrote so well; I always suspected him of going largely on his reputation.

I have a beautiful play that I invented a long time ago when I first learned to read. I put myself to sleep every night by pretending I'm the person (the most important person) in the book I'm reading at the moment.

At present I'm Ophelia—and such a sensible Ophelia! I keep Hamlet amused all the time, and pet him and scold him and make him wrap up his throat when he has a cold. I've entirely cured him of being **melancholy**. The King and Queen are both dead—an accident at sea; no funeral necessary—so Hamlet and I are ruling in Denmark without any bother. We have the kingdom working beautifully. He takes care of the governing, and I look after the charities. I have just founded some first-class orphan asylums. If you or any of the other Trustees would like to visit them, I shall be pleased to show you through. I think you might find a great many helpful suggestions.

I remain, sir,

Yours most graciously,
Ophelia,
Queen of Denmark.

March 24th
maybe the 25th

Dear Daddy-Long-Legs,

I don't believe I can be going to Heaven—I am getting such a lot of good things here; it wouldn't be fair to get them hereafter, too. Listen to what has happened.

Jerusha Abbott has won the short-story contest (a twenty-five dollar prize) that the *Monthly* holds every year. And she a

corking
['kɔ:kiŋ]
adj.【口】很好的

melancholy
['melənkəli]
n. 忧郁

　　说到经典，您读过《哈姆雷特》吗？要是没有，现在开始读吧！绝对是一部巨著！我早就听说过莎士比亚，但不知道他的文笔是如此精妙，我原来以为他是徒有虚名呢！

　　开始阅读的时候，自己总喜欢玩一种游戏。每晚入睡前，我会把自己想象成正在阅读的书中的人物，最重要的那个人物！

　　今晚我是奥菲莉亚——智慧的奥菲莉亚！我要让哈姆雷特每天都很开心，爱他，引导他。他感冒的时候我要给他戴上围巾，不会让他忧伤。国王跟皇后都会死，葬身大海，连葬礼都省了。我跟哈姆雷特统治丹麦，没有任何阻碍。我们会把国家治理得井井有条。他主持政务，我专门负责公益事业。我成立了很多一流的孤儿院，如果您或其他理事想参观的话，我会很乐意带领你们参观的。我想您会有所启发的。

　　此致
敬礼！

您最充满敬意的
丹麦皇后
奥菲莉亚
三月五日

亲爱的长腿叔叔：

　　我相信我上不了天堂。因为活着的时候，老天太眷顾我，给予我太多了，死后再上天堂就有点过分了。听我跟您讲吧：

　　首先，乔茹莎·阿伯特获得了《月刊》杂志年度短篇小说奖（奖金二十五美元）。参赛的大多数

sophomore! The contestants are mostly seniors. When I saw my name posted, I couldn't quite believe it was true. Maybe I am going to be an author after all. I wish Mrs. Lippett hadn't given me such a silly name—it sounds like an **authoress**, doesn't it?

Also I have been chosen for the spring dramatics—As You Like It out of doors. I am going to be Celia, own cousin to Rosalind.

And lastly: Julia and Sallie and I are going to New York next Friday to do some spring shopping and stay all night and go to the theater the next day with "Master Jervie." He invited us. Julia is going to stay at home with her family, but Sallie and I are going to stop at the Martha Washington Hotel. Did you ever hear of anything so exciting? I've never been in a hotel in my life, nor in a theater; except once when the **Catholic** church had a festival and invited the orphans, but that wasn't a real play and it doesn't count.

And what do you think we're going to see? *Hamlet*. Think of that! We studied it for four weeks in Shakespeare class and I know it by heart.

I am so excited over all these prospects that I can scarcely sleep.

Good-bye, Daddy.
This is a very entertaining world.

Yours ever,
Judy

PS. I've just looked at the calendar. It's the 28th.
Another **postscript**.
I saw a streetcar conductor today with one brown eye and one blue. Wouldn't he make a nice **villain** for a detective story?

April 7th

Dear Daddy-Long-Legs,

Mercy! Isn't New York big? Worcester is nothing to it. Do you

authoress
['ɔːθəris]
n. 女作家；女作者

是四年级学生，而我还是个大二的学生。看到自己榜上有名，简直不敢相信是真的！我还真有可能成为作家呢，真希望利皮特太太没给我取这么傻的名字，一听就像女作家，不是吗？

另外，春天我们要进行露天表演，我被选出演赛丽亚，罗赛林的表妹。

最后，朱莉娅、莎莉还有我，下周五要去纽约采购春装，而且要在那儿住一晚。第二天一大早，"杰维少爷"邀请我们一起去看戏。朱莉娅要回家住一宿，莎莉跟我住玛莎·华盛顿饭店。还有比这让人更激动的事吗？我这辈子从没住过饭店，也从没看过演出，只有一次天主教堂举办活动，邀请孤儿们参加。不过那不是真正的演出，不算。

Catholic
['kæθəlik]
adj. 天主教的

您猜我们要看什么演出呢？《哈姆雷特》！想想，我们在莎剧课上读了四周，已经背得滚瓜烂熟了。

简直太兴奋了！几乎睡不着！

晚安，叔叔。

这世界真的太太太好玩儿了！

您永远的
朱蒂
三月二十四日
也可能是二十五日

postscript
['pəustskript]
n.（信末的）附笔，又及（略作P.S.）

补充：我看了一下日历，是二十八号。

还有：我今天发现一个公共汽车售票员的一只眼睛是褐色的，一只眼睛是蓝色的，是不是很像侦探小说里的坏人？

villain
['vilən]
n.（戏剧、小说中的）反派角色，反面人物

亲爱的长腿叔叔：

天啊！纽约真大啊！沃塞斯特简直不值一提。

mean to tell me that you actually live in all that confusion? I don't believe that I shall recover for months from the bewildering effect of two days of it. I can't begin to tell you all the amazing things I've seen; I suppose you know, though, since you live there yourself.

But aren't the streets entertaining? And the people? And the shops? I never saw such lovely things as there are in the windows. It makes you want to devote your life to wearing clothes.

Sallie and Julia and I went shopping together Saturday morning. Julia went into the very most **gorgeous** place I ever saw, white and gold walls and blue carpets and blue silk curtains and **gilt** chairs. A perfectly beautiful lady with yellow hair and a long black silk trailing gown came to meet us with a welcoming smile. I thought we were paying a social call, and started to shake hands, but it seems we were only buying hats—at least Julia was. She sat down in front of a mirror and tried on a dozen, each lovelier than the last, and bought the two loveliest of all.

I can't imagine any joy in life greater than sitting down in front of a mirror and buying any hat you choose without having first to consider the price! There's no doubt about it, Daddy; New York would rapidly **undermine** this fine, stoical character which the John Grier Home so patiently built up.

And after we'd finished our shopping, we met Master Jervie at Sherry's. I suppose you've been in Sherry's? Picture that, then picture the dining room of the John Grier Home with its **oilcloth-covered** tables, and white **crockery** that you can't break, and wooden-handled knives and forks; and fancy the way I felt!

I ate my fish with the wrong fork, but the waiter very kindly gave me another so that nobody noticed.

And after luncheon we went to the theater—it was dazzling, **marvelous**, unbelievable—I dream about it every night.

Isn't Shakespeare wonderful?

gorgeous
['gɔːdʒəs]
adj.【口】令人十分愉快的,极好的

gilt
[gilt]
adj. 镀金的;金色的

undermine
[ˌʌndəˈmain]
v. 损害

oilcloth-covered
铺上油布的

crockery
[ˈkrɔkəri]
n. (总称)陶器,瓦器

marvelous
[ˈmɑːvələs]
adj. 令人惊叹的;非凡的;不可思议的

　　您不会告诉我你就住在那么喧嚣的大城市吧？我才住了两天就晕头转向了，恐怕几个月都缓不过劲儿来。我不知道怎样向您描述我的所见所闻。不过我想您都知道的，您自个儿就住在大城市。

　　城里的街道真有意思，是吧？还有忙碌的人们？琳琅满目的商店？我从来没见过橱窗里有那么多漂亮的东西，恐怕一辈子也穿不了。

　　莎莉、朱莉娅还有我星期六早上一起去购物。朱莉娅带我们进了我生平认为的最漂亮的商场。墙是白色和金色相间，地毯是蓝色的，窗帘是兰色丝织品，椅子是镀金的。一位极为漂亮身穿黑丝拖地裙的金发小姐微笑着招呼我们。我以为需要打个招呼，于是上去和她握手。不过我们似乎只是要买帽子而已，至少是朱莉娅要买。她在镜子前面坐了下来，试了十几项帽子，一项比一项漂亮，她从中选择了两项最漂亮的。

　　还有什么比坐在镜子前面试穿试戴各种物品，然后根本不用考虑价钱买下任何一样心仪的东西还要更快乐的呢？当然这样是最快乐的了！叔叔，纽约腐蚀了我在约翰·格里尔孤儿院里费心培养的各种美好品质啊！

　　购物之后我们到雪莉饭店与杰维少爷会合。您一定去过雪莉饭店吧？您想想它再想想孤儿院饭厅里面铺着的油布桌子、打不碎的白陶盘子和木把刀叉，您就了解我的感受了。

　　中午吃鱼的时候我拿错了叉子，好心的服务员又给了我另一把，没有人注意到。

　　午餐过后，我们前往剧院。剧院真是令人头晕目眩啊！太伟大了！太神奇了！简直无法相信我就坐在剧院里面——我每晚梦见的地方！

　　莎士比亚简直太伟大了！

Hamlet is so much better on the stage than when we analyze it in class; I appreciated it before, but now, dear me!

I think, if you don't mind, that I'd rather be an actress than a writer. Wouldn't you like me to leave college and go into a dramatic school? And then I'll send you a box for all my performances, and smile at you across the footlights. Only wear a red rose in your **buttonhole**, please, so I'll surely smile at the right man. It would be an awfully embarrassing mistake if I picked out the wrong one.

We came back Saturday night and had our dinner in the train, at little tables with pink lamps and Negro waiters. I never heard of meals being served in trains before, and I **inadvertently** said so.

"Where on earth were you brought up?" said Julia to me.

"In a village," said I, meekly to Julia.

"But didn't you ever travel?" said she to me.

"Not till I came to college, and then it was only a hundred and sixty miles and we didn't eat," said I to her.

She's getting quite interested in me, because I say such funny things. I try hard not to, but they do pop out when I'm surprised—and I'm surprised most of the time. It's a dizzying experience, Daddy, to pass eighteen years in the John Grier Home, and then suddenly to be **plunged** into the WORLD.

But I'm getting **acclimated**. I don't make such awful mistakes as I did; and I don't feel uncomfortable any more with the other girls. I used to **squirm** whenever people looked at me. I felt as though they saw right through my sham new clothes to the checked ginghams underneath. But I'm not letting the ginghams bother me anymore. Sufficient unto yesterday is the evil thereof.

I forgot to tell you about our flowers. Master Jervie gave us each a big bunch of violets and lilies of the valley. Wasn't that sweet of him? I never used to care much for men—judging by Trustees—but I'm changing my mind.

buttonhole
['bʌtnhəul]
n. 纽孔；扣眼

inadvertently
[,inəd'və:təntli]
adv. 不慎地

plunge
[plʌndʒ]
v. 投(入)；跳(入)；冲
acclimate
[ə'klaimit]
v. (使)服水土；(使)适应
squirm
[skwə:m]
v. 局促不安

舞台上的《哈姆雷特》比我们在课堂上讲的要有意思多了，我本来就喜欢这部剧，现在，天啦！

您要是不介意，我想当演员，不当作家了。我转去戏剧学院，好吗？我会在演出时为您预留一个包厢，而且从舞台上冲您微笑的。而您呢，只需在外衣纽孔上别上一朵红玫瑰，这样能确定我笑对人。要是笑错了，那可真太尴尬了。

星期六晚上返校，在火车上吃的晚餐，餐桌上摆着粉红色的台灯，还有一个黑人侍者。我以前从没听过火车上有提供餐点的，我无意中说出来的。

"上帝啊，你到底在哪长大的？"朱莉娅问我。

"一个小村庄。"我轻轻地回答道。

"你就没出门旅行过？"她接着问。

"上大学之前没有，再说只有一百六十英里远，不用吃饭的。"

朱莉娅对我很好奇，因为我说了这么可笑的话。其实我已经很小心，可我一激动就管不住嘴巴，而且我又容易激动。这种感觉真奇妙，在约翰·格里尔孤儿院过了十八年，然后一头扎进这个"世界"，着实让人兴奋。

不过我现在慢慢习惯了，不会像以前总犯错了。而且我跟其他女孩子在一起时，也感觉自在了。以前人家一看我，我就浑身不舒服，总感觉他们能透过我的假冒新衣看到里面的花格布衣似的。再也不让花格布衣烦我，再也不让过去烦我了！

忘了告诉您，还有我们的花。杰维少爷送了我们一人一大把紫罗兰和铃兰。他真好，不是吗？我以前对男人就没有好感，主要是受理事的影响，现在逐渐在改变看法。

127

Eleven pages—this *is* a letter! Have courage. I'm going to stop.

>Yours always,
>Judy

>*April 10th*

Dear Mr. Rich-Man,

Here's your check for fifty dollars. Thank you very much, but I do not feel that I can keep it. My allowance is sufficient to afford all of the hats that I need. I am sorry that I wrote all that silly stuff about the **millinery** shop; it's just that I had never seen anything like it before.

However, I wasn't begging! And I would rather not accept any more charity than I have to.

>Sincerely yours,
>Jerusha Abbott

>*April 11th*

Dearest Daddy,

Will you please forgive me for the letter I wrote you yesterday? After I posted it I was sorry, and tried to get it back, but that beastly mail clerk wouldn't give it to me.

It's the middle of the night now; I've been awake for hours thinking what a worm I am—what a thousand-legged worm—and that's the worst I can say! I've closed the door very softly into the study so as not to wake Julia and Sallie, and am sitting up in bed writing to you on paper torn out of my history notebook.

I just wanted to tell you that I am sorry I was so impolite about your check. I know you meant it kindly, and I think you're an old dear to take so much trouble for such a silly thing as a hat. I ought to have returned it very much more graciously.

写了十一页,太长了。不过别担心,我不写了。

您永远的
朱蒂
四月七日

亲爱的大富翁先生:

随信附上您寄的五十元支票。非常感谢您,不过我想我没有理由要收下。我的零用钱足够买自己所需要的所有帽子了。后悔不该写那么多关于帽店的蠢话,其实,我就是看着好奇罢了。

不管怎样,我并不是向您乞求什么!我也不愿接受您额外的仁慈!

您的
乔茹莎·阿伯特
四月十日

最亲爱的叔叔:

您能原谅我昨天写的那封信吗?信一寄出我就后悔了。本来想取回来,可讨厌的邮差不肯还给我。

现在是半夜了,一直睡不着,觉得自己就是条虫!一条可恶的千脚虫!简直是以小人之心度君子之腹!担心吵醒朱莉娅和莎莉,我轻轻地把通往书房的门关上,从历史笔记本上撕下了一页,坐在床上给您写信。

我只想跟您说,您本来是出于好意给我寄支票,可我却如此无礼,真的很抱歉!我知道您是个好人,连帽子这么小的事情都记在心里,我本应该心存感激把支票退回才是。

millinery
['milinəri]
n. 女帽类

But in any case, I had to return it. It's different with me than with other girls. They can take things naturally from people. They have fathers and brothers and aunts and uncles; but I can't be on any such relations with anyone. I like to pretend that you belong to me, just to play with the idea, but of course I know you don't. I'm alone, really—with my back to the wall fighting the world—and I get sort of **gaspy** when I think about it. I put it out of my mind, and keep on pretending; but don't you see, Daddy? I can't accept any more money than I have to, because some day I shall be wanting to pay it back, and even as great an author as I intend to be won't be able to face a perfectly tremendous debt.

I'd love pretty hats and things, but I mustn't **mortgage** the future to pay for them.

You'll forgive me, won't you, for being so rude? I have an awful habit of writing **impulsively** when I first think things, and then posting the letter beyond recall. But if I sometimes seem thoughtless and ungrateful, I never mean it. In my heart I thank you always for the life and freedom and independence that you have given me. My childhood was just a long, **sullen** stretch of revolt, and now I am so happy every moment of the day that I can't believe it's true. I feel like a made-up heroine in a storybook.

It's a quarter past two. I'm going to tiptoe out to the **mail chute** and get this off now. You'll receive it in the next mail after the other; so you won't have a very long time to think bad of me.

Good night, Daddy,

                              I love you always,
                                        Judy

May 4th

Dear Daddy-Long-Legs,

Field Day last Saturday. It was a very spectacular occasion. First

gaspy
['gɑ:spi]
adj. （因惊讶等）倒抽一口气

mortgage
['mɔ:gidʒ]
v.【口】以…作担保，把…许给

impulsively
[im'pʌlsivli]
adv. 冲动地

sullen
['sʌlən]
adj. 不高兴的;绷着脸的;愠怒的

mail chute
邮筒

可是不管怎么说，我还是应该给您的，我跟其他女孩子不同，她们可以理所当然地接受别人的赠予，因为她们有爸爸、哥哥、姑姑还有叔叔，而我却什么也没有。我想象您是我的家人，当然只是想象而已，我知道您不属于我。我独自在这个世界上面对一切——想起来就郁闷。不过我尽量不想，继续假装。但是，叔叔，您看不出来吗？我不能接受您太多的金钱，总有一天我想是要还的。即使我哪天真的成了大作家，我想我也偿还不了欠下的巨债。

我喜欢那些漂亮帽子还有饰品，但是我不能拿我的未来做抵押啊。

叔叔，您会原谅我的无礼，对吗？我有个坏毛病，心里一有事情就有下笔的冲动，而且也没经思考就寄出去了。可是，我也只是偶尔没心没肺、不知感恩，我真的不是那样想的。我从心底感激您给我的新生活、自由还有独立。我的童年很漫长，很忧郁，所以我内心充满了反抗。可现在，我每时每刻都很快乐，我几乎不敢相信这一切都是真的，我觉得自己简直像小说中的女主人公。

现在已经是凌晨两点一刻了，我准备悄悄溜出去寄信。您在上一封信后不久就会收到这封，这样您不会有太多时间把我想得太坏。

晚安，叔叔。

永远爱您的
朱蒂
四月十一日

亲爱的长腿叔叔：

上星期六开运动会，真是让人兴奋啊。一开

we had a parade of all the classes, with everybody dressed in white linen, the seniors carrying blue and gold Japanese umbrellas, and the juniors white and yellow banners. Our class had **crimson** balloons—very fetching, especially as they were always getting loose and **floating** off—and the freshmen wore green tissuepaper hats with long **streamers**. Also we had a band in blue uniforms hired from town. Also about a dozen funny people, like clowns in a circus, to keep the spectators entertained between events.

Julia was dressed as a fat country man with a **linen** duster and **whiskers** and **baggy** umbrella. Patsy Moriarty (Patricia, really. Did you ever hear such a name? Mrs. Lippett couldn't have done better.), who is tall and thin, was Julia's wife in an absurd green **bonnet** over one ear. Waves of laughter followed them the whole length of the course. Julia played the part extremely well. I never dreamed that a Pendleton could display so much comedy spirit— begging Master Jervie's pardon; I don't consider him a true Pendleton though, any more than I consider you a true Trustee.

Sallie and I weren't in the parade because we were entered for the events. And what do you think? We both won! At least in something. We tried for the running broad jump and lost; but Sallie won the pole vaulting (seven feet three inches) and I won the fifty-yard dash (eight seconds).

I was pretty panting at the end, but it was great fun, with the whole class waving balloons and cheering and yelling:

What's the matter with Judy Abbott?

She's all right.

Who's all right?

Judy Ab-bott!

That, Daddy, is true fame. Then trotting back to the dressing tent and being rubbed down with alcohol and having a lemon to suck. You see we're very professional. It's a fine thing to win an event for your class, because the class that wins the most gets the athletic

始，各班同学身着白色校服列队入场，大四学生撑着蓝色和金色的日本阳伞，大三学生举着白黄相间的旗帜，我们班拿的是鲜红的气球——气球离手飘高的时候更是壮观，大一新生戴着绿色纸巾做的帽子，垂着长长的飘带。另外，从城里请来的一队身穿蓝色制服的乐队，还有十多个滑稽的演员，像马戏团的小丑一样，在比赛期间给观众助兴。

朱莉娅扮成肥胖的乡下人，手捏亚麻鸡毛掸子，粘着胡子，撑着一把袋状的伞。又高又瘦的佩齐·莫莉亚蒂（帕特里卡，真的，您听过这样的名儿吗？利皮特太太都得自叹不如。）扮演朱莉娅的妻子，歪戴着一顶滑稽的绿色无边女帽。她们走到哪儿，哪儿就爆笑。朱莉娅演得非常非常成功。真想不到彭莱顿家的人也这么有幽默感——愿杰维少爷原谅我的不敬，我从没把他当成彭莱顿家族的人，就像我从不认为您是孤儿院理事一样。

莎莉跟我都有比赛项目，所以没有参加开场式。您猜结果怎样？我们都获胜了！至少在某个项目上。我们参加跨栏跑，不过没取得好成绩，不过莎莉撑杆跳获胜了（她跳了七英尺三英寸），我赢得了五十米短跑（跑了八秒）。

最后跑得我喘不过气来，不过挺好玩的，全班同学挥舞着气球替我欢呼着，叫着：

朱蒂·阿伯特棒不棒？

真棒！

谁最棒？

朱蒂·阿伯特！

叔叔，那才叫出名呢。跑完之后回到休息室，她们用酒精替我擦身子，还给了我一块儿柠檬含在嘴里。您瞧我们多专业，是吧？能为班级拿奖是件好事儿，因为奖牌最多的班级可以拿到年度冠军

---

crimson
['krimzn]
adj. 深红色的，绯红的

float
[fləut]
v. 浮

streamer
['stri:mə]
n. 横幅；长旗；幡

linen
['linin]
n. 亚麻布，亚麻线(纱)

whisker
['hwiskə]
n. 连鬓胡子，髯

baggy
['bægi]
adj. 袋状的；宽松而下垂的

bonnet
['bɔnit]
n. (有带子的)女帽

cup for the year. The seniors won it this year, with seven events to their credit. The athletic association gave a dinner in the gymnasium to all of the winners. We had fried soft-shell crabs, and chocolate ice cream **molded** in the shape of basketballs.

Judy Wins the Fifty-Yard Dash

I sat up half of last night reading *Jane Eyre*. Are you old enough, Daddy, to remember sixty years ago? And if so, did people talk that way?

The haughty Lady Blanche says to the footman, "Stop your chattering, **knave**, and do my bidding." Mr. Rochester talks about the metal **welkin** when he means the sky; and as for the mad woman who laughs like a **hyena** and sets fire to bed curtains and tears up wedding veils and bites—it's melodrama of the purest, but just the same, you read and read and read. I can't see how any girl could have written such a book, especially any girl who was brought up in a churchyard. There's something about those Brontës that fascinates me. Their books, their lives, their spirit. Where did they get it? When I was reading about little Jane's troubles in the charity school, I got so angry that I had to go out and take a walk. I understood exactly how she felt. Having known Mrs. Lippett, I could see Mr. Brocklehurst.

Don't be outraged, Daddy. I am not **intimating** that the John Grier Home was like the Lowood institute. We had plenty to eat and plenty to wear, sufficient water to wash in, and a furnace in the

奖。今年的年度冠军是大四班,他们一共赢得七个奖牌。组委会在体育馆宴请所有获奖者,吃的有油炸软壳蟹和做成篮球状的巧克力冰淇淋。

mold
[məuld]
v. 用模子做,铸造

朱蒂赢了
五十米短跑

昨晚熬到大半夜才读完《简·爱》。长腿叔叔,您是不是年龄很大呢?还记得六十年前的事吗?当时人们是那样说话的吗?

傲慢的布兰奇夫人对仆人说"仆人,住嘴!照我说的去做!"罗彻斯特先生用"苍穹"指天空。还有一个疯女人——笑起来特别难看,像条鬣狗,她还放火烧蚊帐,撕婚纱,而且还咬——就是一个简单的通俗剧。虽然如此,可我还是读啊读啊读,因为我想不出来什么样的女孩子才会写出这样一本书,特别是作者还是一个在牧师家庭长大的孩子。我对勃朗特姐妹很有兴趣,想了解她们写的小说,她们的生活以及她们的精神。她们的灵感从哪来?每当我读到小简·爱在寄宿学校的种种遭遇时,我感同身受,愤怒极了,气得不得不出去走走,我非常非常理解她的感受。因为太了解利皮特太太,所以不难知道博若克勒赫斯特先生的为人。

别生气啊,叔叔。我不是说约翰·格里尔孤儿院跟洛伍德寄宿学校一样,我们吃得饱,穿得暖,有足够的水洗澡,而且也有暖和的炉火。不过二者

knave
[neiv]
n.【古】小厮;男仆

welkin
['welkin]
n.【诗】天空,苍穹

hyena
[hai'i:nə]
n.【动】鬣狗,土狼

intimate
['intimit]
v. 提示,暗示

cellar. But there was one deadly likeness. Our lives were absolutely monotonous and **uneventful**. Nothing nice ever happened, except ice cream on Sundays, and even that was regular. In all the eighteen years I was there I only had one adventure—when the **woodshed** burned. We had to get up in the night and dress so as to be ready in case the house should catch. But it didn't catch and we went back to bed.

Everybody likes a few surprises; it's a perfectly natural human **craving**. But I never had one until Mrs. Lippett called me to the office to tell me that Mr. John Smith was going to send me to college. And then she broke the news so gradually that it just barely shocked me.

You know, Daddy, I think that the most necessary quality for any person to have is imagination. It makes people able to put themselves in other people's places. It makes them kind and sympathetic and understanding. It ought to be cultivated in children. But the John Grier Home instantly **stamped** out the slightest **flicker** that appeared. Duty was the one quality that was encouraged. I don't think children ought to know the meaning of the word; it's **odious, detestable**. They ought to do everything from love.

Wait until you see the orphan asylum that I'm going to be the head of! It's my favorite play at night before I go to sleep. I plan it out to the littlest detail—the meals and clothes and study and amusements and punishments; for even my superior orphans are sometimes bad.

But anyway, they are going to be happy. I think that everyone, no matter how many troubles he may have when he grows up, ought to have a happy childhood to look back upon. And if I ever have any children of my own, no matter how unhappy I may be, I am not going to let them have any cares until they grow up.

(There goes the chapel bell—I'll finish this letter sometime.)

uneventful
[ˈʌniˈventful]
adj. 平静无事的

woodshed
[ˈwudʃəd]
n. 柴房

craving
[ˈkreiviŋ]
n. 渴望,热望

stamp
[stæmp]
v. 打上(标记等)

flicker
[ˈflikə]
n. 轻快的动作；闪现

odious
[ˈəudjəs]
adj. 可憎的，可恶的,令人作呕的

detestable
[diˈtestəb(ə)l]
adj. 讨厌的，可憎的,可恶的

确实有个很相似的地方，就是我们的生活都很没趣，单调无聊。除了星期天有冰淇淋吃之外，没有任何让人高兴的事情。在孤儿院的十八年里，我只真正高兴过一次。有一次隔壁的柴房着火了，因为担心我们的房子也着火，所以半夜爬起来，穿好衣服，准备逃跑，不过并没有烧到我们那边，只好又爬回去睡觉。

每个人都喜欢惊喜，这是人的天性。不过，在利皮特太太叫我过去，告诉我有位约翰·史密斯的先生要送我上大学之前，我从来没惊喜过，不过当时她说话慢吞吞又很严肃的样子，我只是稍微有点兴奋而已。

叔叔，我觉得一个人最重要的素质就是想象力。想象力能使人们站在别人的角度思考问题，让人变得善良、富有同情心并且理解他人。而想象力应该从童年时代就开始培养，可是约翰·格里尔孤儿院从萌芽就把它扼杀在摇篮中了。义务虽然也是需要培养的重要素质，可是我认为小孩子不需要那么早懂得——这个可恨可憎的字眼，他们应该用爱心去做每一件事情。

您想想，要是我会怎么管理孤儿院呢？这是我上床睡觉前最喜欢玩的游戏。睡觉之前，我总是缜密地想每一个细节——用餐、穿着、读书、游戏，还有处罚，即使是最乖的孤儿也会犯错的。

可是不管怎么说，他们都应该快快乐乐的。我觉得一个人不管他长大后会遇到多少困难，都应该有一个快乐的童年来回首。要是我将来有孩子，不管我自己多么不快乐，都要让孩子们快乐无忧地成长。

（教堂的钟声响了——我会找时间写完这封信的。）

五月四日

Thursday

When I came in from Laboratory this afternoon, I found a squirrel sitting on the tea table helping himself to **almonds**. These are the kind of callers we **entertain** now that warm weather has come and the window stays open—

Saturday morning

Perhaps you think, last night being Friday, with no classes today, that I passed a nice, quiet, readable evening with the set of Stevenson that I bought with my prize money? But if so, you've never attended a girls' college, Daddy dear. Six friends dropped in to make fudge, and one of them dropped the fudge—while it was still liquid—right in the middle of our best rug. We shall never be able to clean up the mess.

I haven't mentioned any lessons of late, but we are still having them every day. It's sort of a relief though, to get away from them and discuss life in the large—rather one-sided discussions that you and I hold, but that's your own fault. You are welcome to answer back anytime you choose.

almond
['ɑːmənd]
n. 杏仁
entertain
[,entə'tein]
v. 招待,款待

今天下午我从实验室回来发现一只松鼠坐在茶几上吃杏仁。天气暖和了,我们出门前打开了窗户,所以常常有这样友好的客人来访。

星期四

"亲爱的蜈蚣夫人,您要一个还是两个?"

周末没课,或许您认为周五晚上我可以安安静静地阅读我用奖金买的那套斯蒂文森的书了?亲爱的叔叔,您要是这样想,那是因为您从没上过女子大学。有六个同学来我们房间一起做牛奶糖,一不小心把糖滴在了我们最好的地毯正中了,再也弄不干净了。

我还没讲最近的学习呢,不过我每天都在学。不谈学习,跟您谈谈生活琐事也可以放松放松。遗憾的是,我们的谈话总是单边的,可这都是您的问题。欢迎您随时给我回信。

I've been writing this letter off and on for three days, and I fear by now *vous êtes bien* bored!

         Good-bye, nice Mr. Man,
              Judy

Mr. Daddy-Long-Legs Smith,

 Sir: Having completed the study of argumentation and the science of dividing a thesis into heads, I have decided to adopt the following form for letter writing. It contains all necessary facts, but no unnecessary **verbiage**.

 Ⅰ. We had written examinations this week in:
  A. Chemistry
  B. History
 Ⅱ. A new dormitory is being built:
  A. Its material is:
   (a) red brick
   (b) gray stone
  B. Its capacity will be:
   (a) one dean, five instructors
   (b) two hundred girls
   (c) one housekeeper, three cooks, twenty waitresses, twenty **chambermaids**
 Ⅲ. We had **junket** for dessert tonight.
 Ⅳ. I am writing a special topic upon the sources of Shakespeare's plays.
 Ⅴ. Lou McMahon slipped and fell this afternoon at basketball, and she:
  A. **Dislocated** her shoulder
  B. Bruised her knee
 Ⅵ. I have a new hat trimmed with:
  A. Blue **velvet** ribbon

这封信断断续续写了三天，担心您可能烦了！
再见，好心先生！

　　　　　　　　　　　　　　　　　朱蒂
　　　　　　　　　　　　　　　　星期六上午

长腿叔叔史密斯先生：

　　先生，我们刚学完立论和列举要点的方法，我今天就采用下面这种形式给您写信，只包括要点，没有多余的词。

　　一、本周进行以下笔试：

　　　　A. 化学

　　　　B. 历史

　　二、正在建设新宿舍：

　　　　A. 所用材料：

　　　　　（a）红砖

　　　　　（b）灰石

　　　　B. 宿舍容量：

　　　　　（a）1位院长，5位导师

　　　　　（b）200名女生

　　　　　（c）1位舍监，3位厨师，20名女服务员，20名清洁女工

　　三、今晚的甜点是奶冻。

　　四、我在写有关莎剧源流的论文。

　　五、今天下午打篮球，卢·麦克马洪摔倒。诊断结果：

　　　　A. 肩胛骨错位

　　　　B. 膝盖摔破

　　六、我买了一顶新帽子，上面镶：

　　　　A. 蓝丝绒缎带

---

verbiage
['və:biidʒ]
n. 废话；冗词

chambermaid
['tʃeimbəmeid]
n.（旅馆等）房间部的女服务生

junket
['dʒʌŋkit]
n. 凝乳食品

dislocate
['disləkeit]
v. 使脱臼

velvet
['velvit]
n. 天鹅绒，丝绒

      B. Two blue quills
      C. Three red pompons
VII. It is half-past nine.
VIII. Good night.

                                      Judy

June 2d

Dear Daddy-Long-Legs,

You will never guess the nice thing that has happened.

The McBrides have asked me to spend the summer at their camp in the Adirondacks! They belong to a sort of club on a lovely little lake in the middle of the woods. The different members have houses made of logs dotted about among the trees, and they go canoeing on the lake, and take long walks through trails to other camps, and have dances once a week in the clubhouse—Jimmie McBride is going to have a college friend visiting him part of the summer, so you see we shall have plenty of men to dance with.

Wasn't it sweet of Mrs. McBride to ask me? It appears that she liked me when I was there for Christmas.

Please excuse this being short. It isn't a real letter; it's just to let you know that I'm **disposed** of for the summer.

                                      Yours,
In a very contented frame of mind,
                                      Judy

June 5th

Dear Daddy-Long-Legs,

Your secretary man has just written to me saying that Mr. Smith prefers that I should not accept Mrs. McBride's invitation, but should return to Lock Willow the same as last summer.

B. 两根蓝色翎毛
   C. 三个红色绒球
七、现在是九点半。
八、晚安。

朱蒂

亲爱的长腿叔叔：
　　又有好事了呢！您猜猜，不过您绝对猜不到！
　　麦克白太太邀请我暑假和他们一起去阿迪朗达克野营呢！他们参加了一家俱乐部，那个俱乐部就在一个美丽的林中湖畔。俱乐部会员们用圆木在山林中四处搭起了营房，他们可以在湖上划船，在山林中长途散步到其他营区去。俱乐部一星期举行一次舞会——吉米·麦克白的一个同学暑假也会来玩一段时间，这样我们就有很多男舞伴了呢。
　　麦克白太太邀请了我，真是太好了呢，是吧？看来上次去她家过圣诞节她对我的印象还不错。
　　请原谅我这封信写得这么简短，这当然不是真正的信，我只是想让您知道今年暑假我有地方去了呢。

dispose
[dis'pəuz]
v. 处理,处置,销毁

您非常心满意足的
朱蒂
六月二日

亲爱的长腿叔叔：
　　您的秘书来信说史密斯先生希望我不要接受麦克白夫人的邀请，而是和上个暑假一样，回洛克威洛农庄。

Why, why, why, Daddy?

You don't understand about it. Mrs. McBride does want me, really and truly. I'm not the least bit of trouble in the house. I'm a help. They don't take up many servants, and Sallie and I can do lots of useful things. It's a fine chance for me to learn housekeeping. Every woman ought to understand it, and I only know asylum-keeping.

There aren't any girls our age at the camp, and Mrs. McBride wants me for a **companion** for Sallie. We are planning to do a lot of reading together. We are going to read all of the books for next year's English and **sociology**. The professor said it would be a great help if we would get our reading finished in the summer; and it's so much easier to remember it, if we read together and talk it over.

Just to live in the same house with Sallie's mother is an education. She's the most interesting, entertaining, companionable, charming woman in the world; she knows everything. Think how many summers I've spent with Mrs. Lippett and how I'll appreciate the contrast. You needn't be afraid that I'll be crowding them, for their house is made of rubber. When they have a lot of company, they just sprinkle tents about in the woods and turn the boys outside. It's going to be such a nice, healthy summer exercising out of doors every minute. Jimmie McBride is going to teach me how to ride horseback and **paddle** a canoe, and how to shoot and—oh, lots of things I ought to know. It's the kind of nice, jolly, carefree time that I've never had; and I think every girl deserves it once in her life. Of course I'll do exactly as you say, but please, please let me go, Daddy. I've never wanted anything so much.

This isn't Jerusha Abbott, the future great author, writing to you. It's just Judy—a girl.

叔叔，为什么？为什么？为什么？

您不明白，麦克白夫人是真心邀请我去的。我不仅不会给他们添麻烦，而且还是个好帮手。他们没带什么佣人，莎莉跟我可以帮很多忙，而且这也是我学习打理家务的好机会，这是每个女孩子都应该懂的，可我只懂得打理孤儿院的事务。

野营地没有和我们年龄相仿的女孩儿，麦克白夫人想我跟莎莉做个伴儿。我们计划要看很多书，要把下一学年的英文和社会学都先看一遍，教授说利用暑假把这些书通读一遍会有很大好处的。两个人一起学习，一起讨论，印象会更深。

而且只跟莎莉的妈妈住一起就能学不少东西了。她是世界上最有趣、最友好而且最有魅力的女士了，她什么都懂。想想，和利皮特太太一起度过了那么多个夏天，我是多么渴望尝试新鲜的事情啊！您也不用担心我会挤到她们，她们的房子是橡胶做的，伸缩性很大，客人多就多搭些露天帐篷，把男孩子都赶出去睡。户外活动有益于身体健康，而且会玩得很开心的。吉米·麦克白要教我骑马、划船，还有——好多我应该学会的事情。这将是我长这么大以来最开心最快乐最放松的时光；我觉得每个女孩子都值得拥有一次这样的机会。不过，叔叔，我当然也会听您的话，可是，叔叔，求求您，求求您让我去吧，我从来没有像这次愿望这么强烈过。

这不是未来的大作家——乔茹莎·阿伯特——给您写的信，只是朱蒂——一个女孩子。

六月五日

June 9th

Mr. John Smith,

Sir: Yours of the 7th inst. at hand. In **compliance** with the instructions received through your secretary, I leave on Friday next to spend the summer at Lock Willow Farm.

I hope always to remain,
(Miss) Jerusha Abbott

August Third

Dear Daddy-Long-Legs,

It has been nearly two months since I wrote, which wasn't nice of me, I know, but I haven't loved you much this summer— you see I'm being frank!

You can't imagine how disappointed I was at having to give up the McBrides' camp. Of course I know that you're my guardian, and that I have to regard your wishes in all matters, but I couldn't see any reason. It was so distinctly the best thing that could have happened to me. If I had been Daddy, and you had been Judy, I should have said, "Bless you, my child, run along and have a good time; see lots of new people and learn lots of new things; live out of doors, and get strong and well and rested for a year of hard work."

But not at all! Just a curt line from your secretary ordering me to Lock Willow.

It's the impersonality of your commands that hurts my feelings. It seems as though, if you felt the tiniest little bit for me the way I feel for you, you'd sometimes send me a message that you'd written with your own hand, instead of those beastly typewritten secretary's notes. If there were the slightest hint that you cared, I'd do anything on earth to please you.

I know that I was to write nice, long, detailed letters without ever expecting any answer. You're living up to your side of the

约翰·史密斯先生：

先生，您七日的信已经收到。据经您秘书转达的命令，我将于下星期五出发，回洛克威洛农庄。

您永远的
乔茹莎·阿伯特（小姐）
六月九日

亲爱的长腿叔叔：

已经快两个月没跟您写信了，是我做得不好。可是，坦白说，这个暑假我不太喜欢您。

您简直无法想象放弃跟麦克白家去野营，我有多么不情愿。当然，您是我的监护人，我知道凡事都得听您的意见，但我真的不知道"为什么"。对我来说，跟麦克白家去野营是最美好的事情了。如果我是叔叔您，您是朱蒂，我就会说："去吧，我的孩子，祝你玩得愉快！多认识一些人，多学习新东西，在户外多住一阵儿，把身体锻炼得壮壮的；努力一年了，好好放松一下吧。"

可是您却不是这样的！您只叫秘书写来一行字就命令我去洛克威洛！

您不通情达理，我很伤心。如果您对我有一点点我对您的感情，您至少也会偶尔写几行字给我啊，而不仅仅是让您的秘书寄来的那些打出来的讨厌字条。如果我能感受到您一点点的关怀，我愿意做任何让您高兴的事情的。

我知道我应该恭恭敬敬认认真真地给您写长长的详尽的信，而不期望您的任何回复。您履行了您

compliance
[kəm'plaiəns]
n. 承诺，顺从，遵从

bargain—I'm being educated—and I suppose you're thinking I'm not living up to mine!

But, Daddy, it is a hard bargain. It is, really. I'm so awfully lonely. You are the only person I have to care for, and you are so shadowy. You're just an imaginary man that I've made up—and probably the real you isn't a bit like my imaginary you. But you did once, when I was ill in the infirmary, send me a message, and now, when I am feeling awfully forgotten, I get out your card and read it over.

I don't think I am telling you at all what I started to say, which was this:

Although my feelings are still hurt, for it is very humiliating to be picked up and moved about by an **arbitrary**, **peremptory**, **unreasonable**, omnipotent, invisible providence, still, when a man has been as kind and generous and thoughtful as you have heretofore been toward me, I suppose he has a right to be an arbitrary, peremptory, unreasonable, invisible providence if he chooses, and so—I'll forgive you and be cheerful again. But I still don't enjoy getting Sallie's letters about the good times they are having in camp!

However—we will draw a veil over that and begin again.

I've been writing and writing this summer; four short stories finished and sent to four different magazines. So you see I'm trying to be an author. I have a workroom fixed in a corner of the attic where Master Jervie used to have his rainy-day playroom. It's in a cool, **breezy** corner with two dormer windows, and shaded by a maple tree with a family of red **squirrels** living in a hole.

I'll write a nice letter in a few days and tell you all the farm news.

We need rain.

Yours as ever,
Judy

的义务——送我上了大学——我想您会认为我没有履行我的义务。

可是，叔叔，这对我太难了，真的太难了。我是如此孤独，您是我唯一能够挂念的人。可是您却只是个幻影而已，您只是我想象中的人——也许您是真实的，一点也不像我想象的那样。不过，您确实也在我住院的时候给过我一张卡片，每当我感到寂寞时，我总会拿出您的卡片，一遍又一遍地阅读。

我可能没有表达清楚自己的意思，我想要说的是：

我不开心，是因为被一个专横的、蛮不讲理而又无所不在隐藏在背后的力量所支配，这让我很受伤害。不过，一个人能像您对我那么好，那么宽容，那么体贴，我想他有权做一个独断专横、不近人情、无所不在却总是隐藏在背后的上帝——所以我原谅您，让自己重新高兴起来。可是，每次收到莎莉描述他们野营玩得很开心的信件时，我又沮丧。

不说这件事了，说点别的。

这个夏天，我不停地写啊写啊写，写了四个短篇小说，分别寄给了四家杂志社。所以您看，我正努力奋斗当大作家呢。我在小阁楼的一个角落里写作，这是杰维少爷小时候下雨天玩耍的地方。夏天角落里凉风习习，很凉爽。两扇天窗被一棵枫树的浓阴遮盖着，枫树上有一个洞，里面还住着一窝红松鼠呢。

过几天会再写一封高兴点的信，跟您说说农庄的见闻。

这里好久不下雨了。

您永远的
朱蒂
八月三日

---

arbitrary
['ɑ:bitrəri]
adj. 任意的，恣意的，专制的

peremptory
[pə'remptəri]
adj. 专横的，不容反抗的

unreasonable
[ʌn'ri:znəbl]
adj. 不合理的，过度的，不切实际的

breezy
['bri:zi]
adj. 有微风的，通风好的，活泼的

squirrel
['skwirəl]
n. 松鼠

August 10th

Mr. Daddy-Long-Legs,

Sir: I address you from the second crotch in the willow tree by the pool in the pasture. There's a frog **croaking** underneath, a locust singing overhead, and two little "devil down-heads" **darting** up and down the trunk. I've been here for an hour: it's a very comfortable **crotch**, especially after being **upholstered** with two sofa cushions. I came up with a pen and tablet hoping to write an immortal short story, but I've been having a dreadful time with my heroine—I can't make her behave as I want her to behave; so I've abandoned her for the moment, and am writing to you. (Not much relief though, for I can't make you behave as I want you to, either.)

If you are in that dreadful New York, I wish I could send you some of this lovely, breezy, sunshiny outlook. The country is heaven after a week of rain.

Speaking of heaven, do you remember Mr. Kellogg that I told you about last summer? —the minister of the little white church at the Corners. Well, the poor old soul is dead—last winter of **pneumonia**. I went half a dozen times to hear him preach and got very well acquainted with his theology. He believed to the end exactly the same things he started with. It seems to me that a man who can think straight along for forty-seven years without changing a single idea ought to be kept in a cabinet as a curiosity. I hope he is enjoying his **harp** and golden crown; he was so perfectly sure of finding them! There's a new young man, very up and coming, in his place. The **congregation** is pretty dubious, especially the faction led by Deacon Cummings. It looks as though there was going to be an awful split in the church. We don't care for **innovations** in religion in this neighborhood.

During out week of rain I sat up in the **attic** and had an orgy of reading—Stevenson, mostly. He himself is more entertaining than any of the characters in his books; I dare say he made himself into the kind of hero that would look well in print. Don't you think it was

croak
[krəuk]
v. 呱呱地叫；发牢骚

dart
[dɑ:t]
v. 投射，疾走，突进

crotch
[krɔtʃ]
n. 分叉处，叉柱

upholster
[ʌp'həulstə]
v. 以帘幕，地毯，家具装饰

pneumonia
[nju(:)'məunjə]
n. 肺炎

harp
[hɑ:p]
n. 竖琴

congregation
[,kɔngri'geiʃən]
n. 集合，会合

innovation
[,inəu'veiʃən]
n. 创新，革新

attic
['ætik]
n. 阁楼

亲爱的长腿叔叔：

先生：我正在牧场水池边的一棵柳树上的第二个树杈上给您写信。蟋蟀在树上唱个不停，青蛙在树下鼓噪不断，还有几只小虫子在树杈间上蹿下跳，爬来爬去。我已经在这儿呆了一个小时了，垫了两只靠垫在树杈上，很舒服。本来带来了笔和练习本，打算写一篇不朽的短篇小说，可女主人公让我很生气，她太不听话了，只好暂时不理她转而给您写信。（其实写信也不能给我太大的安慰，毕竟我也不能让您按照我的想法行事。）

如果您现在还住在可怕的纽约市，我希望能送您一点新鲜空气和风和日丽的天气。下了一周雨之后的乡间简直就是天堂。

说到天堂，您还记得去年夏天我跟你谈到过凯洛格先生吗？就是四角那个白色小教堂里的牧师。唉，他去世了，去年冬天死于肺炎，真可怜。我经常去听他布道，对他的观点也很熟悉。他是一个坚持自己想法的人。我觉得一个人七十多年来从没改变过自己想法简直可以被挂在墙上当古董展览了。希望他还在天堂传道！他相信自己能做到！他确信有熙熙攘攘的年轻人去听他传道。也有怀疑他的教众，特别是卡明斯带领的那帮人，似乎要分出派系来。我们也不在乎这个教区会不会来场宗教改革。

下了一周的雨，我一直窝在阁楼上尽情地阅读斯蒂文森的小说。他本人比小说中的任何人物都有意思。我敢说，要是他把自己写进书去会是一个更有趣的英雄。他用父亲留给他的一万美金买了一艘

perfect of him to spend all the ten thousand dollars his father left for a **yacht** and go sailing off to the South Seas? He lived up to his adventurous **creed**. If my father had left me ten thousand dollars, I'd do it too. The thought of Vailima makes me wild. I want to see the tropics. I want to see the whole world. I am going to some day—I am, really, Daddy, when I get to be a great author, or artist, or actress, or playwright—or whatever sort of a great person I turn out to be. I have a terrible **wanderthirst**; the very sight of a map makes me want to put on my hat and take an umbrella and start. "I shall see before I die the **palms** and temple of the South."

Thursday evening at twilight,
sitting on the doorstep

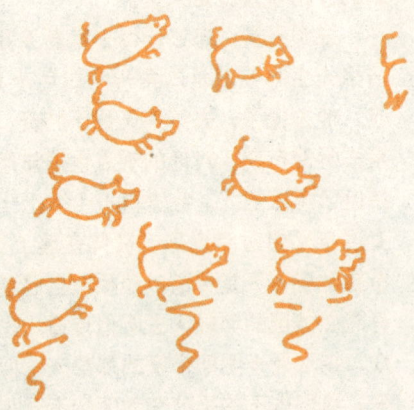

Very hard to get any news into this letter! Judy is becoming so **philosophical** of late that she wishes to **discourse** largely of the world in general, instead of descending to the trivial details of daily life. But if you must have news, here it is:

Our nine young pigs waded across the brook and ran away last Tuesday, and only eight came back. We don't want to accuse anyone **unjustly**, but we suspect that Widow Dowd has one more than she ought to have.

yacht
[jɔt]
n. 游艇，快艇

creed
[kri:d]
n. 信条，教义

wanderthirst
[ˈwɔndəˈθə:st]
n. 渴望旅游的人

palm
[pɑ:m]
n. 棕榈树

游船去畅游南洋去了，他追求理想，喜欢冒险。我父亲要是留给我一万美元，我也会这么做的。我要去领略大千世界的奇妙风光和美景，我要去热带丛林，总有一天，我会去的。叔叔，要是有一天我成了大作家，或者我成了什么伟大人物，我就去周游世界。每当我一看见地图，就想抓起帽子，带着雨伞出游了。我要是在有生之年能见到南洋的棕榈树和庙宇该多好啊！

八月十日

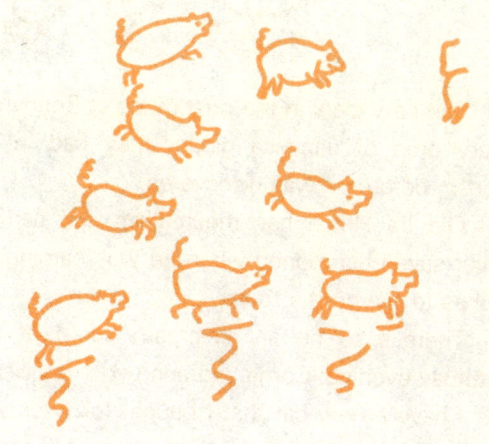

philosophical
[ˌfiləˈsɔfikəl]
adj. 哲学的，冷静的

discourse
[disˈkɔ:s]
v. 讲述，著述

unjustly
[ˈʌnˈdʒʌstli]
adv. 不义地，不法地

没什么新鲜事儿可写了！最近朱蒂变得非常深沉，总想探索大千世界，不仅仅是说说日常生活了。不过，您若是非要听新鲜事儿，只有这些了：

上周四，我们的九只小猪趟过小溪逃跑了，只找回了八只。我们不想冤枉谁，不过还是怀疑寡妇淘德猪圈里的猪比原来多了一只。

Mr. Weaver has painted his barn and his two silos a bright pumpkin yellow—a very ugly color, but he says it will wear.

The Brewers have company this week: Mrs. Brewer's sister and two nieces from Ohio.

One of our Rhode Islands Reds only brought off three chicks out of fifteen eggs. We can't imagine what was the trouble. Rhode Island Reds, in my opinion, are a very inferior breed. I prefer Buff Orpingtons.

The new clerk in the post office at Bonnyrigg Four Corners drank every drop of Jamaica ginger they had in stock—seven dollars' worth—before he was discovered.

Old Ira Hatch has **rheumatism** and can't work anymore; he never saved his money when he was earning good wages, so now he has to live on the town.

There's to be an ice-cream social at the schoolhouse next Saturday evening. Come and bring your families.

I have a new hat that I bought for twenty-five cents at the post office. This is my latest portrait, on my way to rake the hay.

It's getting too dark to see; anyway, the news is all used up.

Good night,
Judy

维弗先生把他的谷仓和两个贮窖漆成了南瓜黄,很难看。不过他说很耐脏。

布鲁尔斯家这周来了客人,布鲁尔斯太太的姐姐和两个外甥女,从俄亥俄州来的。

我们最棒的一只罗德岛母鸡,十五个蛋只孵出了三只小鸡,不知道什么原因。我觉得罗德岛鸡的种不好,我喜欢奥尔平顿的母鸡。

邦尼里格四角邮局的新工作人员把库存的牙买加姜汁啤酒喝得一滴不剩,价值7美元呢,喝完了才发现。

rheumatism
['ru:mətizəm]
n. 风湿症

哈奇老先生的风湿病犯了,干不了活了。他以前挣了不少钱,可他一点积蓄也没有,只得靠救济了。

下周六晚上,校舍有一场冰淇淋晚会。

我花了二十五美分在邮局买了顶新帽子,下面是我的画像——去收割的路上。

天黑了,新闻报道完毕!

晚安,
朱蒂
星期四傍晚,坐在
门口石阶上

Friday

Good morning! Here is some news! What do you think? You'd never, never, never guess who's coming to Lock Willow. A letter to Mrs. Semple from Mr. Pendleton. He's **motoring** through the Berkshires, and is tired and wants to rest on a nice quiet farm—if he climbs out at her doorstep some night will she have a room ready for him? Maybe he'll stay one week, or maybe two, or maybe three; he'll see how **restful** it is when he gets here.

Such a **flutter** as we are in! The whole house is being cleaned and all the curtains washed. I am driving to the Corners this morning to get some new oil cloth for the entry, and two cans of brown floor paint for the hall and back stairs. Mrs. Dowd is engaged to come tomorrow to wash the windows (in the **exigency** of the moment, we **waive** our suspicions in regard to the piglet). You might think, from this account of our activities, that the house was not already **immaculate**; but I assure you it was! Whatever Mrs. Semple's limitations, she is a HOUSEKEEPER.

Old Grove is perfectly safe.

motor
['məutə]
v. 开车

restful
['restful]
adj. 平安的,安静的

flutter
['flʌtə]
n. 摆动,鼓翼;烦扰

exigence
['eksədʒəns]
n. 紧急的需要（危急关头）

waive
[weiv]
v. 免除

immaculate
[i'mækjulit]
adj. 洁白的(无缺点的,无瑕疵的)

早上好！特大新闻！您猜是什么？您永远永远永远都猜不到谁要来洛克威洛了。彭莱顿先生给申普太太来信说他驾车周游柏克郡，累了，想找个宁静的农庄休息。他问要是某天晚上突然出现在申普太太农庄门口，是否能给他留个房间歇息。他可能会待一周，也可能两三周，视情况而定，等他来了再说。

您说我们得有多忙乱！我们把房子收拾了一下，把窗帘都洗了一遍。今天早晨，我驾车去四角买了些油布铺在大门口，还买了两罐棕色地板漆把前厅以及后楼楼梯都漆了一遍。明天请陶德太太来擦窗户（事关重大，我们只能对小猪事件尽弃前嫌了）。您可能会以为就我们忙忙慌慌打扫那两下子，恐怕很难打扫干净，不过我保证它本来就很干净了！虽然申普太太没受过多少教育，可理家还是很不错的。

有老格洛弗，很安全。

But isn't it just like a man, Daddy? He doesn't give the remotest hint as to whether he will land on the doorstep today, or two weeks from today. We shall live in a **perpetual** breathlessness until he comes—and if he doesn't hurry, the cleaning may all have to be done over again.

There's Amasai waiting below with the buckboard and Grover. I drive alone—but if you could see old Grove, you wouldn't be worried as to my safety.

With my hand on my heart—farewell.

Judy

PS. Isn't that a nice ending? I got it out of Stevenson's letters.

Saturday

Good morning again! I didn't get this enveloped yesterday before the postman came, so I'll add some more. We have one mail a day at twelve o'clock. Rural delivery is a blessing to the farmers! Our postman not only delivers letters, but he runs **errands** for us in town, at five cents an errand. Yesterday he brought me some shoestrings and a jar of cold cream (I sunburned all the skin off my nose before I got my new hat) and a blue Windsor tie and a bottle of blacking all for ten cents. That was an unusual bargain, owing to the largeness of my order.

Also he tells us what is happening in the great world. Several people on the route take daily papers, and he reads them as he jogs along, and repeats the news to the ones who don't **subscribe**. So in case a war breaks out between the United States and Japan, or the president is **assassinated**, or Mr. Rockefeller leaves a million dollars to the John Grier Home, you needn't bother to write; I'll hear it anyway.

No sign yet of Master Jervie. But you should see how clean our house is—and with what anxiety we wipe our feet before we step in!

不过,叔叔,他可真男人,行踪完全保密,也不说清楚到底是今天还是两周之后再来。所以我们得一直绷紧神经——他要是不来,我们又得再打扫一遍。

阿马萨备好四轮马车和格洛弗在下面等我了。我自己驾车去——有老格洛弗在,您不用担心我的安全。

把我的手搁在心上,衷心地说声:"再见!"

朱蒂
星期五

补充:这个结尾很不错吧?我从斯蒂文森的书信里学来的。

再说声早上好!昨天一直等到邮差来我才封上的信封,这样我可以再加几行。邮差每天十二点来,乡下邮差对农民来说非常重要,邮差不仅送信,还帮我们从城里带东西回来,每件收费五美分。昨天他帮我带了些鞋带、一瓶凝露(我没买帽子前把鼻子晒脱皮了)、还有温莎领带和一盒黑色鞋油,一共十美分。太便宜了,主要是我买得多。

邮差也会给大家讲一些重大时事。好几家人都订了报纸,他一路送一路看,沿路讲给那些没订报纸的人们听。比如美日开战,总统被刺,洛克菲勒先生给约翰·格里尔孤儿院捐了一百万美元,您不用写信告诉我,邮差都会讲的。

杰维少爷还没有来。不过您真该来看看我们的房子是多么洁净——紧张得我们每次进门都要擦擦脚底的泥土呢!

---

perpetual
[pə'petjuəl]
adj. 永恒的,永久的

errand
['erənd]
n. 差使,差事

subscribe
[səb'skraib]
v. 捐献,赞成,订阅

assassinate
[ə'sæsineit]
v. 暗杀

I hope he'll come soon; I am longing for someone to talk to. Mrs. Semple, to tell you the truth, gets sort of **monotonous**. She never lets ideas interrupt the easy flow of her conversation. It's a funny thing about the people here. Their world is just this single **hilltop**. They are not a bit universal, if you know what I mean. It's exactly the same as at the John Grier Home. Our ideas there were bounded by the four sides of the iron fence, only I didn't mind it so much because I was younger and was so awfully busy. By the time I'd got all my beds made and my babies' faces washed and had gone to school and come home and had washed their faces again and darned their stockings and mended Freddie Perkins's trousers (he tore them every day of his life) and learned my lessons in between—I was ready to go to bed, and I didn't notice any lack of social **intercourse**. But after two years in a conversational college, I do miss it; and I shall be glad to see somebody who speaks my language.

I really believe I've finished, Daddy. Nothing else Occurs to me at the moment—I'll try to write a longer letter next time.

Yours always,
Judy

PS. The lettuce hasn't done at all well this year. It was so dry early in the season.

August 25th

Well, Daddy, Master Jervie's here. And such a nice time as we're having! At least I am, and I think he is too—he has been here ten days and he doesn't show any signs of going. The way Mrs. Semple **pampers** that man is **scandalous**. If she indulged him as much when he was a baby, I don't know how he ever turned out so well.

He and I eat at a little table set on the side porch, or sometimes under the trees, or—when it rains or is cold—in the best

monotonous
[məˈnɔtənəs]
adj. 单调的

hilltop
[ˈhiltɔp]
n. 山顶

希望他能早点来，真想找个人说说话。说实话，申普太太比较乏味，虽然说起话来总是滔滔不绝，但没有什么内涵。这里的人很有意思，他们的天就是这个山顶，他们几乎与世隔绝，您懂我的意思吧？这儿跟约翰·格里尔孤儿院完全一样！在孤儿院，我们的思想被四面铁篱所禁锢，不过当时年龄小，而且每天都很忙碌，所以不太在意。那时候，我每天整理好床铺、给小孩子们洗完脸之后就去学校上课，放学回来再给他们洗一遍脸，把他们的袜子补好，还要给弗雷迪·帕金补裤子（他几乎每天都会把裤子刮破），忙里抽空完成作业，最后累得不行就上床睡觉了，那时候也没觉得缺少社交活动。这两年大学生活让我和更多的人交流了，特别喜欢和有共同语言的人交流，大学生活真是值得怀念啊！

intercourse
[ˈintə(:)kɔ:s]
n. 交往，交流

真得停笔了，这几天也没什么新鲜事发生——下一封信会写得长一点。

您永远的
朱蒂
星期六

补充：今年莴苣长势不好，前段时间太旱了。

叔叔，杰维少爷终于来了。我们玩得特别开心！至少我很开心，我想他也该感觉不错吧——他已经来这儿十天了，还没有要走的意思。申普太太太惯着他了，他要是从小就这么娇生惯养，我真不明白他怎么会变成今天这么好的。

pamper
[ˈpæmpə]
v. 放纵，使吃饱

scandalous
[ˈskændələs]
adj. 不体面的，可耻的，可恶的

我们经常在小阳台上摆上小饭桌吃饭，有时候也在大树下吃，要是下雨或者天冷，就在小客厅里

parlor. He just picks out the spot he wants to eat in and Carrie trots after him with the table. Then if it has been an awful nuisance, and she has had to carry the dishes very far, she finds a dollar under the sugar bowl.

He is an awfully companionable sort of man, though you would never believe it to see him casually; he looks at first glance like a true Pendleton, but he isn't in the least. He is just as simple and **unaffected** and sweet as he can be—that seems a funny way to describe a man, but it's true. He's extremely nice with the farmers around here; he meets them in a sort of man-to-man fashion that disarms them immediately. They were very suspicious at first. They didn't care for his clothes! And I will say that his clothes are rather amazing. He wears **knickerbockers** and pleated jackets and white **flannels** and riding clothes with **puffed** trousers. Whenever he comes down in anything new, Mrs. Semple, beaming with pride, walks around and views him from every angle, and urges him to be careful where he sits down; she is so afraid he will pick up some dust. It bores him dreadfully. He's always saying to her:

"Run along, Lizzie, and tend to your work. You can't boss me any longer. I've grown up."

吃。他随便选个用餐地点，卡莉就会拎着桌子跟着他去。有时候很麻烦，还得把菜端到很远的地方，不过她会在糖罐底下发现他给她的一块钱。

杰维少爷性格随和，虽然看起来不像。乍一看，他就是一典型的彭莱顿家族的人，时间长了就知道他并非如此。他是个很纯真、很可爱的男子——用这些字眼来形容男子好像有点可笑，不过的确如此。他对附近的农民特别友好、真诚，所以人们很快对他消除了疑虑。刚开始人们不相信他，尤其看不惯他的打扮！不过我觉得他打扮挺个性的。他穿着一条灯笼裤，一件褶皱夹克里面套着白绒衣，外面罩着一身儿马服。每次他穿着新衣服下楼，申普太太总是围着他转一边叮嘱他坐下来时要当心沾上灰尘。他总是烦得不行，然后对她说：

"好了，莉莉，去忙你的，我已经长大了，不用管我。"

unaffected
[ˌʌnəˈfektid]
adj. 不矫揉造作的，自然的

knickerbockers
[ˈnikəbɔkəz]
n. 灯笼裤

flannel
[ˈflænl]
n. 法兰绒

puffed
[pʌft]
adj. 夸张的

It's awfully funny to think of that great big, long-legged man (he's nearly as long-legged as you, Daddy) ever sitting in Mrs. Semple's lap and having his face washed. Particularly funny when you see her lap! She has two laps now, and three chins. But he says that once she was thin and wiry and spry and could run faster than he.

Such a lot of adventures we're having! We've explored the country for miles, and I've learned to fish with funny little flies made of feathers. Also to shoot with a rifle and a **revolver**. Also to ride horseback—there's an astonishing amount of life in old Grove. We fed him on oats for three days, and he shied at a calf and almost ran away with me.

Wednesday

We climbed Sky Hill Monday afternoon. That's a mountain near here; not an awfully high mountain, perhaps—no snow on the **summit**—but at least you are pretty breathless when you reach the top. The lower slopes are covered with woods, but the top is just piled rocks and open moor. We stayed up for the sunset and built a fire and cooked our supper. Master Jervie did the cooking; he said he knew how better than me—and he did, too, because he's used to camping. Then we came down by moonlight, and, when we reached the wood trail where it was dark, by the light of a flashlight that he had in his pocket. It was such fun! He laughed and joked all the way and talked about interesting things. He's read all the books I've ever read, and a lot of others besides. It's astonishing how many different things he knows.

We went for a long **tramp** this morning and got caught in a storm. Our clothes were **drenched** before we reached home—but our spirits not even damp. You should have seen Mrs. Semple's face when we dripped into her kitchen.

"Oh, Master Jervie—Miss Judy! You are soaked through. Dear! Dear! What shall I do? That nice new coat is perfectly

遥想现在又高又壮腿还很长的男子（跟您差不多高，叔叔），当年坐在申普太太的腿上让她洗脸，真有意思。特别是当您看到申普太太的腿，更是好笑，她的腿现在粗得吓人。还有她的三下巴，特别好玩。他说她以前也是又高又瘦，活泼可爱，跑得比他还快。

多新鲜啊！我们在乡下到处游逛，我学会了用羽毛做的小苍蝇作诱饵钓鱼，还学会了步枪射击、左轮手枪射击还有骑马——老格洛弗精力充沛之惊人。我们给它喂了三天的燕麦，可它看见一头小牛吓得差点带着我一起逃跑了。

八月二十五日

星期一下午，我们去登了附近的天山。山顶上没有积雪，山也不高，不过爬到山顶也会有点上气不接下气。山坡上有很多树木，山顶则是乱石林立的荒地。我们在山上一直玩到日落，生了一堆篝火，开始做晚餐。杰维少爷做晚饭，他说他比我厨艺好——确实如此，因为他经常露营。饭后，我们借着月光下山，一路走在黑乎乎的林间小道上，多亏他兜里那只手电筒。太好玩儿了！他一路有说有笑，讲了许多有趣的故事，我读过的书他全都读过，他还读过好多别的书，真是博学多才啊！

今天上午，我们一路走了很远的路，恰巧遇上了狂风暴雨。到家后衣服全都湿透了，不过依然很兴奋。您可以想象一下申普太太看见我们淋得跟落汤鸡似的走进厨房时的表情！

"上帝啊，杰维少爷，朱蒂小姐！瞧你们被淋得！瞧瞧！瞧瞧！这可怎么办呀？刚穿的新大衣就

---

revolver
[ri'vɔlvə]
n. 左轮手枪

summit
['sʌmit]
n. 最高级会议

tramp
[træmp]
n. 重步声；流浪者

drench
[drentʃ]
v. 湿透

ruined."

She was awfully funny; you would have thought that we were ten years old, and she a **distracted** mother. I was afraid for a while that we weren't going to get any jam for tea.

Saturday

I started this letter ages ago, but I haven't had a second to finish it.

Isn't this a nice thought from Stevenson?

The world is so full of a number of things,

I'm sure we should all be as happy as kings.

It's true, you know. The world is full of happiness, and plenty to go round, if you are only willing to take the kind that comes your way. The whole secret is in being **pliable**. In the country, especially, there are such a lot of entertaining things. I can walk over everybody's land, and look at everybody's view, and dabble in everybody's **brook**; and enjoy it just as much as though I owned the land—and with no taxes to pay!

. . .

It's Sunday night now, about eleven o'clock, and I am supposed to be getting some beauty sleep, but I had black coffee for dinner, so—no beauty sleep for me!

This morning, said Mrs. Semple to Mr. Pendleton, with a very determined accent:

"We have to leave here at a quarter past ten in order to get to church by eleven."

"Very well, Lizzie," said Master Jervie, "you have the surrey ready, and if I'm not dressed, just go on without waiting."

"We'll wait," said she.

"As you please," said he, "only don't keep the horses standing too long."

Then while she was dressing, he told Carrie to pack up a lunch, and he told me to **scramble** into my walking clothes; and we slipped out the back way and went fishing.

糟蹋成这样了啊!"

她可真有趣,就像我们都是小孩子,她是被惹恼的母亲一样,我担心吃茶点时她会不会惩罚我们不给果酱吃呢。

星期三

我很早就开始写这封信了,可我总是没时间写完。

瞧瞧,我跟斯蒂文森学得怎么样?

世界如此美丽,

我们快乐像皇帝!

的确如此,您知道的,只要你用心体会,其实快乐无所不在,开心的秘诀就在于体验。特别是在乡下,有很多开心的体验,走过每一片土地,享受每一处美景,四处戏水,完全自由,感觉自己就像这片土地的主人——而且根本不用交税!

...

现在是星期天晚上十一点左右,本来早就应该睡美容觉了,可是晚餐时喝了点黑咖啡,睡不着!

今天早上,申普太太跟彭莱顿先生发生了一场激烈的对峙:

"我们必须十点十五分时出发,十一点准时抵达教堂。"

"很好,莉莉,"杰维少爷说,"你把马车备好,到时候要是我还没换好衣服,你就先走,别等我!"

"一定得等。"她说。

"随你的便,"他说,"别让马站得太久就好。"

然后趁申普太太换衣服时,他吩咐卡莉打好午餐包,然后催我快点换上便装,带我从后门溜出去钓鱼去了。

---

distract
[dis'trækt]
v. 转移,分心

pliable
['plaiəbl]
adj. 易曲折的,柔软的,圆滑的

brook
[bruk]
n. 小河,溪

scramble
['skræmbl]
v. 攀缘;搅炒;混杂一起

It **discommoded** the household dreadfully, because Lock Willow of a Sunday dines at two. But he ordered dinner at seven—he orders meals whenever he chooses; you would think the place were a restaurant—and that kept Carrie and Amasai from going driving. But he said it was all the better because it wasn't proper for them to go driving without a **chaperon**; and anyway, he wanted the horses himself to take me driving. Did you ever hear anything so funny?

And poor Mrs. Semple believes that people who go fishing on Sundays go afterwards to a **sizzling** hot hell! She is awfully troubled to think that she didn't train him better when he was small and helpless and she had the chance. Besides—she wished to show him off in church.

Anyway, we had our fishing (he caught four little ones) and we cooked them on a campfire for lunch. They kept falling off our **spiked** sticks into the fire, so they tasted a little **ashy**, but we ate them. We got home at four and went driving at five and had dinner at seven, and at ten I was sent to bed—and here I am, writing to you.

I am getting a little sleepy though.

Good night.

Here is a picture of the one fish I caught.

Ship ahoy, Cap'n Long-Legs!

Avast! Belay! Yo, ho, ho, and a bottle of rum. Guess what I'm reading? Our conversation these past two days has been **nautical** and **piratical**. Isn't *Treasure Island* fun? Did you ever read it, or wasn't it written when you were a boy? Stevenson only got thirty pounds for the serial rights—I don't believe it pays to be a great author. Maybe I'll teach school.

discommode
[ˌdiskəˈməud]
v. 使不方便,使不自由,使为难

chaperon
[ˈʃæpərəun]
n. 女伴

sizzle
[ˈsizl]
v. 发出咝咝声

spike
[spaik]
v. 以大钉钉牢

ashy
[ˈæʃi]
adj. 灰的,覆盖着灰的,苍白的

    这下可乱套了,本来洛克威洛农庄星期天是下午两点用餐的,他却招呼七点才开饭——他想几点吃就几点吃,搞得农庄跟餐馆一样——结果阿马萨和卡莉就不能驾车出去了。他说这样更好,免得他们没女伴跟着出去到处乱跑,关键是他想留着马带我出去兜风。您遇到过这么好玩的事情吗?

    可怜的申普太太,她相信礼拜天溜去钓鱼的人死后肯定会被打入十八层地狱的!她非常恼怒,捶心痛恨自己没从小好好管教他。再说,她本想带他去教堂显摆显摆的。

    不管怎样,我们去钓鱼了,他钓了四条小鱼。后来我们生了火把那些鱼烤来当午餐了,烤的时候,鱼总是掉进火堆,粘满了灰,最后我们还是都吃了。我们四点到家,五点驾车出去玩了一圈,七点回来吃晚饭,十点被催着进屋睡觉——于是,我现在开始给您写信。

    有点困了。

    晚安!

    这是我画的我钓的鱼。

星期六

nautical
[ˈnɔːtikəl]
adj. 海上的,航海的

piratical
[paiˈrætikəl]
adj. 海盗的(非法翻印的)

    噢!船!长腿船长!

    停船!停船!噢!噢!来瓶郎姆酒!猜猜我这些天在读什么?这两天我们谈的都是航海呀,海盗之类的。《金银岛》很有意思,是吧?您读过吗?您还小的时候这本书就出版了,是吗?斯蒂文森的版费只有三十镑——我不相信伟大作家就如此待遇。要不,我还是去当老师吧。

 Excuse me for filling my letters so full of Stevenson; my mind is very much engaged with him at present. He comprises Lock Willow's library.

I've been writing this letter for two weeks, and I think it's about long enough. Never say, Daddy, that I don't give details. I wish you were here, too; we'd all have such a **jolly** time together. I like my different friends to know each other. I wanted to ask Mr. Pendleton if he knew you in New York—I should think he might; you must move in about the same exalted social circles, and you are both interested in reforms and things—but I couldn't, for I don't know your real name.

It's the silliest thing I ever heard of, not to know your name. Mrs. Lippett warned me that you were eccentric. I should think so!

Affectionately,
Judy

PS. On reading this over, I find that it isn't all Stevenson. There are one or two glancing references to Master Jervie.

September 10th

Dear Daddy,

He has gone, and we are missing him! When you get accustomed to people or places or ways of living, and then have them suddenly snatched away, it does leave an awfully empty, **gnawing** sort of sensation. I'm finding Mrs. Semple's conversation pretty **unseasoned** food.

College opens in two weeks and I shall be glad to begin work again. I have worked quite a lot this summer though—six short stories and seven poems. Those I sent to the magazines all came back with the most courteous **promptitude**. But I don't mind. It's

很抱歉，我的信里面总讲到斯蒂文森。主要是我现在满脑子都是他，他的作品就是洛克威洛的图书馆。

这封信我写了两周，已经很长了。长腿叔叔，别说我没——告诉您农庄上的生活。真希望您也在这儿，我喜欢我的朋友们能相互认识。我想问彭莱顿先生在纽约是否认识您——我想他可能认识。你们应该都是上流社会里的人，而且你们俩对改革之类的事务都很感兴趣——可我不知道怎么开口，因为我根本不知道您的真实姓名。

连您的姓名也不知道，这真太稀奇了。利皮特太太说您很有个性，我也这么认为！

您充满感情的
朱蒂

附言：重读了一下这封信，发现并没有都讲斯蒂文森，有一两处讲到了杰维少爷。

jolly
['dʒɔli]
adj. 愉快的,高兴的

亲爱的叔叔：

杰维少爷走了，我们都很想念他！当习惯和某个人一起生活，或者习惯呆在某个地方，或者习惯某种生活方式的时候，忽然变成另外一种生活，人们通常会觉得很失落，心中空荡荡的，而且和申普太太谈话越来越没意思了。

再过两个星期就要开学了，我很高兴又可以继续上课了。这个暑假我很用功，总共写了六篇短篇小说和七首诗。我寄到杂志社的作品全都被退回了，回复非常客气。我并不在意，只当练笔了。杰

gnaw
[nɔ:]
v. 咬,侵蚀

unseasoned
['ʌn'si:znd]
adj. 未干透的(未成熟的,无经验的)

promptitude
['prɔmptitju:d]
n. 敏捷,迅速,机敏

good practice. Master Jervie read them—he brought in the mail, so I couldn't help his knowing—and he said they were dreadful. They showed that I didn't have the slightest idea of what I was talking about. (Master Jervie doesn't let politeness **interfere** with truth.) But the last one I did—just a little sketch laid in college—he said wasn't bad; and he had it typewritten, and I sent it to a magazine. They've had it two weeks; maybe they're thinking it over.

You should see the sky! There's the queerest orange-colored light over everything. We're going to have a storm.

. . .

It commenced just that moment with drops as big as quarters and all the **shutters banging**. I had to run to close windows, while Carrie flew to the attic with an armful of milk pans to put under the places where the roof leaks—and then, just as I was resuming my pen, I remembered that I'd left a cushion and rug and hat and Matthew Arnold's poems under a tree in the orchard, so I dashed out to get them, all quite soaked. The red cover of the poems had run into the inside; "Dover Beach" in the future will be washed by pink waves.

A storm is awfully disturbing in the country. You are always having to think of so many things that are out of doors and getting spoiled.

Thursday

Daddy! Daddy! What do you think? The postman has just come with two letters.

1st—my story is accepted. $50.

Alors! I'm an AUTHOR.

2d—a letter from the college secretary. I'm to have a scholarship for two years that will cover board and tuition. It was founded by an **alumna** for "marked proficiency in English with general excellency in other lines." And I've won it! I applied for it before I left, but I didn't have an idea I'd get it, on account of my freshman bad work in math and Latin. But it seems I've made it up.

interfere
[,ɪntəˈfɪə]
v. 妨碍,冲突,干涉

维少爷读过以后,捎信儿回来说我写得很糟糕,完全不知所云。(杰维少爷向来直爽,怎么想就怎么说。)不过他说我最后一篇——在学校就写了点初稿——短篇小说还行,而且帮我用打字机打了出来,我已经寄给杂志社了。已经有两周了,他们可能在研究呢。

变天了,云层四周聚集着怪异的橘色光晕,暴风雨又要来了!

· · ·

shutter
[ˈʃʌtə]
n. 百叶窗,遮门,快门

bang
[bæŋ]
v. 发巨响,重击

说着还真的就来了! 豆大的雨粒啪嗒啪嗒开始拍打着屋顶,门窗在暴风雨里来回砰砰作响。我赶紧跑去关窗户,这时卡莉拧起好几个奶锅飞奔上小阁楼搁在漏雨的地方接雨水。我正要坐下来开始写作,突然想起我的垫子、小地毯、帽子还有马修·阿罗德的诗集都还搁在果园的果树下,于是我立马飞奔下去取,结果全都湿透了,诗集的红皮儿已经浸到书里面去了,"多佛海滨"要被粉浪冲刷了。

乡下的暴风雨还真说来就来,你得随时想着搁在外面的东西,免得糟蹋了。

九月十日

alumna
[əˈlʌmnə]
n. 女校友,女毕业生

叔叔! 叔叔! 您猜怎么着? 邮差刚送来了两封信。
第一,我的小说被采用了,五十美金稿酬。
哈哈! 我是"作家"了呢!
第二,大学秘书处来信说我可以得到两年的奖学金,包括我的食宿费和学费。该奖学金是奖给"英文特别好以及其他方面也相当出色"的学生的。我得到奖学金了! 这是我放假前申请的,本来没抱什么希望,因为大一时几何学和拉丁文被挂过,不过这似乎说明我补上来了。我高兴极了! 叔叔,以

I am awfully glad, Daddy, because now I won't be such a burden to you. The monthly allowance will be all I'll need, and maybe I can earn that with writing or **tutoring** or something.

I'm *crazy* to go back and begin work.

Yours ever,
Jerusha Abbott,

Author of, "When the Sophomores Won the Game." For sale at all newsstands, price ten cents.

September 26th

Dear Daddy-Long-Legs,

Back at college again and an upper classman. Our study is better than ever this year—faces the south with two huge windows—and, oh! so furnished. Julia, with an unlimited allowance, arrived two days early and was attacked with a fever of settling.

We have new wallpaper and Oriental rugs and mahogany chairs—not painted **mahogany** which made us sufficiently happy last year, but real. It's very **gorgeous**, but I don't feel as though I belonged in it; I'm nervous all the time for fear I'll get an ink spot in the wrong place.

And, Daddy, I found your letter waiting for me—pardon—I mean your secretary's.

Will you kindly convey to me a **comprehensible** reason why I should not accept that scholarship? I don't understand your objection in the least. But anyway, it won't do the slightest good for you to object, for I've already accepted it—and I am not going to change! That sounds a little impertinent, but I don't mean it so.

I suppose you feel that when you set out to educate me, you'd like to finish the work, and put a neat period, in the shape of a diploma, at the end.

后我不再是您的负担了。您每个月只需要寄给我零用钱就行了,不过我也可以写写文章、做做家教或者干点别的什么来挣零用钱。

我兴奋得快疯了,赶紧回学校去吧!

您永远的
乔茹莎·阿伯特

《一个大二学生获奖后》的作者,刊登该文的杂志在每个书报亭均有售,售价为十美分。

星期二

亲爱的长腿叔叔:

我已经返校,现在是高年级学生了。今年的宿舍比以前要好多了——屋子朝南,带两扇大窗户,而且屋里还有很多家具,太好啦!朱莉娅有用不完的零花钱,她两天前就返校了,正热衷于布置房间呢。

我们换了新墙纸,铺上了精致的东方地毯,还有红木椅子呢——不只是去年用漆漆红的那种椅子,是货真价实的红木椅子哦!非常漂亮!不过我总觉得我不配坐这么好的椅子。而且我每天总是神经兮兮,担心把哪儿洒上墨水。

还有,叔叔,一回到学校就收到您的信——重申一下,我说的是您秘书的来信。

能否请您给一个能够接受的理由,为何我不能接受奖学金?我完全不理解您为什么要反对。不过,不管您怎么不同意也没办法了,我已经接受了——而且坚决不改变!这么做似乎很无礼,不过请您谅解,我绝对没有故意冒犯您的意思。

我猜想您可能觉得既然决定供我念大学,就得有始有终,供到我毕业。

But look at it just a second from my point of view. I shall owe my education to you just as much as though I let you pay for the whole of it, but I won't be quite so much **indebted**. I know that you don't want me to return the money, but nevertheless, I am going to want to do it, if I possibly can; and winning this scholarship makes it so much easier. I was expecting to spend the rest of my life in paying my debts, but now I shall only have to spend one-half of the rest of it.

I hope you understand my position and won't be cross. The allowance I shall still most gratefully accept. It requires an allowance to live up to Julia and her furniture! I wish that she had been reared to simpler tastes, or else that she were not my roommate.

This isn't much of a letter; I meant to have written a lot—but I've been **hemming** four window curtains and three **portieres** (I'm glad you can't see the length of the stitches) and polishing a brass desk set with tooth powder (very uphill work) and sawing off picture wire with **manicure** scissors, and unpacking four boxes of books, and putting away two trunkfuls of clothes (it doesn't seem believable that Jerusha Abbott owns two trunks full of clothes, but she does!) and welcoming back fifty dear friends in between.

Opening day is a joyous occasion!

Good night, Daddy dear, and don't be annoyed because your chick is wanting to **scratch** for herself. She's growing up into an awfully energetic little hen—with a very determined cluck and lots of beautiful feathers (all due to you).

Affectionately,
Judy

September 30th

Dear Daddy,

Are you still harping on that scholarship? I never knew a man so **obstinate** and stubborn and unreasonable, and **tenacious**, and

indebt
[in'det]
v. 使负债,使受恩惠

hem
[hem]
v. 缝边,包围,关闭

portiere
[,pɔr'tjɛ]
n. 门帷,门帘

manicure
['mænikjuə]
n. 修指甲

scratch
[skrætʃ]
v. 搔痒,抓,抹掉

obstinate
['ɔbstinit]
adj. 固执的,倔强的

tenacious
[ti'neiʃəs]
adj. 紧粘不放的;固执的,不屈不挠的

可是，请您站在我的角度想一想，即使我接受了奖学金，丝毫没有改变的是，这四年还是您培养我的啊，我只是不想欠您太多债而已。我知道您并不指望我还钱，但我只要有能力，我一定会报答您的。有了那些奖学金，生活就会宽裕许多。我本来打算用一生来还您债的，现在看来半辈子就够了。

希望您明白我的想法，不要生气。我还是会很感激地接受您给我零用钱，和朱莉娅还有她的家具住在一起需要花很多零用钱！真希望她能节约一点，要么别和我住一块儿。

这不太像是封信，我本来打算写长点的——不过我刚装了四个窗帘和三条门帘（幸亏您没看见我做的针线活，太粗糙了），还用牙粉擦了我的铁桌子（相当费劲儿），又缝好了画布的线，还拆了四箱书，还收拾了两大箱衣服。（乔茹莎·阿伯特有满满两大箱衣服呢！听起来不太可能吧？可是她真的有呢！）另外，又要见五十位好朋友了呢。

开学真是很开心呀！

晚安，亲爱的叔叔，别因为您的小鸡要独立生气啊。她已经长大了，充满了活力，已经长成了小母鸡，一身美丽的羽毛，还咯咯大叫呢（这一切都是您的功劳啊）。

爱您的
朱蒂
九月二十六日

亲爱的叔叔：

您还在为奖学金的事情生气吗？我从来没遇到过像您那么倔强、那么固执、那么不讲理、那么刚

bulldoggish, and unable-to-see-other-people's-points-of-view as you.

You prefer that I should not be accepting favors from strangers.

Strangers! —And what are you, pray?

Is there anyone in the world that I know less? I shouldn't recognize you if I met you on the street. Now, you see, if you had been a sane, sensible person and had written nice, cheering, fatherly letters to your little Judy, and had come occasionally and patted her on the head, and had said you were glad she was such a good girl—then, perhaps, she wouldn't have **flouted** you in your old age, but would have obeyed your slightest wish like the dutiful daughter she was meant to be.

Strangers indeed! You live in a glass house, Mr. Smith.

And besides, this isn't a favor; it's like a prize—I earned it by hard work. If nobody had been good enough in English, the committee wouldn't have awarded the scholarship; some years they don't. Also—but what's the use of arguing with a man? You belong, Mr. Smith, to a sex **devoid** of a sense of logic. To bring a man into line there are just two methods: one must either **coax** or be disagreeable. I scorn to coax men for what I wish. Therefore, I must be disagreeable.

I refuse, sir, to give up the scholarship; and if you make any more fuss, I won't accept the monthly allowance either, but will wear myself into a nervous wreck tutoring stupid freshmen.

That is my **ultimatum!**

And listen—I have a further thought. Since you are so afraid that by taking this scholarship I am depriving someone else of an education, I know a way out. You can apply the money that you would have spent for me toward educating some other little girl from the John Grier Home. Don't you think that's a nice idea? Only, Daddy, educate the new girl as much as you choose, but please don't like her any better than me.

I trust that your secretary won't be hurt because I pay so little

bulldoggish
['bul'dɔgiʃ]
adj. 刚愎自用的

flout
[flaut]
v. 嘲笑,愚弄

devoid
[di'vɔid]
adj. 全无的,缺乏的

coax
[kəuks]
v. 哄,诱骗

ultimatum
[,ʌlti'meitəm]
n. 最后通牒

愎自用完全不听别人意见的人!

您不喜欢我接受陌生人的恩惠。

陌生人?!——那么您呢?

这个世界上我还有认识的人吗?恐怕我们在大街上相遇,我也不认识您。如果您是一个理智、讲理的人,并且给小朱蒂回上几封鼓励的信,像父亲一样教导您的小朱蒂,时不时地再来看看她,拍拍她的小脑袋,说说您很喜欢这个小女孩儿——那么,她可能还不会冒犯您老人家,而是像一个孝顺的女儿一样满足您小小的愿望。

真的是陌生人啊!您就是住在玻璃房子里的陌生人啊,史密斯先生!

另外,奖学金并不是恩惠,是奖励——我是通过自己的努力得到的。要是英语不好,评定委员会也不会批准我的申请,前些年也没给我啊。而且——跟一个固执的老人争论有什么用呢?史密斯先生,您是一个完全没有理智的人。要使这样的人恢复理智只有两个办法:要么循循善诱,要么发脾气!我不屑循循善诱说服您,所以只好发脾气!

先生,我拒绝放弃奖学金,您要是再有意见,我就不再接受您每月给的零用钱了,我只好牺牲健康去辅导一年级那些笨学生挣零花钱了!

这是我的最后通牒!

我还想说:您那么不想我接受奖学金,怕我剥夺了其他人接受教育的机会,我有一个办法,您可以把资助我的费用给约翰·格里尔孤儿院别的女孩子,供她们上学。您不觉得这是个好办法吗?而且,叔叔,您可以自由选择,只是不要更喜欢她就好。

我相信您的秘书不会因为我不接受您的意见而

attention to the suggestions offered in his letter, but I can't help it if he is. He's a spoiled child, Daddy. I've meekly given in to his **whims** heretofore, but this time I intend to be FIRM.

Yours,
With a mind completely and irrevo-
cably and world-without-end
made-up,
Jerusha Abbott

November 9th

Dear Daddy-Long-Legs,

I started downtown today to buy a bottle of shoe blacking and some collars and the material for a new **blouse** and a jar of violet cream and a cake of castile soap—all very necessary; I couldn't be happy another day without them—and when I tried to pay the carfare, I found that I had left my purse in the pocket of my other coat. So I had to get out and take the next car, and was late for gymnasium.

It's a dreadful thing to have no memory and two coats!

Julia Pendleton has invited me to visit her for the Christmas holidays. How does that strike you, Mr. Smith? Fancy Jerusha Abbott, of the John Grier Home, sitting at the tables of the rich. I don't know why Julia wants me—she seems to be getting quite attached to me of late. I should, to tell the truth, very much prefer going to Sallie's, but Julia asked me first, so if I go anywhere it must be to New York instead of to Worcester. I'm rather awed at the prospect of meeting Pendletons en masse, and also I'd have to get a lot of new clothes—so, Daddy dear, if you write that you would prefer having me remain quietly at college, I will bow to your wishes with my usual sweet **docility**.

I'm engaged at odd moments with the *Life and Letters of Thomas Huxley*—it makes nice, light reading to pick up between times. Do

whim
[(h)wim]
n. 一时的兴致，反复无常，怪念头

生气的，可他真要生气，我也没办法。叔叔，您的秘书被您宠坏了，我以前一直都很温顺，总是听话，这次我一定要坚决！

　　　　　您下定决心的、意志坚定的、决不改变的
　　　　　　　乔茹莎·阿伯特
　　　　　　　九月三十日

亲爱的长腿叔叔：

　　今天我去城里买了一盒鞋油、做衬衫的衣领还有布料、一瓶面霜、橄榄香皂等——都是生活必需品。我简直高兴坏了！糟糕的是，等我上车付费的时候，发现钱包忘在了另外一件外套兜儿里。所以我不得不回去取然后赶下一班，结果去健身又晚了。

blouse
[blauz]
n. 女衬衫

　　我简直太健忘了！连自己有两件外套都不记得！

　　朱莉娅·彭莱顿邀请我去她家过圣诞节。史密斯先生，您一定很惊讶吧？想想，约翰·格里尔孤儿院的乔茹莎·阿伯特跟豪门家族同桌用餐。我不知道为什么朱莉娅邀请我——她最近似乎对我友好了很多。说实话，我宁愿去莎莉家。不过朱莉娅先邀请我的，要去也只能是去纽约而不是沃塞斯特。想想要跟彭莱顿家族的人见面，心里就很忐忑，而且我还得添几件新衣服——所以，亲爱的叔叔，您要是来信希望我假期乖乖地留在学校，我会像平时一样温顺听话的。

docility
[dəuˈsiləti]
n. 顺从，温顺

　　《托马斯·赫胥黎的生平和书信集》这本书读来很轻松很愉快，所以我只要有空就会拿出来读一读。您知道"archaeopteryx"是什么吗？它是一种

you know what an archaeopteryx is? It's a bird. And a **stereognathus**? I'm not sure myself but I think it's a missing link, like a bird with teeth or a **lizard** with wings. No, it isn't either; I've just looked in the book. It's a **mesozoic** mammal.

I've elected economics this year—very illuminating subject. When I finish that I'm going to take Charity and Reform; then, Mr. Trustee, I'll know just how an orphan asylum ought to be run. Don't you think I'd make an admirable voter if I had my rights? I was twenty-one last week. This is an awfully wasteful country to throw away such an honest, educated, conscientious, intelligent citizen as I would be.

Yours always,
Judy

December 7th

Dear Daddy-Long-Legs,

Thank you for permission to visit Julia—I take it that silence means **consent**.

Such a social **whirl** as we've been having! The founder's dance came last week—this was the first year that any of us could attend, only upperclassmen being allowed.

stereognathus
n. 始祖鸟

lizard
['lizəd]
n. 蜥蜴

mesozoic
[ˌmesəu'zəuik]
adj. 中生代的

古代的始祖鸟。"stereognathus"呢？我也不知道，好像是一种过渡物种，比如说长牙的鸟类或长翅膀的蜥蜴等。也不一定，有可能都不是，是一种中生代的哺乳动物。

这只是一幅stereognathus的画，他长着一副蛇的头，狗的耳朵，奶牛的脚，蜥蜴的尾巴，天鹅的翅膀；还长着一身软软的毛，像小猫身上的那种

我今年选修了经济学——让我大开眼界。修完之后，我要写一篇"论慈善事业的改革"的论文。瞧，叔叔，我很快就能知道如何管理一家孤儿院了。要是我有资格投票的话，您不觉得我会是一个很棒的选举人吗？我上周满二十一岁了。国家抛弃我这样一个诚实、受过教育而又聪明的公民，简直太浪费了！

您永远的
朱蒂
十一月九日

亲爱的长腿叔叔：

谢谢您批准我去朱莉娅家——我想您保持沉默就表示同意。

这段时间的活动真是太多了！上星期学校举行了一年一度的舞会——今年是第一次参加，以往只有高年级同学可以参加的。

consent
[kən'sent]
n. 同意，许可

whirl
[(h)wə:l]
n. 回旋，旋转，急走

I invited Jimmie McBride, and Sallie invited his roommate at Princeton, who visited them last summer at their camp—an awfully nice man with red hair—and Julia invited a man from New York, not very exciting, but socially **irreproachable**. He is connected with the de la Mater Chichesters. Perhaps that means something to you? It doesn't illuminate me to any extent.

However—our guests came Friday afternoon in time for tea in the senior corridor, and then dashed down to the hotel for dinner. The hotel was so full that they slept in rows on the **billiard** tables, they say. Jimmie McBride says that the next time he is bidden to a social event in this college, he is going to bring one of their Adirondack tents and **pitch** it on the campus.

At seven thirty they came back for the president's reception and dance. Our functions commence early! We had the men's cards all made out ahead of time, and after every dance, we'd leave them in groups under the letter that stood for their names, so that they could be readily found by their next partners. Jimmie McBride, for example, would stand patiently under M until he was claimed. (At least, he ought to have stood patiently, but he kept wandering off and getting mixed with R's and S's and all sorts of letters.) I found him a very difficult guest; he was **sulky** because he had only three dances with me. He said he was bashful about dancing with girls he didn't know!

The next morning we had a **glee** club concert—and who do you think wrote the funny new song composed for the occasion? It's the truth. She did. Oh, I tell you, Daddy, your little foundling is getting to be quite a **prominent** person!

Anyway, our gay two days were great fun, and I think the men enjoyed it. Some of them were awfully **perturbed** at first at the prospect of facing one thousand girls; but they got **acclimated** very quickly. Our two Princeton men had a beautiful time—at least they politely said they had, and they've invited us to their dance next spring. We've accepted, so please don't object, Daddy dear.

irreproachable [ˌiri'prəutʃəbl] *adj.* 不可非难的,无缺点的,无过失的	我邀请了吉米·麦克白,莎莉邀请了吉米的大学室友,他去年暑假参加过麦克白家的露营活动,满头红发,人很和蔼。朱莉娅则邀请了一位纽约上流社会人士,从社交的角度看,没什么可说的,因为他是德拉马特·奇切斯特家的人。这对您可能还有点意思,对我而言,一点意义也没有。

我们的客人星期五下午到齐,先聚在高年级生宿舍吃茶点,然后再赶回旅馆吃晚餐。旅馆住不下,他们只好横着睡台球桌——他们后来自己说的。吉米·麦克白说下次再被邀参加大学生活动,一定要把帐篷睡袋带来,好在校园里露营。

billiard ['biljəd] *adj.* 撞球的

pitch [pitʃ] *v.* 投,向前倾跌,扎牢

校长招待会和舞会七点半开始的,联欢会提早开始了!我们事先将卡片做好,每跳完一支曲子,就让男士们按姓氏字母的顺序列队等候,以方便随后的女舞伴找到。比如,吉米·麦克白需要站在M组耐心等候,一直得等到有人来请他(至少他应该耐心等,不过他总是蹿来蹿去,经常混进R或者S组)。我发现他真是很难对付,还因为只和我跳了三支舞曲生气了,他说自己不好意思跟不认识的女孩子跳舞!

sulky ['sʌlki] *adj.* 生气的(阴沉的)

glee [gli:] *n.* 欢乐,高兴

prominent ['prɔminənt] *adj.* 杰出的,显著的,突出的

第二天早上有一场合唱音乐会——您猜那滑稽搞笑的新歌是谁写的呢?是她!噢!告诉您吧,叔叔,是您的小弃儿!她现在很出名了呢!

perturb [pə'tə:b] *v.* 扰乱,使混乱,使心慌

acclimate [ə'klaimit] *v.* 使习惯于新环境

不管怎么说,这两天玩得很开心,我想男士们也应该很开心吧!面对一千个女孩子,有些男宾刚开始非常拘束,不过很快就适应了。普林斯顿来的两位客人也十分开心——至少他们是出于礼貌这样说的,还邀请我们明年春天去参加他们的舞会。我们接受了邀请,所以亲爱的叔叔,请您别反对啊。

Julia and Sallie and I all had new dresses. Do you want to hear about them? Julia's was cream satin and gold embroidery, and she wore purple orchids. It was a dream and came from Paris, and cost a million dollars.

Sallie's was pale blue trimmed with Persian **embroidery**, and went beautifully with red hair. It didn't cost quite a million, but was just as effective as Julia's.

Mine was pale pink crepe de chine trimmed with ecru lace and rose satin. And I carried crimson roses which J. McB. sent (Sallie having told him what color to get). And we all had satin slippers and silk stockings and **chiffon scarfs** to match.

You must be deeply impressed by these millinery details!

One can't help thinking, Daddy, what a colorless life a man is forced to lead, when one reflects that chiffon and **venetian** point and hand embroidery and Irish **crochet** are to him mere empty words. Whereas a woman whether she is interested in babies or **microbes** or husbands or poetry or servants or **parallelograms** or gardens or Plato or bridge—is fundamentally and always interested in clothes.

It's the one touch of nature that makes the whole world kin. (That isn't original. I got it out of one of Shakespeare's plays.)

However, to resume. Do you want me to tell you a secret that I've lately discovered? And will you promise not to think me vain? Then listen:

I'm pretty.

I am, really. I'd be an awful idiot not to know it with three looking glasses in the room.

A Friend

PS. This is one of those wicked anonymous letters you read about in novels.

embroidery
[imˈbrɔidəri]
n. 刺绣品；粉饰；刺绣

chiffon
[ˈʃifɔn]
adj. 薄而软的

scarf
[skɑ:f]
n. 围巾

venetian
[viˈni:ʃən]
adj. 威尼斯城的

crochet
[ˈkrəuʃei]
n. 编织器

microbe
[ˈmaikrəub]
n. 微生物

parallelogram
[ˌpærəˈleləgræm]
n. 平行四边形

朱莉娅、莎莉还有我都穿了新裙子。您想听听我们怎样打扮的吗？朱莉娅穿的是乳白色缎面衣服，上面有金色刺绣，她还带着紫色兰花。她的衣服是在巴黎定做的，穿上很梦幻哦，估计得值上百万美元。

莎莉穿的是天蓝色裙装，镶有波斯花边，跟她的头发很搭配。虽然不值百万，但是丝毫不比朱莉娅逊色。

我穿的是淡粉色的裙子，缀着玫瑰花边，手里捧着吉米·麦克白送我的玫瑰花（莎莉提前告诉他要带什么颜色的花）。我们都穿着长统丝袜、缎面鞋、披着颜色相配的薄纱披巾。

这些服饰的细节肯定会给您留下深刻印象吧！

叔叔，我真为男人们单调枯燥的生活感到遗憾。想想看，薄纱、威尼斯花边和爱尔兰钩针编织，这些对男人们来说毫无意义。而女人，不管她们是喜欢孩子、微生物、丈夫、诗歌、仆人、平行四边形、花园、柏拉图，还是喜欢桥牌，服装永远是她们最喜欢的。

四海一家亲（并非我首创，摘自莎士比亚的戏剧）。

另外，您想知道我最近刚发现的秘密吗？不过您得保证不会认为我很虚荣才行，好吗？告诉您吧：

我很漂亮。

真的！房里有三面镜子，我不会傻到连这一点都看不出来。

一位友人
十二月七日

补充：这是一封像您在小说里读到过的邪恶的匿名信之一。

December 20th

Dear Daddy-Long-Legs,

I've just a moment, because I must attend two classes, pack a trunk and a suitcase, and catch the four-o'clock train—but I couldn't go without sending a word to let you know how much I appreciate my Christmas box.

I love the furs and the necklace and the liberty scarf and the gloves and handkerchiefs and books and purse—and most of all I love you! But Daddy, you have no business to spoil me this way. I'm only human—and a girl at that. How can I keep my mind **sternly** fixed on a **studious** career when you **deflect** me with such worldly frivolities?

I have strong suspicions now as to which one of the John Grier trustees used to give the Christmas tree and the Sunday ice cream. He was nameless, but by his works I know him! You deserve to be happy for all the good things you do.

Good-bye, and a very merry Christmas.

Yours always,
Judy

PS. I am sending a slight token, too. Do you think you would like her if you knew her?

January 11th

I meant to write to you from the city, Daddy, but New York is an **engrossing** place.

I had an interesting—and illuminating—time, but I'm glad I don't belong in such a family! I should truly rather have the John Grier Home for a background. Whatever the drawbacks of my bringing up, there was at least no pretense about it. I know now what people mean when they say they are weighted down by things. The material

亲爱的长腿叔叔：

我只有一点时间，要先去上两节课，还要收拾一个行李箱和一个大手提袋，得去赶四点的火车——不过走之前还是想写几句，告诉您我非常喜欢您送的圣诞礼物。

貂皮大衣、项链、头巾、手套、手绢、书还有手提包，所有的我都喜欢——当然，最喜欢的还是您！不过，叔叔，您没有义务把我宠坏呀！我只是个普通人——一个再普通不过的女孩子。您用这些凡尘俗物来腐化我的心灵，我又怎么能专心念书呢？

我现在终于知道是谁每年给约翰·格里尔孤儿院提供圣诞树和每周一次的冰淇淋了。虽然他从不提自己的姓名，我也能猜出来。您所做的这一切，一定会带给您一生快乐的！

再见，祝您圣诞快乐！

您永远的
朱蒂
十二月二十日

附言：这是我送给您的小礼物，假如您认识她的话，希望您能喜欢她！

叔叔，本来打算在纽约给您写信的，可是纽约实在太让人眼花缭乱了。

我在纽约度过了一段很有意义的日子，简直让我大开眼界！我庆幸自己没有出生在那样的家庭，我宁愿在孤儿院里长大。不管出身多么不好，至少过得简单而真诚。我现在终于明白为何人们总说他

---

sternly
['stə:nli]
adv. 严格地，严肃地，严厉地

studious
['stju:djəs]
adj. 爱好学问的，努力于…的，热心的

deflect
[di'flekt]
v. 打歪，使偏，歪

engross
[in'grəus]
v. 占去，使全神贯注

atmosphere of that house was crushing; I didn't draw a deep breath until I was on an express train coming back. All the furniture was carved and upholstered and gorgeous; the people I met were beautifully dressed and low-voiced and well-bred, but it's the truth, Daddy, I never heard one word of real talk from the time we arrived until we left. I don't think an idea ever entered the front door.

Mrs. Pendleton never thinks of anything but jewels and dressmakers and social engagements. She did seem a different kind of mother from Mrs. McBride! If I ever marry and have a family, I'm going to make them as exactly like the McBrides as I can. Not for all the money in the world would I ever let any children of mine develop into Pendletons. Maybe it isn't polite to criticize people you've been visiting. If it isn't, please excuse. This is very **confidential**, between you and me.

I only saw Master Jervie once when he called at tea time, and then I didn't have a chance to speak to him alone. It was sort of disappointing after our nice time last summer. I don't think he cares much for his relatives—and I am sure they don't care much for him! Julia's mother says he's unbalanced. He's a socialist—except, thank heaven, he doesn't let his hair grow and wear red ties. She can't imagine where he picked up his queer ideas; the family have been Church of England for generations. He throws away his money on every sort of crazy reform, instead of spending it on such sensible things as yachts and automobiles and **polo ponies**. He does buy candy with it though! He sent Julia and me each a box for Christmas.

You know, I think I'll be a socialist too. You wouldn't mind, would you, Daddy? They're quite different from **anarchists**; they don't believe in blowing people up. Probably I am one by rights; I belong to the **proletariat**. I haven't determined yet just which kind I am going to be. I will look into the subject over Sunday, and declare my principles in my next.

们不堪重负。她家浓重的金钱味儿憋得我简直喘不过起来。一直到我登上了特快专列返回校园才松了口气。她家所有的家具都精雕细琢，屋内装饰得富丽堂皇；所见的人都是衣着讲究、低声交谈，显得很有品味的样子。不过，叔叔，说实话，我打从进她家到离开，始终没有听到过一句真心话。

跟麦克白太太完全不同，彭莱顿太太满脑子都是金钱、珠宝、裁缝还有宴会。有朝一日，我要是结婚生子，我会像麦克白家一样培养自己的孩子，就是全世界的钱都给我，我也不会让我的任何一个孩子像彭莱顿家的那样。这样说也许对一个刚刚拜访过的家庭很不礼貌，可是请您原谅，我只不过是想跟您说说心里话。

我只在吃茶点的时候见过杰维少爷，也没机会跟他单独交流，真遗憾！去年夏天，我们玩得非常开心的！看起来他对他那些亲戚没有太多好感，而且他们也不大理他。朱莉娅的妈妈说他是个愤世嫉俗的人。他是一个社会主义者——不过，感谢上帝，他没留长发，也没扎红领带。她简直不知道他那些奇怪的想法是哪儿学来的。他们家世代都是国教徒，可他偏偏不爱享受游艇啊、汽车啊、赌马之类的，偏偏喜欢花钱在疯狂的社会改革上。不过他也买糖的！圣诞节的时候他还分别送给我和朱莉娅礼物！

我想我也快成社会主义者了。叔叔，您不介意吧？社会主义者跟无政府主义者完全不同，他们不会煽动大众反抗。我可能也是其中一员，不过我是无产阶级，我还没想好我到底朝哪个方向发展。周日我要仔细研究研究这个主题，下次再表达我的看法。

---

confidential
[kɔnfi'denʃəl]
adj. 机密的；获他人信赖的，易于信任他人的

polo pony
马球马

anarchist
['ænəkist]
n. 无政府主义者

proletariat
[,prəule'tɛəriət]
n.（古罗马社会中的）最下层阶级，工人阶级

I've seen loads of theaters and hotels and beautiful houses. My mind is a confused **jumble** of **onyx** and **gilding** and **mosaic** floors and palms. I'm still pretty breathless but I am glad to get back to college and my books—I believe that I really am a student; this atmosphere of academic calm I find more bracing than New York. College is a very satisfying sort of life; the books and study and regular classes keep you alive mentally, and then when your mind gets tired, you have the gymnasium and outdoor athletics, and always plenty of **congenial** friends who are thinking about the same things you are. We spend a whole evening in nothing but talk—talk—talk—and go to bed with a very uplifted feeling, as though we had settled permanently some pressing world problems. And filling in every **crevice**, there is always such a lot of nonsense—just silly jokes about the little things that come up—but very satisfying. We do appreciate our own **witticisms**!

It isn't the great big pleasures that count the most; it's making a great deal out of the little ones—I've discovered the true secret of happiness, Daddy, and that is to live in the now. Not to be forever regretting the past, or anticipating the future; but to get the most that you can out of this very instant. It's like farming. You can have extensive farming and intensive farming; well, I am going to have intensive living after this. I'm going to enjoy every second, and I'm going to know I'm enjoying it while I'm enjoying it. Most people don't live; they just race. They are trying to reach some goal far away on the horizon, and in the heat of the going they get so breathless and panting that they lose all sight of the beautiful, tranquil country they are passing through; and then the first thing they know, they are old and worn out, and it doesn't make any difference whether they've reached the goal or not. I've decided to sit down by the way and pile up a lot of little happinesses, even if I never become a great author. Did you ever know such a

jumble
['dʒʌmbl]
n. 混杂，混乱

onyx
['ɔniks]
n. 缟玛瑙

gilding
['gildiŋ]
n. 镀金术（假象）

mosaic
[mɔ'zeiik]
n. 马赛克；镶嵌细工，镶木细工

congenial
[kən'dʒi:njəl]
adj. 同性质的，适意的，趣味相同的

crevice
['krevis]
n.（岩石、墙等）裂缝

witticism
['witisizəm]
n. 名言，机敏，妙语

　　我见了数不清的大剧院、饭店和豪宅，脑子里全是玛瑙、镀金、镶木地板和棕榈树，这一切璀璨夺目的东西久久停留在我的脑海。然而，我却很高兴又回到宁静的学校，回来读我的书，变回原来那个单纯的学生。校园的宁静比纽约的喧嚣更迷人，大学生活才是惬意的。书籍、学习还有上课让我们的思想活跃。疲劳的时候，可以到体育馆或操场上运动运动，还有那么多志同道合的同学们，可以和他们秉烛畅谈，然后舒舒服服地睡上一觉，就仿佛我们彻底地解决了什么世界难题似的。谈论中时而穿插一些笑话，胡扯一通，虽然没谈什么，但是心情格外舒畅，而且还经常妙语连珠、洋洋得意的样子呢！

　　其实，最有意思的不是谈惊天动地的大事，而是生活琐事。我觉得自己发现了快乐的真谛——品味历程，活在当下。不要总是懊悔过去或者展望未来，而是要充分享受今天。比如种田，可以分为粗放耕作和精耕细作。今后，我要过精细的生活，享受人生的每一刻，而且在享受的同时能清醒地意识到自己是在享受。现实生活中，许多人不是在生活，而是在跟时间赛跑。他们一直努力攀登生命地平线上的最高峰，拼命地奔跑着，可他们却忘记了欣赏一路上美轮美奂的旖旎风光。有一天，自己老了，倦了，猛然发现原来实不实现目标结果都一样。不过，我是打算漫步人生的，一路走一路游，累积人生，享受生活中的点点滴滴，就算永远当不了伟大的作家也无所谓。您见过像我

philosopheress as I am developing into?

>Yours ever,
>Judy

PS. It's raining cats and dogs tonight. Two puppies and a kitten have just landed on the windowsill.

Dear Comrade,

Hooray! I'm a Fabian.

That's a socialist who's willing to wait. We don't want the social **revolution** to come tomorrow morning; it would be too upsetting. We want it to come very gradually in the distant future, when we shall all be prepared and able to sustain the shock.

In the meantime we must be getting ready, by instituting industrial, educational, and orphan asylum reforms.

>Yours, with fraternal love,
>Judy
>Monday, 3d hour

February 11th

Dear D. L. L.,

Don't be insulted because this is so short. It isn't a letter; it's just a line to say that I'm going to write a letter pretty soon when examinations are over. It is not only necessary that I pass, but pass WELL. I have a scholarship to live up to.

>Yours, studying hard,
>J. A.

March 5th

Dear Daddy-Long-Legs,

President Cuyler made a speech this evening about the modern

这样的哲学家吗?

您永远的

朱蒂

一月十一日

附言：今晚倾盆大雨，两只狗和一只猫跳到窗台上躲雨。

亲爱的同志：

万岁！我决定当个费边社会主义者！

社会主义者期待改革。可我们也不想明天早上就来一场社会革命。太惊心动魄了！我们希望它慢慢地来，时间长一点也没关系，这样好让我们有点心理准备。

同时，我们得准备好进行工业改革、教育改革还有孤儿院管理体制改革等等。

亲切问候您的

朱蒂

周一第三节课

revolution
[ˌrevəˈluːʃən]
n. 革命

亲爱的长腿叔叔：

别介意这封信太短啊。其实这算不上是封信，我只是想告诉您，等考试结束，我会很快给您写信的。为了我的奖学金，我不仅要及格，而且还得考高分。

您努力学习的

朱蒂

二月十一日

亲爱的长腿叔叔：

库勒校长今晚讲话时谈到现代青年过于轻薄过

generation being **flippant** and superficial. He says that we are losing the old ideals of earnest **endeavor** and true scholarship; and particularly is this falling off noticeable in our disrespectful attitude toward organized authority. We no longer pay a seemly deference to our superiors.

I came away from chapel very sober.

Am I too familiar, Daddy? Ought I to treat you with more dignity and **aloofness**? —Yes, I'm sure I ought. I'll begin again.

. . .

My dear Mr. Smith,

You will be pleased to hear that I passed successfully my midyear examinations, and am now **commencing** work in the new semester. I am leaving chemistry—having completed the course in qualitative analysis—and am entering upon the study of biology. I approach this subject with some hesitation, as I understand that we dissect angleworms and frogs.

An extremely interesting and valuable lecture was given in the chapel last week upon Roman Remains in Southern France. I have never listened to a more illuminating exposition of the subject.

We are reading Wordsworth's *Tintern Abbey* in connection with our course in English Literature. What an exquisite work it is, and how adequately it embodies his conception of Pantheism! The Romantic movement of the early part of the last century, **exemplified** in the works of such poets as Shelley, Byron, Keats, and Wordsworth, appeals to me very much more than the Classical period that preceded it. Speaking of poetry, have you ever read that charming little thing of Tennyson's called *"Locksley Hall"*?

I am attending gymnasium very regularly of late. A **proctor** system has been devised, and failure to comply with the rules causes a great deal of inconvenience. The gymnasium is equipped with a very beautiful swimming tank of cement and **marble**, the gift of a former graduate. My roommate, Miss McBride, has given me

flippant
['flipənt]
adj. 轻率的,没礼貌的,嘴碎的

endeavor
[in'devə]
n. 努力,尽力

aloofness
[ə'lu:fnis]
n. 远离(隔开)

commence
[kə'mens]
v. 开始

exemplify
[ig'zemplifai]
v. 例证,例示

proctor
['prɔktə]
n. 代理人,学监

marble
['mɑ:bl]
n. 大理石

于肤浅,说我们逐渐失去了勤奋刻苦、认真做学问的优秀品质。这一点尤其体现在不尊重权威、不尊敬前辈上。

从大讲堂回来,我一直都在思考这个问题。

叔叔,我跟您是不是太不见外了呢?是否应该对您更恭敬保持距离好些呢?没错,我确实应该这么做。那我就重新开始吧。

. . .

亲爱的史密斯先生:

期末考试全部通过,您一定很高兴吧。现在要开始为新学年做准备了。我要停修化学——已学完了定性分析——改修生物学。这门课要解剖蚯蚓和青蛙,选课的时候我还犹豫了一阵。

上周在大讲堂听关于南部法国的古罗马遗迹,讲座非常有趣,很有价值。我从来没听过这么别开生面的主题讲座。

最近我们一直在读华兹华斯的《丁登寺旁》,跟我们的英国文学课有关的。简直是太精妙的诗歌了!完全体现他诗人泛神论的思想!上世纪早期的浪漫主义运动孕育了雪莱、拜伦、济慈以及华兹华斯这些伟大的诗人。相对于古典时期,我更喜欢浪漫主义时期。说到诗歌,您读过丁尼森的《洛克斯莱大厅》吗?特别迷人。

最近,我经常去体育馆锻炼身体。体育馆里有一个漂亮的游泳池,水泥和大理石砌起来的,是校友捐赠的。我的室友麦克白小姐把她的泳衣给了我

her bathing suit (it shrank so that she can no longer wear it) and I am about to begin swimming lessons.

We had delicious pink ice cream for dessert last night. Only vegetable dyes are used in coloring the food. The college is very much opposed, both from **esthetic** and **hygienic** motives, to the use of **aniline** dyes.

The weather of late has been ideal—bright sunshine and clouds **interspersed** with a few welcome snowstorms. I and my companions have enjoyed our walks to and from classes—particularly from.

Trusting, my dear Mr. Smith, that this will find you in your usual good health,

I remain,
Most cordially yours,
Jerusha Abbott

April 24th

Dear Daddy,

Spring has come again! You should see how lovely the campus is. I think you might come and look at it for yourself. Master Jervie

(因为缩水她穿不了了),我要开始学游泳了。

昨晚晚餐后的甜点——粉色冰淇淋——真好吃。出于美容和健康的考虑,学校禁止使用色素,规定食物只用蔬菜着色。

最近天气挺好的,常常阳光灿烂,偶尔下了几场雪。我和同学喜欢步行上下课,特别是下课的时候更喜欢步行。

亲爱的史密斯先生,祝您永远身体健康!

此致

您最真诚的
乔茹莎·阿伯特
三月五日

亲爱的叔叔:

春天又来了!您真该亲自来看看校园风光是多么美丽!杰维少爷上星期五来访——可惜他来得不

esthetic
[iːsˈθetik]
adj. 审美的

hygienic
[haiˈdʒiːnik]
adj. 卫生学的,卫生的

aniline
[ˈæniliːn]
n. 苯胺

intersperse
[ˌintə(ː)ˈspəːs]
v. 散布,点缀

dropped in again last Friday—but he chose a most unpropitious time, for Sallie and Julia and I were just running to catch a train. And where do you think we were going? To Princeton, to attend a dance and a ball game, if you please! I didn't ask you if I might go, because I had a feeling that your secretary would say no. But it was entirely regular; we had leave of absence from college, and Mrs. McBride **chaperoned** us. We had a charming time—but I shall have to omit details; they are too many and complicated.

Saturday

Up before dawn! The night watchman called us—six of us—and we made coffee in a **chafing** dish (you never saw so many grounds!) and walked two miles to the top of One Tree Hill to see the sun rise. We had to **scramble** up the last slope! The sun almost beat us! And perhaps you think we didn't bring back appetites to breakfast!

Dear me, Daddy, I seem to have a very **ejaculatory** style today; this page is peppered with exclamations.

This is Prexy's kitten. You can see from the picture how Angora he is.

I meant to have written a lot about the budding trees and the new cinder path in the athletic field, and the awful lesson we have in biology for tomorrow, and the new canoes on the lake, and Catherine Prentiss who has pneumonia, and Prexy's Angora kitten

是时候,正赶上莎莉、朱莉娅和我去赶火车。您猜我们去哪儿了?是去普林斯顿参加舞会和球赛。我没有征求您的意见就离开,因为我觉得您的秘书不会同意我去。不过我们是履行手续了的,我们向学校请了假,而且同行的还有麦克白太太。玩得开心极了!细节我就不详述了,发生太多故事了,讲起来也复杂。

chaperone
['ʃæpərəun]
v. 伴护

四月二十四日

我们天还没亮就上山了!守夜的人叫醒了我们六个。我们煮了咖啡喝,留一大堆咖啡渣在锅里!随后,我们步行大约两英里上独树山山顶看日出。我们一路连滚带爬,差点错过了日出!回来吃的早餐,您简直无法想象我们狼吞虎咽的样子!

天啦!叔叔,这页怎么这么多感叹号!真是感慨万分啊!

chafe
[tʃeif]
v. 摩擦,擦痛;激怒

scramble
['skræmbl]
v. 攀缘,搅炒,混杂一起

ejaculatory
[i'dʒækjulətəri]
adj. 突然喊叫的;感叹的;射出性的

这是蕾里克茜的小猫,您可以瞧瞧他长得多么安哥拉!

本来打算多写写发新芽的树木和运动场里新的煤渣跑道的,或者多写一些关于明天要上的糟糕的生物课、湖上的新游船、凯瑟琳·普兰蒂丝患了肺炎、普里克茜的安哥拉小猫找不着家了,在弗格森

that strayed from home and has been boarding in Fergussen Hall for two weeks until a chambermaid reported it, and about my three new dresses—white and pink and blue polka dots with a hat to match—but I am too sleepy. I am always making this an excuse, am I not? But a girls' college is a busy place and we do get tired by the end of the day! Particularly when the day begins at dawn.

Affectionately,
Judy

May 15th

Dear Daddy-Long-Legs,

Is it good manners when you get into a car just to stare straight ahead and not see anybody else?

A very beautiful lady in a very beautiful velvet dress got into the car today, and without the slightest expression sat for fifteen minutes and looked at a sign advertising **suspenders**. It doesn't seem polite to ignore everybody else as though you were the only important person present. Anyway, you miss a lot. While she was absorbing that silly sign, I was studying a whole car full of interesting human beings.

大厦呆了两周才被打扫卫生的女工发现。还有我的三件新裙子：白色的、粉色的以及天蓝色圆点花纹裙和配的帽子——可我太困了，我经常拿这个当借口，是吧？大学其实挺忙的，一整天下来真的很累！而且今天天一亮就起床了。

您充满感情的
朱蒂
星期六

亲爱的长腿叔叔：

坐车的时候眼睛直盯着前方，旁若无人的样子，您不觉得这样做不礼貌吗？

今天，一位身穿非常漂亮的天鹅绒衣服的漂亮小姐上了车之后，面无表情坐了十五分钟，一直盯着裤子背带的广告牌看，简直目中无人，似乎就她一个人很重要的样子，这样似乎太不礼貌了。不管怎么说，您没看到。她一直欣赏着蠢乎乎的广告牌，而我则琢磨着这车上所有那些有意思的人。

suspender
[sə'spendə(r)]
n. 吊裤带

The accompanying illustration is hereby reproduced for the first time. It looks like a **spider** on the end of a string, but it isn't at all; it's a picture of me learning to swim in the tank in the gymnasium.

The instructor hooks a rope into a ring in the back of my belt, and runs it through a **pulley** in the ceiling. It would be a beautiful system if one had perfect confidence in the **probity** of one's instructor. I'm always afraid, though, that she will let the rope get slack, so I keep one anxious eye on her and swim with the other, and with this divided interest I do not make the progress that I otherwise might.

Very **miscellaneous** weather we're having of late. It was raining when I commenced and now the sun is shining. Sallie and I are going out to play tennis—thereby gaining exemption from gym.

A week later

I should have finished this letter long ago, but I didn't. You don't mind, do you, Daddy, if I'm not very regular? I really do love to write to you; it gives me such a respectable feeling of having some family. Would you like me to tell you something? You are not the only man to whom I write letters. There are two others! I have been receiving beautiful long letters this winter from Master Jervie (with typewritten envelopes so Julia won't recognize the writing). Did you ever hear anything so shocking? And every week or so a very **scrawly** epistle, usually on yellow tablet paper, arrives from Princeton. All of which I answer with businesslike promptness. So you see, I am not so different from other girls—I get mail too.

Did I tell you that I have been elected a member of the Senior Dramatic Club? Very recherché organization. Only seventy-five members out of one thousand. Do you think as a consistent socialist that I ought to belong?

What do you suppose is at present engaging my attention in sociology? I am writing (*figurez vous!*) a paper on the *Care of Dependent Children*. The professor **shuffled** up his subjects and dealt

spider
['spaidə]
n. 蜘蛛

pulley
['puli]
n. 滑车,滑轮

probity
['prəubiti]
n. 诚实,廉洁,正直

miscellaneous
[misi'leinjəs]
adj. 各种的，多方面的

　　附上图画再现情景。看起来像一只蜘蛛吊在一条绳子上，其实完全不是，这是我学游泳的样子。

　　学游泳的时候，教练用挂在天花板滑轮上的绳子穿过我的腰带。如果对教练的教法完全充满信心，这种办法倒是挺不错的。可是我总怕她松开绳子，所以只好一只眼睛紧张地盯着她，另一只眼睛注意游泳。一心二用，自然进步很慢了。

　　这几天天气变化无常，刚开始写信时还阴雨连绵，现在已经是阳光明媚了。莎莉约我去打网球，我就不去体育馆锻炼了。

五月十五日

　　这封信早就该写完的。叔叔，您不介意我写信这么没有规律吧？我真的很喜欢写信给您，这让我感到有亲人的存在。您知道吗？您已不再是我唯一的通信对象了，还有另外两个哦！今年冬天，杰维少爷给我写了一封很长很漂亮的信（信封是用打字机打印的，主要是为了不让朱莉娅认出笔迹来）。多有趣呀！另外，每周也会收到一封从普林斯顿寄来的信，用的是学校的黄色信笺，字很潦草，我都

scrawl
[skrɔ:l]
n. 瞎画

及时回复了，所以您瞧——我现在跟别的女孩子一样能收到不同的信了呢。

　　我告诉过您我入选高年级戏剧社的会员了吗？这个社团非常受欢迎，每一千人中才选七十五人呢。

　　您知道我最近对什么社会学问题感兴趣吗？我正在写一篇《如何照顾依赖性强的孩子》的论文（多棒!），老师把题目写在纸条上让我们抽签，我

shuffle
['ʃʌfl]
v. 拖曳,慢吞吞地走

them out **promiscuously**, and that fell to me. *C'est drôle ça n'est pas?*
There goes the gong for dinner. I'll mail this as I pass the chute.

Affectionately,
J.

June 4th

Dear Daddy,

Very busy time—commencement in ten days, examinations tomorrow; lots of studying, lots of packing, and the outdoors world so lovely that it hurts you to stay inside.

But never mind, vacation's coming. Julia is going abroad this summer—it makes the fourth time. No doubt about it, Daddy, goods are not distributed evenly. Sallie, as usual, goes to the Adirondacks. And what do you think I am going to do? You may have three guesses. Lock Willow? Wrong. The Adirondacks with Sallie? Wrong. (I'll never attempt that again; I was discouraged last year.) Can't you guess anything else? You're not very inventive. I'll tell you, Daddy, if you'll promise not to make a lot of objections. I warn your secretary ahead of time that my mind is made up.

I am going to spend the summer at the seaside with a Mrs. Charles Paterson and tutor her daughter who is to enter college in the autumn. I met her through the McBrides, and she is a very charming woman. I am to give lessons in English and Latin to the younger daughter, too, but I shall have a little time to myself, and I shall be earning fifty dollars a month! Doesn't that impress you as a perfectly **exorbitant** amount? She offered it; I should have blushed to ask more than twenty-five.

I finish at Magnolia (that's where she lives) the first of September and shall probably spend the remaining three weeks at Lock Willow—I should like to see the Semples again and all the friendly animals.

正好抽到了这个题目。很有意思,不是吗?

晚餐铃响了,我一会儿路过邮筒就把信寄出去。

充满深情的

J.

一周后

亲爱的叔叔:

这段时间非常忙碌,因为再过十天就是毕业典礼了,明天还要考试,大家忙着复习,忙着收拾行李。外面的世界是如此精彩,总呆着不出门真让人憋屈啊。

不过没关系,暑假快到了。朱莉娅今年暑假要出国旅行——这是第四次了。叔叔,人各有天命啊。跟往常一样,莎莉去阿迪朗达克。我呢?您可以猜猜,最多猜三次哦。洛克威洛?错!跟莎莉去阿迪朗达克?错!(不敢奢望,去年已经很受打击了)。猜不到别的了吗?您太缺乏想象力了吧。告诉您,叔叔,您答应不极力反对的话,我事先向您的秘书说明我已经打定主意了。

夏天我要跟查尔斯·帕特尔森夫人去海边,辅导她即将上大学的女儿。查尔斯·帕特尔森夫人是我在麦克白家认识的,她是位非常有魅力的女士。我还要教她的小女儿英文和拉丁文,不过我还留了一点时间给自己。每月可赚五十元。您不觉得太高了吗?是她先提出来的,我本来觉得要二十五元就挺难开口的了。

所以我整个九月都将在麦格诺利亚度过,她家在那儿。剩下三周我可能要去洛克威洛——很高兴再见到申普夫妇,还有那些可爱的小动物。

---

promiscuously
[prəˈmiskjuəs]
adv. 杂乱地,混杂地

exorbitant
[igˈzɔːbitənt]
adj. 过高的

How does my program strike you, Daddy? I am getting quite independent, you see. You have put me on my feet and I think I can almost walk alone by now.

Princeton commencement and our examinations exactly coincide—which is an awful blow. Sallie and I did so want to get away in time for it, but of course that is utterly impossible.

Good-bye, Daddy. Have a nice summer and come back in the autumn rested and ready for another year of work. (That's what you ought to be writing to me!) I haven't an idea what you do in the summer, or how you amuse yourself. I can't visualize your surroundings. Do you play golf or hunt or ride horseback or just sit in the sun and meditate?

Anyway, whatever it is, have a good time and don't forget Judy.

June tenth

Dear Daddy,

This is the hardest letter I ever wrote, but I have decided what I must do, and there isn't going to be any turning back. It is very sweet and generous and dear of you to wish to send me to Europe this summer—for the moment I was **intoxicated** by the idea; but sober second thoughts said no. It would be rather illogical of me to refuse to take your money for college, and then use it instead just for amusement! You mustn't get me used to too many luxuries. One doesn't miss what one has never had; but it is awfully hard going without things after one has commenced thinking they are his—hers (English language needs another pronoun) by natural right. Living with Sallie and Julia is an awful strain on my social philosophy. They have both had things from the time they were babies; they accept happiness as a matter of course. The world, they think, owes them everything they want. Maybe the world does—in any case, it seems to acknowledge the debt and pay up. But as for me, it owes me nothing and distinctly told me so in the

叔叔,您觉得我安排得怎么样?您瞧我现在变得很独立了呢。您让我站稳了脚步,现在我可以独自行走了呢。

普林斯顿举行毕业典礼时我们还在考试,非常郁闷,莎莉和我都想去参加,可根本没时间去。

再见,叔叔!祝您暑假快乐!秋天回来时精神百倍,投入新一年的工作!(这好像是您该写给我的),因为您夏天都要做些什么,在哪儿度假休闲,我完全不知道。您打高尔夫吗?还是打猎?骑马?抑或只是坐着晒晒太阳遐想一阵儿?

不管您做什么,祝您开心!别忘了朱蒂。

六月四日

亲爱的叔叔:

这是最难写的一封信。不管怎样,我决心已定,决不反悔。您说夏天送我去欧洲旅游,您真是太好太慷慨了!一开始我真的高兴坏了,三思之后,还是决定拒绝您。我拒绝用您的钱来缴学费,反倒是去玩,这太不符合逻辑了,您不能培养我过奢侈的生活啊。对于不属于我的,我从来不去想;可一想到这些奢侈的东西是他或她(英文需要再有一个代词)与生俱来的,就觉得很难不去想。跟莎莉还有朱莉娅住在一起,对我来说就是一种挑战。她们从小就拥有这一切,她们理所当然接受这一切与生俱来的幸福。对她们来说,这个世界欠着她们想要的一切,也许真的欠她们的——无论如何,这个世界似乎承认了这笔债而且也偿还了。而我呢,

intoxicate
[in'tɔksikeit]
v. 使…陶醉,醉人

beginning. I have no right to borrow on credit, for there will come a time when the world will repudiate my claim.

I seem to be floundering in a sea of metaphor—but I hope you grasp my meaning? Anyway, I have a very strong feeling that the only honest thing for me to do is to teach this summer and begin to support myself.

Magnolia,
Four days later

I'd got just that much written when—what do you think happened? The maid arrived with Master Jervie's card. He is going abroad too this summer; not with Julia and her family but entirely by himself. I told him that you had invited me to go with a lady who is chaperoning a party of girls. He knows about you, Daddy. That is, he knows that my father and mother are dead, and that a kind gentleman is sending me to college; I simply didn't have the courage to tell him about the John Grier Home and all the rest. He thinks that you are my guardian and a perfectly legitimate old family friend. I have never told him that I didn't know you—that would seem too queer!

Anyway, he insisted on my going to Europe. He said that it was a necessary part of my education and that I mustn't think of refusing. Also, that he would be in Paris at the same time, and that we would run away from the chaperon occasionally and have dinner together at nice, funny, foreign restaurants.

Well, Daddy, it did appeal to me! I almost weakened; if he hadn't been so **dictatorial**, maybe I should have entirely weakened. I can be enticed step by step, but I won't be forced. He said I was a silly, foolish, irrational, **quixotic**, **idiotic**, stubborn child (those are a few of his abusive adjectives; the rest escape me) and that I didn't know what was good for me; I ought to let older people judge. We almost quarreled—I am not sure but that we entirely did!

In any case, I packed my trunk fast and came up here. I

世界并不欠我什么,从一开始就很清楚。我无权欠债,某一天世界会拒绝我的要求。

我好像一直在打比喻——希望您明白我的意思。总之,我深深地感到这个夏天我应该做的就是去教课,开始自力更生。

六月十日

刚写完上面那些——您猜怎么了?女仆送来了杰维少爷的名片。他今年夏天也要出国,不是和朱莉娅一家同去,而是他自己去。我告诉他您邀请我跟一位会照顾女孩子的女士同去。他知道您,叔叔。他也知道我父母双亡,是一位好心的老先生送我上的大学,但我没勇气跟他讲约翰·格里尔孤儿院的事。他以为您是我的远亲或者我家的世交什么的。我从没说过不认识您,要不然太奇怪了!

然而,他坚持要我去欧洲,他说这是我学习的一部分,我不该拒绝。而且,他说他也要去巴黎,然后我偶尔可以从陪同我的夫人身边溜掉,一起去精致的法国餐厅享用美食。

叔叔,我真的挺动心的!我差点动摇了,要不是他那么专制,也许我真的会改变主意。我可以慢慢被说服,但是绝不能被强迫。他说我是个傻瓜、笨蛋、不可理喻、脾气古怪、性格固执的小孩子(只记得他骂我那些词,还有好多我都记不得了),还说我什么不知好歹,应该听长者的话。我们差点吵了起来——我记不清了,不过好像是吵了。

不管怎样,我已经收拾行李来到这里了。在我

dictatorial
[ˌdɪktəˈtɔːriəl]
adj. 独裁的
quixotic
[kwɪkˈsɒtɪk]
adj. 堂吉诃德式的,狂想家的
idiotic
[ˌɪdiˈɒtɪk]
adj. 愚蠢的

thought I'd better see my bridges in flames behind me before I finished writing to you. They are entirely reduced to ashes now. Here I am at Cliff Top (the name of Mrs. Paterson's cottage) with my trunk unpacked and Florence (the little one) already struggling with first **declension** nouns. And it bids fair to be a struggle! She is a most uncommonly spoiled child; I shall have to teach her first how to study—she has never in her life concentrated on anything more difficult than ice-cream soda water.

We use a quiet corner of the cliffs for a schoolroom—Mrs. Paterson wishes me to keep them out of doors—and I will say that I find it difficult to concentrate with the blue sea before me and ships a-sailing by! And when I think I might be on one, sailing off to foreign lands—but I won't let myself think of anything but Latin grammar.

The prepositions a or ab, absque, coram, cum, de, e or ex, prae, pro, sine, tenus, in, subter, sub, and super govern the ablative.

So you see, Daddy, I am already **plunged** into work with my eyes persistently set against temptation. Don't be cross with me, please, and don't think that I do not appreciate your kindness, for I do—always—always. The only way I can ever repay you is by turning out a Very Useful Citizen (Are women citizens? I don't suppose they are) . Anyway, a Very Useful Person. And when you look at me you can say, "I gave that Very Useful Person to the world."

That sounds well, doesn't it, Daddy! But I don't wish to mislead you. The feeling often comes over me that I am not at all remarkable; it is fun to plan a career, but in all probability, I shan't turn out a bit different from any other ordinary person. I may end by marrying an undertaker and being an inspiration to him in his work.

                                                   Yours ever,
                                                      Judy

declension
[dɪˈklenʃən]
n. 语尾变化，格变化；倾斜

给您写完信之前，我想我已经自断退路了。我现在在崖顶（帕特森夫人海边别墅的名字），刚把衣服收拾出来挂好。弗罗伦斯（她的小女儿）已经开始努力学习名词词尾变化了。她被宠坏了，我得先教她如何学习——以前除了冰淇淋和苏打水，她从未专注于任何东西。

我们在崖顶找了个安静的角落上课——帕特森太太希望我专心教她女儿——我想说的是要在轮船行驶的大海边专心学习真的挺困难的，特别是一想到自己可能坐在某艘船上，驶向异国——不过，除了拉丁文法，我不会让自己瞎想别的的。

The prepositions a or ab, absque, coram, cum, de, e or ex, prae, pro, sine, tenus, in, subter, sub, and super govern the ablative.

plunge
[plʌndʒ]
v. 投入，跳进，使…陷入

叔叔，您看，我完全抵制了诱惑，专心致志地工作呢。请您别生我的气啊，别误解我不知感恩，我从心底很感激您，真的——永远——永远感激您。唯一能报答您的就是当个非常有用的公民（女孩子也算是公民吗？我想不算）。总之，做一个非常有用的人。当您见到我的时候，您可以自豪地说："我为社会培养了一个非常有用的人。"

听起来不错吧，叔叔？不过您千万别被误导啊。我常常觉得自己很平庸，这种感觉一直徘徊在我心中。对未来职业的规划可真有意思，可是，到头来我可能还是跟多数人一样普通——结婚生子。

您永远的
朱蒂
于麦格诺利亚
四天后

August 19th

Dear Daddy-Long-Legs,

My window looks out on the loveliest landscape—ocean-scape rather—nothing but water and rocks.

The summer goes. I spend the morning with Latin and English and **algebra** and my two stupid girls. I don't know how Marion is ever going to get into college, or stay in after she gets there. And as for Florence, she is hopeless—but, oh! such a little beauty. I don't suppose it matters in the least whether they are stupid or not so long as they are pretty. One can't help thinking though how their conversation will bore their husbands, unless they are fortunate enough to obtain stupid husbands. I suppose that's quite possible; the world seems to be filled with stupid men; I've met a number this summer.

In the afternoon we take a walk on the cliffs, or swim, if the tide is right. I can swim in salt water with the utmost ease—you see my education is already being put to use!

A letter comes from Mr. Jervis Pendleton in Paris, rather a short, concise letter; I'm not quite forgiven yet for refusing to follow his advice. However, if he gets back in time, he will see me for a few days at Lock Willow before college opens, and if I am very nice and sweet and docile, I shall (I am led to infer) be received into favor again.

Also a letter from Sallie. She wants me to come to their camp for two weeks in September. Must I ask your permission, or haven't I yet arrived at the place where I can do as I please? Yes, I am sure I have—I'm a senior, you know. Having worked all summer, I feel like taking a little healthful recreation; I want to see the Adirondacks; I want to see Sallie; I want to see Sallie's brother—he's going to teach me to canoe—and (we come to my chief motive, which is mean) I want Master Jervie to arrive at Lock Willow and find me not there.

algebra
['ældʒibrə]
n. 代数学

亲爱的长腿叔叔：

　　凭窗远眺，海上风平浪静，只有海水和岩石相拥，真是美不胜收啊！

　　夏日依旧。我教了那两个笨孩子一上午的拉丁文、英文和代数。真不知道玛莉恩如何考上大学的，或者真的上了又怎么能顺利完成学业；至于弗罗伦斯，更是没得救了——她幸好长得很漂亮！还好，只要人长得漂亮，管她笨不笨。除非她们有幸嫁个蠢男人，否则她无聊的谈话会烦死她老公的。这样的人也很可能嫁给蠢男人，因为这个世界上蠢男人也多，今年夏天我就遇到了不少。

　　下午，我们去海边散步，不涨潮时就游泳。我现在可以轻松自在遨游大海了呢。您看看，我上的游泳课终于派上了用场。

　　我收到一封来自杰维·彭莱顿先生的信，信是从巴黎写来的，很短，语气很强硬，说我不听他劝，他还在生气呢。不过，他说要是他能及时回来，开学前他可以到洛克威洛来见我，再呆上几天，如果我又乖，嘴巴又甜，还听话，他会原谅我的（他的信好像是这个意思）。

　　对了，还有一封莎莉写来的信。要我九月份跟他们去露营地玩两周。我是应该征得您的同意还是我可以自由选择呢？可以，我相信我可以自己选择的——我已经是大四的学生了。工作了一个夏天，我觉得自己也该休息休息了。我要去爬爬山，去看看莎莉，还想见见她哥哥——他说要带我去划船——还有，我要让杰维少爷到洛克威洛时发现我不在（这才是最主要的理由，我很坏吧）。

I must show him that he can't dictate to me. No one can **dictate** to me but you, Daddy—and you can't always! I'm off for the woods.

              Judy

           Camp McBride
           September 6th

Dear Daddy,

Your letter didn't come in time (I am pleased to say). If you wish your instructions to be obeyed, you must have your secretary **transmit** them in less than two weeks. As you observe, I am here, and have been for five days.

The woods are fine, and so is the camp, and so is the weather, and so are the McBrides, and so is the whole world. I'm very happy!

There's Jimmie calling for me to come canoeing. Good-bye—sorry to have disobeyed, but why are you so persistent about not wanting me to play a little? When I've worked all summer I deserve two weeks. You are awfully dog-in-the-mangerish.

However—I love you still, Daddy, in spite of all your faults.

              Judy

             October 3rd

Dear Daddy-Long-Legs,

Back at college and a senior—also editor of the *Monthly*. It doesn't seem possible, does it, that so sophisticated a person, just four years ago, was an inmate of the John Grier Home? We do arrive fast in America!

dictate
[dik'teit]
v. 听写,口述,口授

　　我一定要让他明白他无权对我发号施令,除了叔叔您,没有人可以命令我——而且您也不能事事都命令我!我要出发去山里了。

朱蒂
八月十九日

亲爱的叔叔:
　　真高兴没有及时收到您的信。您要是希望我听您的话,您至少应该提前两周叫您的秘书寄信出来。您瞧,我已经在山上呆五天了。

transmit
[trænz'mit]
v. 传输,转送,传达

　　森林真美,露营地很舒服,天气非常好,麦克白一家人也都很好,整个世界都是如此美好。我开心极了!
　　吉米叫我去划船了,再见!——很抱歉没听您的话,可是您为什么不想让我玩一下呢?我工作了一个夏天,也应该放两周的假啊。您真残忍,自己不玩还不让我玩!
　　不管怎样——我还是爱您的,叔叔,虽然您很不讲理。

朱蒂
于麦克白露营地
九月六日

亲爱的长腿叔叔:
　　我已经返校,我现在是大四毕业生了呢,而且还当上了《月刊》的编辑,听起来挺不可思议吧?四年前还是约翰·格里尔孤儿院孤儿的我,如今担任这个职位,真是一夜成名啊!

What do you think of this? A note from Master Jervie directed to Lock Willow and forwarded here. He's sorry but he finds that he can't get up there this autumn; he has accepted an invitation to go yachting with some friends. Hopes I've had a nice summer and am enjoying the country.

And he knew all the time that I was with the McBrides, for Julia told him so! You men ought to leave **intrigue** to women; you haven't a light enough touch. Julia has a trunkful of the most **ravishing** new clothes—an evening gown of rainbow Liberty crepe that would be fitting **raiment** for the angels in paradise. And I thought that my own clothes this year were unprecedentedly (is there such a word?) beautiful. I copied Mrs. Paterson's wardrobe with the aid of a cheap dressmaker, and though the gowns didn't turn out quite twins of the originals, I was entirely happy until Julia unpacked. But now—I live to see Paris!

Dear Daddy, aren't you glad you're not a girl? I suppose you think that the fuss we make over clothes is too absolutely silly? It is. No doubt about it. But it's entirely your fault.

Did you ever hear about the learned Herr Professor who regarded unnecessary adornment with **contempt**, and favored sensible, **utilitarian** clothes for women? His wife, who was an obliging creature, adopted "dress reform". And what do you think he did? He eloped with a chorus girl.

                                                Yours ever,
                                                Judy

PS. The chambermaid on our corridor wears blue checked gingham aprons. I am going to get her some brown ones instead, and sink the blue ones in the bottom of the lake. I have a **reminiscent** chill every time I look at them.

您觉得呢?洛克威洛转来了杰维少爷的信。他很抱歉秋天赶不回来了,说他受几个朋友邀约乘快艇出游,希望我度过一个美好的夏天,好好享受乡间生活。

他明明知道我一直和麦克白家在一起,肯定是朱莉娅告诉他的!你们男人可真不如女人,应该多向女人学习学习,多长个心眼儿。朱莉娅有满满一箱令人羡慕的漂亮新衣服——特别是那件彩虹色的晚礼服,穿起来简直像天堂里的天使。我以为我今年的衣服是史无前例的(有这个词儿吗?)漂亮。我的衣服是请一位普通的女裁缝仿帕特森太太的服装做的,虽然跟原版不是一模一样,可在朱莉娅打开箱子之前我都还万分高兴,而现在——我真想去巴黎看看了。

亲爱的叔叔,您是不是庆幸自己不是个女孩子呢?我猜您肯定觉得我们傻乎乎地比衣服非常可笑。没办法,女孩子就是这样的,不过这也不能怪您。

您听说过学识渊博的赫尔教授吗?就是那位号称不喜欢女人那些无用的打扮,认为有理智的女人应该合理打扮、着装讲究实用。他的妻子乐于顺从,接受他的"衣着革命"。结果呢?他跟一个歌舞团的女人私奔了。

您永远的
朱蒂
十月三日

附言:给我们扫走廊的清洁工围的是蓝格围裙,我要去给她换上褐色的,让那蓝色永远沉入湖底。我每每看到他们都会觉得一阵心寒。

---

intrigue
[in'tri:g]
n. 阴谋,复杂的事

ravishing
['ræviʃiŋ]
adj. 令人陶醉的

raiment
['reimənt]
n. 衣服

contempt
[kən'tempt]
n. 轻视,轻蔑

utilitarian
[,ju:tili'tɛəriən]
adj. 功利的,实利的

reminiscent
[remi'nis(ə)nt]
adj. 回忆的,怀旧的,耽于回想的

November 17th

Dear Daddy-Long-Legs,

Such a **blight** has fallen over my literary career. I don't know whether to tell you or not, but I would like some sympathy—silent sympathy, please; don't reopen the wound by referring to it in your next letter.

I've been writing a book, all last winter in the evenings, and all summer when I wasn't teaching Latin to my two stupid children. I just finished it before college opened and sent it to a publisher. He kept it two months and I was certain he was going to take it; but yesterday morning an express parcel came (thirty cents due) and there it was back again with a letter from the publisher, a very nice, fatherly letter—but frank! He said he saw from the address that I was still in college, and if I would accept some advice, he would suggest that I put all of my energy into my lessons and wait until I graduated before beginning to write. He enclosed his reader's opinion. Here it is:

"Plot highly improbable. **Characterization** exaggerated. Conversation unnatural. A good deal of humor but not always in the best of taste. Tell her to keep on trying, and in time she may produce a real book."

Not on the whole flattering, is it, Daddy? And I thought I was making a notable addition to American literature, I did truly. I was planning to surprise you by writing a great novel before I graduated. I collected the material for it while I was at Julia's last Christmas. But I dare say the editor is right. Probably two weeks was not enough in which to observe the manners and customs of a great city.

I took it walking with me yesterday afternoon, and when I came to the gas house, I went in and asked the engineer if I might borrow his furnace. He politely opened the door, and with my own hands I **chucked** it in. I felt as though I had **cremated** my only child!

I went to bed last night utterly **dejected**; I thought I was never going to amount to anything, and that you had thrown away your

亲爱的长腿叔叔：

我的写作事业遭受打击了。不知道是否应该告诉您，不过我期望得到您的同情——默默地同情，请您在回信时别提及此事，以免再次伤害我。

整整一个冬天的晚上加上整整一个夏天教那两个笨学生拉丁文的空闲时间写了一部长篇小说，开学前才写完，寄给了出版社。两个月没有回信，我确信他们应该接受了。可是昨天早上，邮政快递（欠费三毛）送了回来，还附上了一封出版商的信，信写得很温和很客气——而且非常坦率！信上说从我的住址来看我还是大学在读，他建议等我毕业之后再写。他引用某编辑的意见如下：

"情节甚是荒诞，角色也够夸张，对话有点儿生硬。有一定幽默感，但品味不高。如果她继续努力，或许可以写出一本真正像样的书。"

叔叔，被他们说得一无是处，是吧？我还自以为能为美国文学史谱写新的篇章呢。我当时确实这么想的，原本计划在毕业之前写本大作给您惊喜的。素材是去年在朱莉娅家作客时收集的。不过我承认编辑意见是合理的，只用两周来看一个大城市的习俗和风貌是远远不够的。

昨天，我带着书稿外出散步，走到气站时，我进去问里面的工人是否可以借用一下火炉。他很礼貌地打开了炉门，我亲手把书稿扔了进去，感觉像是在火化自己的孩子。

昨晚睡觉时心如刀绞，觉得自己很难有所作为，白白浪费了您的钱。可是，您猜怎么着？今天

---

blight
[blait]
n. 枯萎病

characterization
[ˌkæriktərai'zeiʃən]
n. 描绘，刻画

chuck
[tʃʌk]
v. 轻叩，抛掷

cremate
[kri'meit]
v. 烧成灰，火葬

deject
[di'dʒekt]
v. 使沮丧，使灰心

money for nothing. But what do you think? I woke up this morning with a beautiful new plot in my head, and I've been going about all day planning my characters, just as happy as I could be. No one can ever accuse me of being a pessimist! If I had a husband and twelve children **swallowed** by an earthquake one day, I'd bob up smilingly the next morning and commence to look for another set.

> Affectionately,
> Judy

December 14th

Dear Daddy-Long-Legs,

I dreamed the funniest dream last night. I thought I went into a bookstore and the clerk brought me a new book named *The Life and Letters of Judy Abbott*. I could see it perfectly plainly—red cloth binding with a picture of the John Grier Home on the cover, and my portrait for a **frontispiece** with "Very truly yours, Judy Abbott" written below. But just as I was turning to the end to read the inscription on my tombstone, I woke up. It was very annoying! I almost found out whom I'm going to marry and when I'm going to die.

Don't you think it would be interesting if you really could read the story of your life—written perfectly truthfully by an **omniscient** author? And suppose you could only read it on this condition: that you would never forget it, but would have to go through life knowing ahead of time exactly how everything you did would turn out, and foreseeing to the exact hour the time when you would die. How many people do you suppose would have the courage to read it then? Or how many could suppress their curiosity sufficiently to escape from reading it, even at the price of having to live without hope and without surprises?

Life is monotonous enough at best; you have to eat and sleep about so often. But imagine how deadly monotonous it would be if

早上一觉醒来，满脑子都是美妙的新故事，妙极了！这一整天我都在安排我的角色，非常兴奋。我绝不是悲观主义者！即使有一天我的丈夫和十二个孩子全都在地震中丧生，第二天我依然会振作精神，开始寻找新的生活。

充满感情的
朱蒂
十一月十七日

亲爱的长腿叔叔：

昨晚我做了一个非常奇怪的梦。梦到我走进了一家书店，营业员给我一本新书，书名叫《朱蒂·阿伯特的生平与书信》。我清楚地看见——红色的封面上印着约翰·格里尔孤儿院的照片，扉页是我的照片，还题写着"朱蒂·阿伯特敬献"。正当要翻到最后一页看自己的墓志铭时，我醒了。太恼人了！差点就可以知道自己嫁给谁了，什么时候去世的呢！

如果能读到博学之士为自己写下的生平传记，您不觉得很有意思吗？！假如规定您读后必须记住将会发生的一切并且去经历这一切，而且了解自己去世的准确时间，会有多少人有勇气去读呢？即使是无聊无望地过一生，又有多少人能够忍住好奇不去读它呢？

生活是单调乏味的，每天除了吃饭就是睡觉，可一日三餐之间没有什么奇妙的事情发生，怎么能

nothing unexpected could happen between meals. Mercy! Daddy, there's a blot, but I'm on the third page and I can't begin a new sheet.

I'm going on with biology again this year—very interesting subject; we're studying the **alimentary** system at present. You should see how sweet a cross section of the **duodenum** of a cat is under the microscope.

Also we've arrived at philosophy—interesting but **evanescent**. I prefer biology where you can pin the subject under discussion to a board. There's another! And another! This pen is weeping copiously. Please excuse its tears.

Do you believe in free will? I do—unreservedly. I don't agree at all with the philosophers who think that every action is the absolutely inevitable and automatic **resultant** of an aggregation of remote causes. That's the most immoral doctrine I ever heard—nobody would be to blame for anything. If a man believed in **fatalism**, he would naturally just sit down and say, "The Lord's will be done," and continue to sit until he fell over dead.

I believe absolutely in my own free will and my own power to accomplish—and that is the belief that moves mountains. You watch me become a great author! I have four chapters of my new book finished and five more drafted.

This is a very abstruse letter—does your head ache, Daddy? I think we'll stop now and make some **fudge**. I'm sorry I can't send you a piece; it will be unusually good, for we're going to make it with real cream and three butter balls.

Yours affectionately,
Judy

PS. We're having fancy dancing in gymnasium class. You can see by the accompanying picture how much we look like a real ballet. The one on the end accomplishing a graceful **pirouette** is me— I mean I.

不单调、不乏味呢？可怜的上帝啊！啊！叔叔，落了一滴墨水儿！可是我已经写到第三页了，不能另起新页了，太长了！

今年我将继续修生物学，生物是非常有趣的科目，现在我们正学到消化系统，可以在显微镜下看到小猫可爱的十二指肠剖面。

今年也学哲学，非常有趣，但是太抽象了。我更喜欢生物，因为生物学的东西可以拿到黑板上讨论，很具体的。又掉了！又掉墨水儿了！这支笔时不时地抽泣一下，请您原谅它的泪水哦！

您相信自由意志吗？我相信的——绝对相信。我一点也不相信凡事都有其因其果的因果论，这是我所听过的最不道德的信条，没有谁注定就该为什么负责。要是一个人只相信命运，他只需要坐下来说"听天由命"，然后等死就可以了。

我完全相信自由意志，相信我自己力量所能及——这种信念可以移山填海，开天辟地。您等着瞧吧，我一定会成为伟大的作家！我已经写完新书的前四章了，另外五章的初稿也出来了。

这封信很玄妙吧？叔叔，您看了会头疼吗？就写到这儿吧，我要做点麦芽糖吃，可惜没法给您寄一块儿，真的非常好吃呢！

充满感情的
朱蒂
十二月十四日

附言：我们在体操课上学舞蹈了，您可以看看下面这幅画，瞧瞧我们多像芭蕾舞演员！最后一个脚尖立地旋转的、跳着优雅舞姿的就是我呢！

---

alimentary
[ˌæliˈmentəri]
adj. 食物的，滋养的

duodenum
[ˌdju(:)əuˈdi:nəm]
n. 十二指肠

evanescent
[ˌi:vəˈnesnt]
adj. 逐渐消失的，容易消散的；会凋零的

resultant
[riˈzʌltənt]
adj. 合成的（有结果的）

fatalism
[ˈfeitəliz(ə)m]
n. 宿命论

fudge
[fʌdʒ]
n. 软糖

pirouette
[piruˈet]
n.（舞蹈）脚尖立地的旋转

December 26th

My dear, dear Daddy,

Haven't you any sense? Don't you know that you mustn't give one girl seventeen Christmas presents? I'm a socialist, please remember; do you wish to turn me into a **plutocrat**?

Think how embarrassing it would be if we should ever quarrel! I should have to engage a moving van to return your gifts.

I am sorry that the necktie I sent was so **wobbly**; I knit it with my own hands (as you doubtless discovered from internal evidence. You will have to wear it on cold days and keep your coat buttoned up tight.

Thank you, Daddy, a thousand times. I think you're the sweetest man that ever lived—and the foolishest!

Judy

Here's a four-leaf clover from Camp McBride to bring you good luck for the new year.

我亲爱亲爱的叔叔:

您失去理智了吗?难道您不知道不该送给一个女孩子十七件圣诞礼物吗?别忘了,我是个社会主义者,难道您想把我变成富家小姐吗?

想想,我们要是吵架,得有多尴尬!我可能要雇一辆大货车才能全部退还您送的礼物!

很抱歉我送给您的领巾织得不够好,不过是我亲手织的,您应该从织工也看得出来。不过天冷的时候,您可以围上保暖,记得把外衣扣子扣好就行。

谢谢您,叔叔,万分感谢!您是世上最可爱的人——也是最傻的人!

朱蒂
十二月二十六日

随信附上一株跟麦克白家露营时摘的四叶幸运草,祝您在新的一年里好运连连!

---

plutocrat
['plu:təkræt]
n. 富豪(财阀)

wobbly
['wɔbli]
adj. 摆动的,不稳定的

January 9th

Do you wish to do something, Daddy, that will insure your eternal **salvation**? There is a family here who are in awfully desperate straits. A mother and father and four visible children—the two older boys have disappeared into the world to make their fortune and have not sent any of it back. The father worked in a glass factory and got consumption—it's awfully unhealthy work—and now has been sent away to a hospital. That took all of their savings, and the support of the family falls upon the oldest daughter who is twenty-four. She dressmakes for $1.50 a day (when she can get it) and embroiders centerpieces in the evening. The mother isn't very strong and is extremely ineffectual and pious. She sits with her hands folded, a picture of patient resignation, while the daughter kills herself with overwork and responsibility and worry; she doesn't see how they are going to get through the rest of the winter—and I don't either. One hundred dollars would buy some coal and some shoes for the three children so that they could go to school, and give a little margin so that she needn't worry herself to death when a few days pass and she doesn't get work.

You are the richest man I know. Don't you suppose you could spare one hundred dollars? That girl deserves help a lot more than I ever did. I wouldn't ask it except for the girl; I don't care much what happens to the mother—she is such a **jellyfish**.

The way people are forever rolling their eyes to heaven and saying "Perhaps it's all for the best" when they are perfectly dead sure it's not, makes me enraged. Humility or resignation or whatever you choose to call it, is simply impotent inertia. I'm for a more militant religion!

We are getting the most dreadful lessons in philosophy—all of Schopenhauer for tomorrow. The professor doesn't seem to realize that we are taking any other subject. He's a queer old duck; he goes about with his head in the clouds and blinks dazedly when occasionally he strikes solid earth. He tries to lighten his lectures

salvation
[sæl'veiʃən]
n. 得救,拯救

　　叔叔,您愿意当救世主做点好事吗?有一家人很穷,父母身边剩下四个孩子——另外两个大一点的男孩子已经外出谋生了,一去不回。父亲在一家快要倒闭的玻璃厂工作,因为工作很伤身体,住院之后,家里的积蓄全花光了。家庭的重担全落在二十四岁的大女儿肩上。她白天帮别人做针线活,一天挣一块五,这还是找得到活儿的时候;晚上熬夜刺绣。母亲体弱多病,什么活儿也干不了,只是坐着等人伺候,基本上跟病休差不多。女儿每天过度工作,为家里的事儿忧心忡忡。她简直不知道后半个冬天该怎么过——我也不知道。如果有一百元,她就可以买些煤和几双鞋给另外三个要上学的孩子,这样还可以剩点钱,她就不会为好几天找不到工作犯愁了。

　　叔叔,您是我认识的最富有的人了。您可不可以省下一百元资助一下那个女孩呢?她比我更需要帮助。要不是为了她,我不会跟您开口的,我才懒得管那个母亲呢!她简直就是个窝囊废!

　　当人们经历苦难时,他们心里是非常肯定日子不会好起来的,可他们还是会溜动眼睛转向上天祈祷"一切都会好起来的!",这让我非常不舒服。

jellyfish
['dʒelifiʃ]
n. 水母,海蜇;意志薄弱的人

　　哲学课上到最难懂的部分了——明天讲叔本华(译者注:1788~1860,德国哲学家)。教授似乎没意识到我们没有上过其他课程,他是个老顽固,性格古怪。他十分理想,一会儿扯天一会儿扯地,听得我们晕乎乎的。他偶尔还用一些幽默语言活跃课

with an occasional **witticism**—and we do our best to smile, but I assure you his jokes are no laughing matter. He spends his entire time between classes in trying to figure out whether matter really exists or whether he only thinks it exists.

I'm sure my sewing girl hasn't any doubt but that it exists!

Where do you think my new novel is? In the wastebasket. I can see myself that it's no good on earth, and when a loving author realizes that, what would be the judgment of a critical public?

Later

I address you, Daddy, from a bed of pain. For two days I've been laid up with swollen **tonsils**; I can just swallow hot milk and that is all. "What were your parents thinking of not to have those tonsils out when you were a baby?" the doctor wished to know. I'm sure I haven't an idea, but I doubt if they were thinking much about me.

Yours,
J. A.

Next morning

I just read this over before sealing it. I don't know why I cast such a misty atmosphere over life. I hasten to assure you that I am young and happy and exuberant; and I trust you are the same. Youth has nothing to do with birthdays, only with aliveness of spirit, so even if your hair is gray, Daddy, you can still be a boy.

Affectionately,
Judy

witticism
['witisizəm]
n. 名言,机敏,妙语

堂,我们是尽量配合他挤出点笑容。说实话,我确实没觉得他讲的好笑。他一堂又堂地分析物质是否存在或者他认为存在。

毋庸置疑,我相信那个做针线活儿的女孩是存在的!

您觉得我的新小说现在在哪儿呢?我扔到垃圾桶了。我终于明白自己不行了。当一个富有爱心的作者意识到这一点时,带有批判眼光的读者会怎么评论呢?

稍后

tonsil
['tɔnsil]
n. 扁桃体,扁桃腺

叔叔,这封信是我在病床上给您写的。扁桃体又发炎了,已经在医院躺了两天。除了热牛奶,别的都不能吃。医生问我:"小时候你爸妈为什么没有替你摘去扁桃体?"我怎么知道呢,我怀疑他们是否为我操过半点心。

您的
J.A.
一月九日

信在寄出之前我又重读了一遍,不知为何写得如此忧郁。不过我向您保证,我很年轻、很开心、很有活力!相信您也一样!青春跟年龄没什么关系,青春是一种精神状态,所以叔叔,即使您头发花白,您依然可以是个小男孩。

充满感情的
朱蒂
第二天早上

Jan. 12th

Dear Mr. Philanthropist,

Your check for my family came yesterday. Thank you so much! I cut gymnasium and took it down to them right after luncheon, and you should have seen the girl's face! She was so surprised and happy and relieved that she looked almost young; and she's only twenty-four. Isn't it pitiful?

Anyway, she feels now as though all the good things were coming together. She has steady work ahead for two months—someone's getting married, and there's a **trousseau** to make.

"Thank the good Lord!" cried the mother, when she grasped the fact that that small piece of paper was one hundred dollars.

"It wasn't the good Lord at all," said I, "it was Daddy-Long-Legs." (Mr. Smith, I called you.)

"But it was the good Lord who put it in his mind," said she.

"Not at all! I put it in his mind myself," said I.

But anyway, Daddy, I trust the good Lord will reward you suitably. You deserve ten thousand years out of **purgatory**.

            Yours most gratefully,
            Judy Abbott

Feb. 15th

May it please Your Most Excellent Majesty:

This morning I did eat my breakfast upon a cold turkey pie and a goose, and I did send for a cup of tee (a china drink) of which I had never drank before.

Don't be nervous, Daddy—I haven't lost my mind; I'm merely quoting Sam'l Pepys. We're reading him in connection with English History, original sources. Sallie and Julia and I converse now in the language of 1660. Listen to this:

亲爱的慈善家：

您给那一家人的支票昨天收到了，非常感谢您！我翘了下午的体操课，把支票给他们送了过去，您真该看看那女孩当时激动的样子！她太惊讶了，开心得不得了，终于长长地松了口气！瞬间，她似乎变得年轻了许多，其实她才二十四岁，可怜的孩子，是吧？

不管怎样，最近她觉得似乎好事连连，接连两个月都会有活儿干，因为有人要办嫁妆。

"感谢上帝啊！"她母亲看到那一小张纸片上写的一百元时大声叫道。

我说"不是上帝，是长腿叔叔。"（史密斯先生，我指的是您。）

"是上帝让他这样做的。"她接着说道。

"才不是呢！是我让他这样做的！"我回答道。

不管怎么说，叔叔，相信仁慈的上帝会保佑您一生幸福！相信您将永远享受天堂般的快乐！

最感激您的
朱蒂·阿伯特
一月十二日

我尊敬的皇帝陛下：

今天早上我吃了一块火鸡派和一只鹅，还要了一杯以前从来没喝过的中国茶。

别紧张，叔叔——我思维还清楚。我只是引用塞缪尔·佩普斯（译者注：十七世纪英国散文家）的话，他的个人日志跟我们学的英国历史有很大关系。莎莉、朱莉娅还有现在都用1660年的语言讲话，请看下面这段：

---

trousseau
['truːsəu]
n. 嫁妆

purgatory
['pəːgətəri]
n. 灵魂的净化，涤罪，炼狱

"I went to Charing Cross to see Major Harrison hanged, drawn and quartered: he looking as cheerful as any man could do in that condition." And this: "Dined with my lady who is in handsome mourning for her brother who died yesterday of spotted fever".

Seems a little early to commence entertaining, doesn't it? A friend of Pepys devised a very cunning manner whereby the king might pay his debts out of the sale to poor people of old decayed provisions. What do you, a reformer, think of that? I don't believe we're so bad today as the newspapers make out.

Samuel was as excited about his clothes as any girl; he spent five times as much on dress as his wife—that appears to have been the golden age of husbands. Isn't this a touching entry? You see he really was honest. "Today came home my fine Camlett cloak with gold buttons, which cost me much money, and I pray God to make me able to pay for it."

Excuse me for being so full of Pepys; I'm writing a special topic on him.

What do you think, Daddy? The Self-Govern-ment Association has abolished the ten-o'clock rule. We can keep our lights all night if we choose, the only requirement being that we do not disturb others—we are not supposed to entertain on a large scale. The result is a beautiful **commentary** on human nature. Now that we may stay up as long as we choose, we no longer choose. Our heads begin to nod at nine o'clock, and by nine thirty the pen drops from our nerveless grasp. It's nine thirty now. Good night.

Sunday

Just back from church—preacher from Georgia. We must take care, he says, not to develop our intellects at the expense of our emotional natures—but methought it was a poor, dry sermon (Pepys again). It doesn't matter what part of the United States or Canada they come from, or what denomination they are, we

"我去查林十字街看见梅杰·哈里逊被吊了起来,一拖,然后被分成了四块:在那种情况下,他只能表现得很高兴。"还有:"跟一个昨天刚因为患斑疹热死掉哥哥的、极度悲痛的女人一起吃饭"。

搞笑有点早了,对吧?佩普斯的一个朋友想出了一个可以借以让国王向旧时代的贫苦人民偿还债务的办法。作为一个改革家,您怎么想?我相信并没有今天的报纸写得那么糟糕。

塞缪尔跟女孩子一样喜欢他的衣服,他常常买衣服花的钱是他妻子的五倍——好像是一个男人的黄金年代。难道不是挺好的社交基础吗?您看得出来他真的很诚实。"今天我的漂亮的卡姆勒特大外套送来了,扣子是金色的,花了我不少钱,我祈祷着能支付得起。"

很抱歉一直用佩普斯的语言给您写信,不过我正在写一篇关于他的文章。

您觉得怎么样,叔叔?管理处取消了十点熄灯的规定,我们可以自己控制开关时间,只要不影响别的同学,想通宵就可以通宵——不管怎么说,我们不该亮着灯一直玩。虽然我们可以想熬到什么时候就什么时候,不再受约束,可人的天性是没办法改变的,到了九点脑袋就不清醒了,开始瞌睡了,到九点半的时候笔就不听使唤了。现在就是九点半了。晚安!

commentary
['kɔməntəri]
n. 注释,评论,批评

二月十五日

我刚从教堂回来——听佐治亚教堂的牧师布道去了。牧师说我们不必以牺牲情商为代价来培养我们的智商——不过我觉得他讲得挺没劲的(又是模仿佩普斯的风格)。无论美国还是加拿大的牧师,

always get the same sermon. Why on earth don't they go to men's colleges and urge the students not to allow their manly natures to be crushed out by too much mental application?

It's a beautiful day—frozen and icy and clear. As soon as dinner is over, Sallie and Julia and Marty Keen and Eleanor Pratt (friends of mine, but you don't know them) and I are going to put on short skirts and walk 'cross country to Crystal Spring Farm and have a fried chicken and **waffle** supper, and then have Mr. Crystal Spring drive us home in his **buckboard**. We are supposed to be inside the campus at seven, but we are going to stretch a point tonight and make it eight.

Farewell, kind sir.

I have the honour of subscribing myself,

Your most loyall, dutiful, faithful and obedient servant,

J. Abbott

March fifth

Dear Mr. Trustee,

Tomorrow is the first Wednesday in the month—a weary day for the John Grier Home. How relieved they'll be when five o'clock comes and you pat them on the head and take yourselves off! Did you (individually) ever pat me on the head, Daddy? I don't believe so—my memory seems to be concerned only with fat trustees.

Give the Home my love, please—my truly love. I have quite a feeling of tenderness for it as I look back through a haze of four years. When I first came to college I felt quite resentful because I'd been robbed of the normal kind of childhood that the other girls had had; but now, I don't feel that way in the least. I regard it as a very unusual adventure. It gives me a sort of **vantage** point from which to stand aside and look at life. Emerging full-grown, I get a perspective on the world that other people who have been brought up in the

无论什么教派,他们说得都一样。他们为什么不去男子大学教导那些学生不要让他们的情感战胜理性呢?

今天天气很好——虽然外面结冻结冰,但是天空晴朗。吃完中午饭之后,莎莉、朱莉娅、玛蒂·克恩、伊莲诺·普拉特(我的朋友们,不过您可能不认识)还有我要换上便衣短裙要散步到水晶泉农场,晚上一边吃炸鸡块儿,一边聊天。完了之后水晶泉的男主人赶他的四轮马车送我们回家。我们大概七点到学校,不过我们没定那么死,也可能是八点。

再见,好心的先生,很荣幸跟您写信!

您最忠实的、有责任感的、忠诚的以及听您话的仆人,

朱蒂·阿伯特
星期日

waffle
['wɔfl]
v. 闲聊

buckboard
['bʌkbɔ:d]
n. 四轮马车的一种

亲爱的理事:

明天是本月第一个周三——对约翰·格里尔孤儿院的孩子来说是很讨厌的一天。五点钟声一响就得起床,一直要忙到等你们拍拍孩子们小脑袋准备离去,他们才会长长地松一口气!您拍过我的头吗?我记得好像没有,印象中只有胖理事。

拜托您转达我对孤儿院的问候——真诚的问候。回首四年的大学生活,再想起以前在孤儿院的日子,心中的暖意油然而生。刚上大学时,我为自己被剥夺了的美好童年而满腹不平,因为别的女孩子都有幸福的童年。而今,我再也不这么想了。我只是觉得那是一段不同寻常的人生经历,让我能从不同的角度去审视生命,好像是逐渐成熟了,而我对世界的独特认识正是那些正常家庭出身的孩子所

vantage
['vɑ:ntidʒ]
n. 优势,有利情况

thick of things entirely lack.

I know lots of girls (Julia, for instance) who never know that they are happy. They are so accustomed to the feeling that their senses are deadened to it, but as for me—I am perfectly sure every moment of my life that I am happy. And I'm going to keep on being, no matter what unpleasant things turn up. I'm going to regard them (even toothaches) as interesting experiences, and be glad to know what they feel like. "Whatever sky's above me, I've a heart for any fate."

However, Daddy, don't take this new affection for the J. G. H. too literally. If I have five children, like Rousseau, I shan't leave them on the steps of a foundling asylum in order to insure their being brought up simply.

Give my kindest regards to Mrs. Lippett (that, I think, is truthful; love would be a little strong) and don't forget to tell her what a beautiful nature I've developed.

Affectionately,
Judy

Lock Willow,
April 4th

Dear Daddy,

Do you observe the postmark? Sallie and I are embellishing Lock Willow with our presence during the Easter vacation. We decided that the best thing we could do with our ten days was to come where it is quiet. Our nerves had got to the point where they wouldn't stand another meal in Fergussen. Dining in a room with four hundred girls is an **ordeal** when you are tired. There is so much noise that you can't hear the girls across the table speak unless they make their hands into a **megaphone** and shout. That is the truth.

We are tramping over the hills and reading and writing, and having a nice, restful time. We climbed to the top of Sky Hill this

缺乏的。

我认识的很多女孩子（比如朱莉娅），永远都感觉不到什么是幸福，因为她们太习惯于拥有的一切了，她们早已麻木。而我，确信自己能感受到生命中每时每刻的幸福和快乐。无论以后发生多么不快的事情，我依然会觉得自己是幸福的。我会把一切不幸——就算是牙疼——看作是有趣的人生经历，乐观地去感受一切。不论风吹雨打，胜似闲庭信步！

不过叔叔，请不要简单从字面上理解我对孤儿院生活的新感受，我要是像卢梭一样有五个孩子，我也不会为了让他们接受教育而送他们到孤儿院去的。

请您代我问候利皮特太太（"问候"似乎确切些，"爱"这个字太沉重了），别忘了告诉她，我现在品性很好。

充满深情的
朱蒂
三月五日

亲爱的叔叔：

您看邮戳了吗？莎莉跟我复活节来到了洛克威洛。我们最想做的事情就是找个安静的地方度过这十天假。再多吃一顿弗格森楼的饭简直要脾胃崩溃。和四百个女同学挤一个餐厅简直就是活受罪，饭堂特别吵，连桌子对面的人讲话都听不清，真的，除非把两手合拢做话筒放在嘴边喊着说。

我们爬山、读书、写作、聊天，好好放松了几天。我们爬到了以前我和杰维少爷做过晚餐的天山

---

ordeal
[ɔːˈdiːl]
n. 严酷的考验，痛苦的经验

megaphone
[ˈmeɡəfəun]
n. 扩音器

morning where Master Jervie and I once cooked supper—it doesn't seem possible that it was nearly two years ago. I could still see the place where the smoke of our fire blackened the rock. It is funny how certain places get connected with certain people, and you never go back without thinking of them. I was quite lonely without him—for two minutes.

What do you think is my latest activity, Daddy? You will begin to believe that I am **incorrigible**—I am writing a book. I started it three weeks ago and am eating it up in chunks. I've caught the secret. Master Jervie and that editor man were right; you are most convincing when you write about the things you know. And this time it is about something that I do know—exhaustively. Guess where it's laid? In the John Grier Home! And it's good, Daddy, I actually believe it is—just about the tiny little things that happened every day. I'm a realist now. I've abandoned romanticism; I shall go back to it later though, when my own adventurous future begins.

This new book is going to get itself finished—and published! You see if it doesn't. If you just want a thing hard enough and keep on trying, you do get it in the end. I've been trying for four years to get a letter from you—and I haven't given up hope yet.

Good-bye, Daddy dear.

(I like to call you Daddy dear; it's so alliterative.)

Affectionately,
Judy

PS. I forgot to tell you the farm news, but it's very distressing. Skip this postscript if you don't want your sensibilities all **wrought up**.

Poor old Grove is dead. He got so he couldn't chew and they had to shoot him.

Nine chickens were killed by a **weasel** or a **skunk** or a rat last week.

顶——时间真快，一晃已经两年了。不过当时生火烤黑的石块依然清晰可见。触景生情，挺有意思的，有些地方总是和某人联系在一起。他不在这里我的确觉得有些孤单——两分钟而已。

您猜我最近在做什么，叔叔？您一定会觉得我很固执——我在写一本小说。三周前就开始了，进展得挺顺利。杰维爷爷与那个编辑说的没错，只有自己最熟悉的才会写得感人。这次我写的是我熟悉的题材——熟得不能再熟了。猜猜故事发生在哪儿？是约翰·格里尔孤儿院。故事挺好的，至少我认为挺好的——都是生活琐事。我不再浪漫了，现在要做个现实主义者。不过等我将来开始冒险，我会再做回浪漫主义者的。

这本书一定得写完、出版！您等着吧！我相信下定决心做一件事，只要坚持到底就一定会成功。这四年来，我一直希望能收到您一封回信——到现在我还坚持等待着。

再见，亲爱的叔叔。

（我喜欢叫您亲爱的叔叔，挺押头韵的。）

您充满感情的

朱蒂

于洛克威洛

四月四日

附言：忘记告诉您农庄的事儿了，很郁闷。您要是不想受刺激的话，就别读这个消息了。

可怜的老格洛弗死了，因为老得连东西也没法吃了，所以他们只好杀了它。

上周有九只小鸡不知道被黄鼠狼还是臭鼬还是老鼠什么的给弄死了。

---

incorrigible
[inˈkɔridʒəbl]
adj. 无药可救的，积习难改的，固执的

wrought up
神经紧张（兴奋，气愤）

weasel
[ˈwiːzl]
n. 鼬鼠，狡猾的人

skunk
[skʌŋk]
n. 臭鼬鼠，其皮毛，讨厌鬼

One of the cows is sick, and we had to have the **veterinary** surgeon out from Bonnyrigg Four Corners. Amasai stayed up all night to give her **linseed** oil and whisky. But we have an awful suspicion that the poor sick cow got nothing but linseed oil.

Sentimental Tommy (the tortoiseshell cat) has disappeared; we are afraid he has been caught in a trap.

There are lots of troubles in the world!

May 17th

Dear Daddy-Long-Legs,

This is going to be extremely short because my shoulder aches at the sight of a pen. Lecture notes all day, immortal novel all evening makes too much writing.

Commencement three weeks from next Wednesday. I think you might come and make my acquaintance—I shall hate you if you don't! Julia's inviting Master Jervie, he being her family, and Sallie's inviting Jimmie McB., he being her family, but who is there for me to invite? Just you and Mrs. Lippett, and I don't want her. Please come.

Yours, with love and writer's cramp,

Judy

Lock Willow,
June 19th

Dear Daddy-Long-Legs,

I'm educated! My diploma is in the bottom bureau drawer with my two best dresses. Commencement was as usual, with a few showers at vital moments. Thank you for your rosebuds. They were lovely. Master Jervie and Master Jimmie both gave me roses, too, but I left theirs in the **bathtub** and carried yours in the class procession.

还有一头奶牛病了，我们只好请邦尼里格四角的兽医来给它看病。阿马萨整个晚上都在给她喂亚麻籽油跟威士忌，不过我们怀疑可怜的病奶牛除了亚麻籽油什么也吃不了。

多愁善感的汤米（花斑猫）不见了，我们担心他可能被谁抓住了。

总是祸不单行！

亲爱的长腿叔叔：

这将是一封非常非常简短的信，因为我一动笔肩膀就疼。做了一天的课堂笔记，后来又写了一晚上的"不朽"作品，写得太久了。

三周后的星期三就是毕业典礼了。真希望您能来，——您要是不来，我会恨您的！朱莉娅邀请了杰维少爷代表家人出席，莎莉则邀请了吉米·麦克白代表家人出席，我邀请谁呢？只有您和利皮特太太，我可不想请她！请您来吧！

您手都写抽筋了的作家
朱蒂
五月十七日

亲爱的长腿叔叔：

毕业了！毕业证书搁在我放最好的两套裙子的五斗柜抽屉里。毕业典礼一如往常，在高潮时掉了几滴眼泪。谢谢您送的玫瑰花，非常漂亮。杰维少爷和吉米都送我了玫瑰花，不过我都留在浴缸里了，排队入场时我捧的是您送的花。

Here I am at Lock Willow for the summer—forever maybe. The board is cheap, the surroundings quiet and conducive to a literary life. What more does a struggling author wish? I am mad about my book. I think of it every waking moment, and dream of it at night. All I want is peace and quiet and lots of time to work (interspersed with nourishing meals).

Master Jervie is coming up for a week or so in August, and Jimmie McBride is going to drop in sometime through the summer. He's connected with a bond house now, and goes about the country selling bonds to banks. He's going to combine the Farmers' National at the Corners and me on the same trip.

You see that Lock Willow isn't entirely lacking in society. I'd be expecting to have you come motoring through—only I know now that that is hopeless. When you wouldn't come to my commencement, I tore you from my heart and buried you forever.

> Judy Abbott, A. B.

> *July 24th*

Dearest Daddy-Long-Legs,

Isn't it fun to work—or don't you ever do it? It's especially fun when your kind of work is the thing you'd rather do more than anything else in the world. I've been writing as fast as my pen would go every day this summer, and my only quarrel with life is that the days aren't long enough to write all the beautiful and valuable and entertaining thoughts I'm thinking.

I've finished the second draft of my book and am going to begin the third tomorrow morning at half-past seven. It's the sweetest book you ever saw—it is, truly. I think of nothing else. I can barely wait in the morning to dress and eat before beginning; then I write and write and write till suddenly I'm so tired that I'm limp all over. Then I go out with Colin (the new sheep dog) and **romp** through

今年我在洛克威洛过暑假——也许会永远留在这儿吧。食宿便宜，环境幽雅，有利于写作。一个正在努力的作家还能奢求什么呢？我痴迷于我的小说，每天一睁开眼睛就想着它，晚上做梦也梦着它。我需要一个宁静的地方和充足的时间来写作（还要加上营养丰富的食物）。

　　杰维少爷八月会来玩一周，吉米·麦克白夏天也会顺便来访——吉米在一家证券交易所上班，要到各地向银行销售债券。他打算在拜访四角的国家农业银行时来看我。

　　您瞧，洛克威洛也挺热闹的，我也希望您能开车经过这儿——现在我知道是不可能的了。当您没来参加毕业典礼的时候，我就将您永远抹去了，永远埋藏了。

文学院学士
朱蒂·阿伯特
于洛克威洛
六月十九日

最亲爱的长腿叔叔：

　　工作真是有意思啊，您有过这种感受吗？做自己喜欢的工作更是其乐无穷。暑假以来，我每天快笔疾书，下笔如神，唯一不满的是时光飞逝，不能将一切美好的、有价值的、有意思的想法通通写出。

　　我已经完成第二稿，明天早上七点半开始第三稿。它将是您读过的最好的一本书——相信我，真的。我几乎满脑子都是它。天一亮，我等不及穿衣吃饭就想动笔，然后就写啊写啊写啊，一直写到手脚发软，于是才跟柯林斯（新的牧羊犬）一起去田

romp
[rɔmp]
v. 嬉闹玩耍

the fields and get a fresh supply of ideas for the next day. It's the most beautiful book you ever saw—oh, pardon—I said that before.

You don't think me conceited, do you, Daddy dear?

I'm not, really, only just now I'm in the enthusiastic stage. Maybe later on I'll get cold and critical and sniffy. No, I'm sure I won't! This time I've written a real book. Just wait till you see it.

I'll try for a minute to talk about something else. I never told you, did I, that Amasai and Carrie got married last May? They are still working here, but so far as I can see it has spoiled them both. She used just to laugh when he tramped in mud or dropped ashes on the floor, but now—you should hear her scold! And she doesn't curl her hair any longer. Amasai, who used to be so obliging about beating rugs and carrying wood, **grumbles** if you suggest such a thing. Also his neckties are quite dingy—black and brown, where they used to be **scarlet** and purple. I've determined never to marry. It's a deteriorating process, evidently.

There isn't much of any farm news. The animals are all in the best of health. The pigs are unusually fat, the cows seem contented, and the hens are laying well. Are you interested in **poultry**? If so, let me recommend that invaluable little work 200 Eggs per Hen per Year. I am thinking of starting an **incubator** next spring and raising **broilers**. You see, I'm settled at Lock Willow permanently. I have decided to stay until I've written 114 novels like Anthony Trollop's mother. Then I shall have completed my life work and can retire and travel.

Mr. James McBride spent last Sunday with us. Fried chicken and ice cream for dinner, both of which he appeared to appreciate. I was awfully glad to see him; he brought a momentary reminder that the world at large exists. Poor Jimmie is having a hard time peddling his bonds. The Farmers' National at the Corners wouldn't have anything to do with them in spite of the fact that they pay six percent interest and sometimes seven. I think he'll end by going

间散步,思考第二天的内容。它是您看过的最好的一本书——对不起——我已经说过了。

亲爱的叔叔,您不会觉得我太骄傲吧?

绝不是,真的。现在是脑子发热的阶段,也许过会儿冷静下来,重新审视就会厌烦它呢,不,我相信不会的!我这回写了本像样的书,您等着瞧吧。

谈点别的什么吧。我还没跟您说吧,阿马萨和卡莉五月份结婚了!他们还在这儿做工,不过我觉得人结婚后都会变的。以前阿马萨腿上沾满泥或是把灰弄在了地板上,卡莉只是一笑了之,而今,您瞧瞧她厉声呵斥的样子!卡莉现在也不卷头发了,阿马萨以前总爱打扫地毯、搬运木材,现在叫他干什么就嘟囔不停。而且现在也不爱收拾领结了,以前他喜欢用鲜红色或者紫色的,而现在不是黑色就是棕色。我决定不结婚了,结婚让人越来越颓废。

乡下没有什么新闻。牲口都很健壮,猪都异常肥壮,奶牛们似乎也过得很不错,鸡也下了不少蛋。您对家禽感兴趣吗?要喜欢的话,我给您介绍一下这平凡而有价值的工作吧,每只母鸡每年能产二百只蛋。我在考虑明年春天建个养鸡场,开始养鸡产蛋。你瞧,我打算永远呆在洛克威洛了呢。像安东尼·特罗洛普的母亲一样,我决定要呆到写完114本小说,这是我一生的工作,完成之后我就可以退休出去旅行了。

詹姆士·麦克白先生上星期天来访。晚餐吃的鸡肉和冰淇淋,他似乎两样都很喜欢。见到他挺高兴的,他让我感觉外面还有个世界存在。可怜的吉米兜售债券并不顺利,他们尽管肯付6%甚至7%的利息,农业银行仍不愿意接受。我想,他可能得回

---

grumble
['grʌmbl]
v. 呻吟,喃喃地说出

scarlet
['skɑːlit]
adj. 鲜红色的

poultry
['pəultri]
n. 家禽

incubator
['inkjubeitə]
n. 孵卵器,细菌培养器,早产儿保育器

broiler
['brɔilə(r)]
n. 烤器(酷暑)

home to Worcester and taking a job in his father's factory. He's too open and confiding and kindhearted ever to make a successful financier. But to be the manager of a flourishing overalls factory is a very desirable position, don't you think? Just now he turns up his nose at overalls, but he'll come to them.

I hope you appreciate the fact that this is a long letter from a person with writer's **cramp**. But I still love you, Daddy dear, and I'm very happy. With beautiful scenery all about, and lots to eat and a comfortable four-post bed and a ream of blank paper and a pint of ink—what more does one want in the world?

Yours, as always,
Judy

PS. The postman arrives with some more news. We are to expect Master Jervie on Friday next to spend a week. That's a very pleasant prospect—only I am afraid my poor book will suffer. Master Jervie is very demanding.

August 27th

Dear Daddy-Long-Legs,

Where are you, I wonder?

I never know what part of the world you are in, but I hope you're not in New York during this awful weather. I hope you're on a mountain peak (but not in Switzerland; somewhere nearer) looking at the snow and thinking about me. Please be thinking about me. I'm quite lonely and I want to be thought about. Oh, Daddy, I wish I knew you! Then when we were unhappy we could cheer each other up.

I don't think I can stand much more of Lock Willow. I'm thinking of moving. Sallie is going to do settlement work in Boston next winter. Don't you think it would be nice for me to go with her, then we could have a studio together? I could write while she settled and we could be together in the evenings. Evenings are very

沃赛斯特，去他爸爸的工厂里谋个职位了。吉米为人直爽，心地善良，并不适合做金融。当个工装制衣厂的经理却是不错，您觉得呢？不过他现在对工装制造还嗤之以鼻，相信他慢慢会变得现实些的。

一个手抽筋的人给您写这么长的信，希望您能喜欢。我是爱您的，亲爱的叔叔，我非常快乐。窗外是美景，吃得很丰盛，还有一张舒服的四脚床、一叠白纸和一瓶墨水——我还有什么可求的呢？

cramp
[kræmp]
n. 抽筋，腹部绞痛；铁箍

您一如既往的

朱蒂

于洛克威洛

七月二十四日

附言：邮差送来了信，杰维少爷下周五到，呆一周。真是让人兴奋不已！不过我的写作日程又得受影响了，杰维少爷可不是个好伺候的人。

亲爱的长腿叔叔：

我在想，您会在哪儿呢？

我从来都不知道您在哪儿，不过希望您别在这炎热的夏天呆在纽约就好，希望您是呆在山上（不是瑞士哦，近一点的吧）看看雪，想想我。请想想我吧，我很孤独，希望有人挂念。噢，叔叔，要是能认识您该多好！不高兴的时候，我们还可以相互打打气。

恐怕我不能继续住在洛克威洛了，真的想换个环境。莎莉明年冬天要去波士顿从事社会工作。您不觉得我跟她一起去挺好吗？我们可以合住一个小屋，她去工作时我可以写作，晚上还可以做伴。这里除了申普夫妇、卡莉还有阿马萨，没有任何人可

long when there's no one but the Semples and Carrie and Amasai to talk to. I know ahead of time that you won't like my studio idea. I can read your secretary's letter now:

Miss Jerusha Abbott.

Dear Madam,
Mr. Smith prefers that you remain at Lock Willow.

Yours truly,
Elmer H. Griggs

I hate your secretary. I am certain that a man named Elmer H. Griggs must be horrid. But truly, Daddy, I think I shall have to go to Boston. I can't stay here. If something doesn't happen soon, I shall throw myself into the **silo** pit out of sheer desperation.

Mercy! but it's hot. All the grass is burnt up and the brooks are dry and the roads are dusty. It hasn't rained for weeks and weeks.

This letter sounds as though I had **hydrophobia**, but I haven't. I just want some family.

Good-bye, my dearest Daddy.
I wish I knew you.

Judy

Lock Willow,
September 19th

Dear Daddy,

Something has happened and I need advice. I need it from you, and from nobody else in the world. Wouldn't it be possible for me to see you? It's so much easier to talk than to write; and I'm afraid your secretary might open the letter.

Judy

以说话，晚上可真难熬啊。不过我早就知道您不会同意的，我都能想出您秘书的信的内容了：

致乔茹莎·阿伯特小姐：
　　亲爱的女士，
　　史密斯先生希望你留在洛克威洛。

您真挚的
埃尔莫·H·格里格斯

　　我讨厌您的秘书！敢说叫埃尔莫·H·格里格斯这个名字的人肯定很可恶！说真的，叔叔，我真的希望能去波士顿。我不想留在这儿了，再这样下去，我可能会抑郁去跳贮窖了。
　　可怜啊！热死啦！好几周没下雨了，草木干枯，小溪干涸，灰尘漫天。
　　看起来我好像得了狂犬病似的，不过没有。我只是希望有点家的感觉。
　　再见，我最亲爱的叔叔。真希望能跟您认识！

朱蒂
八月二十七日

亲爱的叔叔：
　　发生了一些事情，我需要听听您的意见，就需要您的意见。我有可能见您吗？这事儿讲起来比写容易点，主要是担心您的秘书会拆我的信。

朱蒂
于洛克威洛
九月十九日

---

silo
['sailəu]
n. 筒仓，导弹地下仓库

hydrophobia
[,haidrəu'fəubjə]
n. 恐水病，狂犬病

PS. I'm very unhappy.

Lock Willow,
October 3d

Dear Daddy-Long-Legs,

Your note written in your own hand—and a pretty wobbly hand! —came this morning. I am so sorry that you have been ill; I wouldn't have bothered you with my affairs if I had known. Yes, I will tell you the trouble, but it's sort of complicated to write, and very private. Please don't keep this letter, but burn it.

Before I begin—here's a check for one thousand dollars. It seems funny, doesn't it, for me to be sending a check to you? Where do you think I got it?

I've sold my story, Daddy. It's going to be published serially in seven parts, and then in a book! You might think I'd be wild with joy, but I'm not. I'm entirely **apathetic**. Of course I'm glad to begin paying you—I owe you over two thousand more. It's coming in installments. Now don't be **horrid**, please, about taking it, because it makes me happy to return it. I owe you a great deal more than the mere money, and the rest I will continue to pay all my life in gratitude and affection.

And now, Daddy, about the other thing; please give me your most worldly advice, whether you think I'll like it or not.

You know that I've always had a very special feeling toward you; you sort of represented my whole family; but you won't mind, will you, if I tell you that I have a very much more special feeling for another man? You can probably guess without much trouble who he is. I suspect that my letters have been very full of Master Jervie for a very long time.

I wish I could make you understand what he is like and how entirely companionable we are. We think the same about everything—I am afraid I have a tendency to make over my ideas to

附言：我很痛苦。

亲爱的长腿叔叔：

今天上午收到您写的亲笔信，可是感觉笔迹颤抖得很厉害，您病了？我很担心。早知道的话，就不拿我的事情烦您了。是的，我得跟您讲讲我的烦恼，可事情非常隐私，很难起笔。请您看完后不要保存，立即烧掉吧。

在讲之前——先给您附上一张一千元的支票。我寄支票给您，很好笑，是吧？您想我从哪儿来这么多钱呢？

我卖掉我的小说了，叔叔。小说分七部分刊登，然后成书出版！您可能觉得我会欣喜若狂，可是我没有，一点兴奋的感觉也没有。当然，能回报您我很开心——我欠您两千多块呢，慢慢还吧。请您别拒绝，请求您，回报您是我最大的快乐！我欠您的不是仅仅用金钱就能偿还，我会用一生的感激和爱来报答您的。

叔叔，现在说另一件事情。请您给我一个世俗的建议吧，不用考虑我是否接受得了。

您知道我一直对您有种很特殊的感情，因为您代表了我整个家庭。如果我告诉您我对另一位男子有更强烈的、更特殊的情感，您不会介意的，对吧？您应该很容易就能猜出他是谁。这段时间以来，我给您的每封信里都提到了他——杰维少爷。

我是希望能告诉您他是一个什么样的人，我们在一起有多么快乐。我们对所有事情的看法都相同——也可能是我潜意识改变想法去迎合他！不过

apathetic
[ˌæpəˈθetik]
adj. 缺乏感情的，缺乏兴趣的，无动于衷的

horrid
[ˈhɔrid]
adj. 可怕的，极可厌的，毛骨悚然的

match his! But he is almost always right; he ought to be, you know, for he has fourteen years' start of me. In other ways, though, he's just an overgrown boy, and he does need looking after—he hasn't any sense about wearing rubbers when it rains. He and I always think the same things are funny, and that is such a lot; it's dreadful when two people's senses of humor are **antagonistic**. I don't believe there's any bridging that gulf!

And he is—Oh, well! He is just himself, and I miss him, and miss him, and miss him. The whole world seems empty and aching. I hate the moonlight because it's beautiful and he isn't here to see it with me. But maybe you've loved somebody, too, and you know? If you have, I don't need to explain; if you haven't, I can't explain.

Anyway, that's the way I feel—and I've refused to marry him.

I didn't tell him why; I was just dumb and miserable. I couldn't think of anything to say. And now he has gone away imagining that I want to marry Jimmie McBride—I don't in the least, I wouldn't think of marrying Jimmie; he isn't grown up enough. But Master Jervie and I got into a dreadful muddle of misunderstanding, and we both hurt each other's feelings. The reason I sent him away was not because I didn't care for him, but because I cared for him so much. I was afraid he would regret it in the future—and I couldn't stand that! It didn't seem right for a person of my lack of **antecedents** to marry into any such family as his. I never told him about the orphan asylum, and I hated to explain that I didn't know who I was. I may be dreadful, you know. And his family are proud—and I'm proud too!

Also, I felt sort of bound to you. After having been educated to be a writer, I must at least try to be one; it would scarcely be fair to accept your education and then go off and not use it. But now that I am going to be able to pay back the money, I feel that I have partially discharged that debt—besides, I suppose I could keep on

他几乎都是对的,这不奇怪,因为他比我长十四岁。虽然年龄比我大,可在生活方面简直像个大小孩,什么事都需要人提醒。譬如,连下雨天要穿雨鞋都不知道。不过我们常常为一件事情笑得乐翻天,而且很多事情都这样。两个人要是价值观不相似,幽默感不同,那是挺可怕的,而且我相信价值观上的冲突是很难沟通的!

antagonistic
[æn,tægəˈnistik]
adj. 对抗性的

就是他——唉!可他就是他!我想他,想他,想他,非常想念他!非常孤独、心痛!我恨自己不能和他一起欣赏如此美好的月色!您要是爱过某人,您就会明白我的感觉的。如果您爱过,那我无需解释;您要是没有,那我也无法解释。

不管怎样,这是我的感觉——可是,我却拒绝了他。

我没有告诉他原因,只是沉默,暗自伤心。其实我也不知道该说什么。他以为我要嫁给吉米·麦克白,于是独自离开了。我没想啊,我从来都没想过要嫁给吉米,他还小啊。杰维少爷跟我有很严重的误会,伤害了彼此的感情。我赶他走不是因为我不在乎他,是因为我太在乎了。我怕他将来后悔——我会受不了的!像我这样没有来历的人嫁入他那样的家庭太不合适了!我从没跟他讲过约翰·格里尔孤儿院的事,也讨厌讲连我自己都不知道我是谁。我可能很可怕的,您知道的。他的家庭是那么高贵——我也是有自尊的!

antecedent
[,ænti'si:dənt]
n. 前情,先行词

还有,我对您有责任的。您送我上大学接受教育,想把我培养成作家,所以我必须要努力奋斗。接受了教育而不继续努力,对您太不公平了。从另一方面讲,我开始回报您了,已经偿还了一部

255

being a writer even if I did marry. The two professions are not necessarily exclusive.

I've been thinking very hard about it. Of course he is a socialist, and he has unconventional ideas; maybe he wouldn't mind marrying into the proletariat so much as some men might. Perhaps when two people are exactly in accord, and always happy when together and lonely when apart, they ought not to let anything in the world stand between them. Of course I want to believe that! But I'd like to get your **unemotional** opinion. You probably belong to a Family also, and will look at it from a worldly point of view and not just a sympathetic, human point of view—so you see how brave I am to lay it before you.

Suppose I go to him and explain that the trouble isn't Jimmie, but is the John Grier Home—would that be a dreadful thing for me to do? It would take a great deal of courage. I'd almost rather be miserable for the rest of my life.

This happened nearly two months ago; I haven't heard a word from him since he was here. I was just getting sort of acclimated to the feeling of a broken heart, when a letter came from Julia that stirred me all up again. She said—very casually—that "Uncle Jervis" had been caught out all night in a storm when he was hunting in Canada, and had been ill ever since with pneumonia. And I never knew it. I was feeling hurt because he had just disappeared into blankness without a word. I think he's pretty unhappy, and I know I am!

What seems to you the right thing for me to do?

Judy

October 6th

Dearest Daddy-Long-Legs,

Yes, certainly I'll come—at half-past four next Wednesday afternoon. Of course I can find the way. I've been in New York three

分——而且即使结了婚也同样可以成为作家,两件事情并没有多大的冲突。

　　我也想了很久。当然,他是个社会主义者,想法不俗。他也可能跟别的一些男子一样不在乎娶个无产者。也许只要两个人心有灵犀,在一起的时候都很开心,不在一起都很寂寞,这样的两个人之间不应该有障碍的。当然,我也想相信!可是我想听听您的客观建议。您可能也是出身豪门,能用世俗的眼光来看这件事情,而不仅仅是同情。唉,您瞧瞧在您面前我是多么勇敢!

　　我是否应该去找他,然后告诉他问题不在于吉米而是在约翰·格里尔孤儿院,这对我来说不是挺糟糕的事情吗?这需要多大的勇气啊!我宁愿孤老一生!

　　这件事发生快两个月了,他走后音信全无。朱莉娅的来信让我的心几乎支离破碎。她无意中提到杰维少爷在加拿大打猎被暴风雪整整困了一夜,最后患了肺炎,现在还卧床不起。我却一点都不知道,我还怨他走了就没音儿了呢。我想他一定很痛苦,至少我知道我非常非常不开心!

　　叔叔,您说我该怎么办才好呢?

朱蒂
于洛克威洛
十月三日

最亲爱的长腿叔叔:

　　我一定去——下周三下午四点半。我已经去过纽约三次了,不再是个小孩了,我当然能找到地

---

unemotional
['ʌnɪ'məʊʃɪnl]
adj. 不诉诸感情的,非感情的

times and am not quite a baby. I can't believe that I am really going to see you—I've been just thinking you so long that it hardly seems as though you are a tangible flesh-and-blood person.

You are awfully good, Daddy, to bother yourself with me, when you're not strong. Take care and don't catch cold. These fall rains are very damp.

Affectionately,
Judy

PS. I've just had an awful thought. Have you a butler? I'm afraid of butlers, and if one opens the door I shall faint upon the step. What can I say to him? You didn't tell me your name. Shall I ask for Mr. Smith?

Thursday morning

My very dearest Master-Jervie-Daddy-Long-Legs-Pendleton-Smith,

Did you sleep last night? I didn't. Not a single **wink**. I was too amazed and excited and bewildered and happy. I don't believe I ever shall sleep again—or eat either. But I hope you slept; you must, you know, because then you will get well faster and can come to me.

Dear man, I can't bear to think how ill you've been—and all the time I never knew it. When the doctor came down yesterday to put me in the cab, he told me that for three days they gave you up. Oh, dearest, if that had happened, the light would have gone out of the world for me. I suppose that some day—in the far future—one of us must leave the other; but at least we shall have had our happiness and there will be memories to live with.

I meant to cheer you up—and instead I have to cheer myself. For in spite of being happier than I ever dreamed I could be, I'm also **soberer**. The fear that something may happen to you rests like a

方。简直不敢相信真的要去见您了——这么多年以来,我一直想着世界上有个您,可如今,我似乎很难想象您是个有血有肉的真人。

您真是太好了,叔叔,身体不好还为我操心。请多保重,秋天容易着凉。

深情的
朱蒂
十月六日

附言:我突然害怕起来。您的秘书在吗?我很怕您的秘书,如果他开门的话,我可能会晕倒在门口。我该对他说些什么呢?您也不曾告诉我您的名字。我该请求见史密斯先生吗?

我最最亲爱的杰维少爷——长腿叔叔——彭莱顿·史密斯:

昨晚你睡了吗?我一夜没睡。我简直太激动,太兴奋,太糊涂,太高兴了!我想我再也睡不好吃不香了!不过我希望你睡,你必须睡,这样你才能很快好起来,才能很快回到我的身边。

亲爱的,一想到你病得如此严重,我的心就痛,我怎么会就一点都不知道呢?!昨天医生送我下楼上车时,告诉我说这三天以来他们几乎都放弃了。噢!我最亲爱的,要果真如此,我活着就简直也没有希望了。假如有一天——遥远的未来的某一天——其中有一人不得不先离开了,至少我们曾经幸福地在一起过了,还有许多值得回忆。

我希望你能振作起来,不过我得让我自己先打起精神起来。虽然我做梦都没现在这么开心过,可是我还是清醒的,总担心你会有事,这个念头像愁

---

wink
[wiŋk]
n. 眨眼,使眼色

soberer
['səubə]
adj. 清醒的,稳重的

shadow on my heart. Always before I could be frivolous and carefree and unconcerned, because I had nothing precious to lose. But now—I shall have a Great Big Worry all the rest of my life. Whenever you are away from me I shall be thinking of all the automobiles that can run over you, or the signboards that can fall on your head, or the dreadful, squirmy germs that you may be swallowing. My peace of mind is gone forever—but anyway, I never cared much for just plain peace.

Please get well—fast—fast—fast. I want to have you close by where I can touch you and make sure you are tangible. Such a little half hour we had together! I'm afraid maybe I dreamed it. If I were only a member of your family (a very distant fourth cousin) then I could come and visit you every day, and read aloud and plump up your pillow and smooth out those two little wrinkles in your forehead and make the corners of your mouth turn up in a nice cheerful smile. But you are cheerful again, aren't you? You were yesterday before I left. The doctor said I must be a good nurse, that you looked ten years younger. I hope that being in love doesn't make everyone ten years younger. Will you still care for me, darling, if I trun out to be only eleven?

Yesterday was the most wonderful day that could ever happen. If I live to be ninety-nine I shall never forget the tiniest detail. The girl that left Lock Willow at dawn was a very different person from the one who came back at night. Mrs. Semple called me at half-past four. I started wide awake in the darkness and the first thought that popped into my head was "I am going to see Daddy-Long-Legs!" I ate breakfast in the kitchen by candlelight, and then drove the five miles to the station through the most glorious October coloring. The sun came up on the way, and the swamp maples and dogwood glowed crimson and orange and the stone walls and cornfields sparkled with hoarfrost; the air was keen and clear and full of promise. I knew something was going to happen. All the way in the

frivolous
['frivələs]
adj. 轻佻的，妄动的，琐碎的

tangible
['tændʒəbl]
adj. 可触知的；明确的

plump
[plʌmp]
v. 突然放下

swamp
[swɔmp]
n. 沼泽，湿地

dogwood
['dɔgwud]
n. 山茱萸

hoarfrost
['hɔː'frɔst]
n. 霜，白霜

云惨雾般笼罩在我心上。以前我了无牵挂，对什么都不在乎，不曾拥有过什么所以也不害怕失去。可现在，以后的日子恐怕都得在担心在乎中度过了。只要你一离开，我就会担心你可能被汽车撞到，可能被招牌砸到，或者又感染了什么可怕的细菌。我的心恐怕很难安定了，本来我也不喜欢平淡的安宁。

请快好起来吧，快点，快点，再快点！我要你在我身边，可以触摸到你，确信你是真实的你。我们才相聚短短半小时啊！我深怕是在做梦。我要是你家族一员该多好啊（一个遥远的第四代表亲），我就可以每天去看你，念书给你听，帮你理好靠枕，抚平你额头上的皱纹，让你的嘴角露出笑容。你现在感觉好些了吗？昨天我走的时候你还挺好的，医生说我是个好护士，你看起来一下子年轻了十岁呢。恋爱可不要让所有人都年轻十岁。亲爱的，如果我只有十一岁，你还喜欢我吗？

昨天是我一生中最美好的一天！即使我活到九十九岁，我也永远忘不了那一幕。早上离开洛克威洛时的那个女孩儿跟晚上回来的简直判若两人。申普太太四点半就叫我起床，我在黑暗中醒来，闪入脑海的第一个念头就是："我就要见长腿叔叔啦！"借着厨房的烛光吃过早餐，穿越十月的美景，坐着马车走了五里路终于到了火车站。一路上伴着太阳慢慢升起，枫树和山茱萸红遍山野，石墙上和玉米地里结了一层霜，碧空如洗，一切生机盎然，充满了希望。我总感觉有什么事会发生。一路上，连火

train the rails kept singing "You're going to see Daddy-Long-Legs."
It made me feel secure. I had such faith in Daddy's ability to set
things right. And I knew that somewhere another man—dearer than
Daddy—was wanting to see me, and somehow I had a feeling that
before the journey ended I should meet him too. And you see!

When I came to the house on Madison Avenue it looked so big
and brown and forbidding that I didn't dare go in, so I walked
around the block to get up my courage. But I needn't have been a
bit afraid; your butler is such a nice, fatherly old man that he made
me feel at home at once. "Is this Miss Abbott?" he said to me,
and I said, "Yes," so I didn't have to ask for Mr. Smith after all.
He told me to wait in the drawing room. It was a very somber,
magnificent, man's sort of room. I sat down on the edge of a big
upholstered chair and kept saying to myself: "I'm going to see
Daddy-Long-Legs! I'm going to see Daddy-Long-Legs!"

Then presently the man came back and asked me please to step
up to the library. I was so excited that really and truly my feet would
hardly take me up. Outside the door he turned and whispered,
"He's been very ill, miss. This is the first day he's been allowed to
sit up. You'll not stay long enough to excite him?" I knew from the
way he said it that he loved you—and I think he's an old dear!

Then he knocked and said, "Miss Abbott," and I went in and
the door closed behind me.

It was so dim coming in from the brightly lighted hall that for a
moment I could scarcely make out anything; then I saw a big easy
chair before the fire and a shining tea table with a smaller chair
beside it. And I realized that a man was sitting in the big chair
propped up by pillows with a rug over his knees. Before I could stop
him he rose—sort of shakily—and steadied himself by the back of
the chair and just looked at me without a word. And then—and
then—I saw it was you! But even with that I didn't understand. I
thought Daddy had had you come there to meet me for a surprise.

车轮子都不断地唱着:"你就要见到长腿叔叔啦!你就要见到长腿叔叔啦!"心里感觉特别温暖。我对叔叔的为人处事很有信心,我也知道,在某个地方还有一位男子——比长腿叔叔更亲爱的——正等着要见我,我预感不用等到下火车就能见到他!结果,你看!

到了麦迪逊大街的寓所,高大雄伟的棕色房子让人望而生畏,都不敢随便进去,我在外面徘徊了很久才鼓足勇气。其实我根本不用怕,您的秘书是个挺好挺和蔼的人,他让我觉得挺自在的。"是阿伯特小姐吗?"他问我。我回答说:"是的。"我根本没提史密斯先生。于是他叫我在客厅等候。这是一间庄严而华丽的男人住的屋子。我坐在一张舒服的大软椅上,心里不断叨念着:"我就要见到长腿叔叔啦!我就要见到长腿叔叔啦!"

不一会儿,秘书请我到书房去。我简直激动得路都快不会走了。走到书房门口,他回头低声对我说:"小姐,他病得很严重。医生今天才同意他下床。请别呆太长时间,让他太激动。"从你秘书说话的样子就知道他很爱你,所以我对他也产生了好感。

他敲门说道:"阿伯特小姐来了。"于是我走了进去,随手关上了门。

从亮堂堂的走廊走进黑乎乎的书房,瞬间,我的眼睛模糊了。渐渐地,我看见壁炉前有一张大安乐椅,还有一张锃亮的茶桌和一把椅子。我看到有个人坐在大椅子上,靠着靠枕,膝上还搭着一条毯子。我还没来得及阻止,他就已经站了起来——有点颤抖——靠着椅子站稳了,然后一直看着我,什么话也没说。然后……然后……我看到的居然是你!不过我还是晕乎乎的,完全没明白怎么回事儿!我以为是长腿叔叔让你来见我的,给我个惊喜。

prop up
支撑,支持

Then you laughed and held out your hand and said, "Dear little Judy, couldn't you guess that I was Daddy-Long-Legs?"

In an instant it flashed over me. Oh, but I have been stupid! A hundred little things might have told me, if I had had any wits. I wouldn't make a very good detective, would I, Daddy? —Jervie? What must I call you? Just plain Jervie sounds **disrespectful** and I can't be disrespectful to you!

It was a very sweet half hour before your doctor came and sent me away. I was so dazed when I got to the station that I almost took a train for St. Louis. And you were pretty dazed too. You forgot to give me any tea. But we're both very, very happy, aren't we? I drove back to Lock Willow in the dark—but, oh, how the stars were shining! And this morning I've been out with Colin visiting all the places that you and I went to together, and remembering what you said and how you looked. The woods today are burnished bronze and the air is full of frost. It's climbing weather. I wish you were here to climb the hills with me. I am missing you dreadfully, Jervie dear, but it's a happy kind of missing; we'll be together soon. We belong to each other now really and truly, no make-believe. Doesn't it seem queer for me to belong to someone at last? It seems very, very sweet.

And I shall never let you be sorry for a single instant.

                                        Yours, forever and ever,
                                                Judy

PS. This is the first love letter I ever wrote. Isn't it funny that I know how?

车轮子都不断地唱着:"你就要见到长腿叔叔啦!你就要见到长腿叔叔啦!"心里感觉特别温暖。我对叔叔的为人处事很有信心,我也知道,在某个地方还有一位男子——比长腿叔叔更亲爱的——正等着要见我,我预感不用等到下火车就能见到他!结果,你看!

到了麦迪逊大街的寓所,高大雄伟的棕色房子让人望而生畏,都不敢随便进去,我在外面徘徊了很久才鼓足勇气。其实我根本不用怕,您的秘书是个挺好挺和蔼的人,他让我觉得挺自在的。"是阿伯特小姐吗?"他问我。我回答说:"是的。"我根本没提史密斯先生。于是他叫我在客厅等候。这是一间庄严而华丽的男人住的屋子。我坐在一张舒服的大软椅上,心里不断叨念着:"我就要见到长腿叔叔啦!我就要见到长腿叔叔啦!"

不一会儿,秘书请我到书房去。我简直激动得路都快不会走了。走到书房门口,他回头低声对我说:"小姐,他病得很严重。医生今天才同意他下床。请别呆太长时间,让他太激动。"从你秘书说话的样子就知道他很爱你,所以我对他也产生了好感。

他敲门说道:"阿伯特小姐来了。"于是我走了进去,随手关上了门。

从亮堂堂的走廊走进黑乎乎的书房,瞬间,我的眼睛模糊了。渐渐地,我看见壁炉前有一张大安乐椅,还有一张锃亮的茶桌和一把椅子。我看到有个人坐在大椅子上,靠着靠枕,膝上还搭着一条毯子。我还没来得及阻止,他就已经站了起来——有点颤抖——靠着椅子站稳了,然后一直看着我,什么话也没说。然后……然后……我看到的居然是你!不过我还是晕乎乎的,完全没明白怎么回事儿!我以为是长腿叔叔让你来见我的,给我个惊喜。

prop up
支撑,支持

Then you laughed and held out your hand and said, "Dear little Judy, couldn't you guess that I was Daddy-Long-Legs?"

In an instant it flashed over me. Oh, but I have been stupid! A hundred little things might have told me, if I had had any wits. I wouldn't make a very good detective, would I, Daddy? —Jervie? What must I call you? Just plain Jervie sounds **disrespectful** and I can't be disrespectful to you!

It was a very sweet half hour before your doctor came and sent me away. I was so dazed when I got to the station that I almost took a train for St. Louis. And you were pretty dazed too. You forgot to give me any tea. But we're both very, very happy, aren't we? I drove back to Lock Willow in the dark—but, oh, how the stars were shining! And this morning I've been out with Colin visiting all the places that you and I went to together, and remembering what you said and how you looked. The woods today are burnished bronze and the air is full of frost. It's climbing weather. I wish you were here to climb the hills with me. I am missing you dreadfully, Jervie dear, but it's a happy kind of missing; we'll be together soon. We belong to each other now really and truly, no make-believe. Doesn't it seem queer for me to belong to someone at last? It seems very, very sweet.

And I shall never let you be sorry for a single instant.

                              Yours, forever and ever,
                                         Judy

PS. This is the first love letter I ever wrote. Isn't it funny that I know how?

可你笑着伸出手,说道:"亲爱的小朱蒂,你没猜到我就是长腿叔叔吧?"

一个念头闪过脑海。噢!我简直笨死了!我要是聪明的话,有一百件小事都可能说明这一点。我要是做警探肯定做不好,是吧?叔叔——杰维?我该怎么称呼你呢?叫你杰维显得不够尊敬吧,我应该对您表示敬意的。

disrespectful
[ˌdisrisˈpektful]
adj. 失礼的,无礼的

那半小时太甜蜜了,可是医生进来把我赶走了。我恍恍惚惚到了车站,差点错赶了去往圣路易斯的火车。你也激动得连茶都忘了请我喝。我们都太太太开心了,不是吗?我坐着车一路趁着月光伴着星星回到了洛克威洛——哇!星光闪耀!今天早上,我带着柯林斯走遍我们一起去过的所有地方,回忆起当时的情景,想起你说的话。今天树林里一片青铜色,空气清新,真适合登山!真希望你能陪我爬山啊!我太想你了,亲爱的杰维。思念也是快乐的、兴奋的、激动的。我们会很快就在一起了!我们的心已相属,真真切切、完完全全!我终于有了归属感,挺奇怪的吧?但是这种感觉的确很甜蜜很甜蜜很甜蜜。

我绝不会让你有片刻伤心了!

你曾经的永远的
朱蒂
星期四早晨

附言:这是我第一次写情书,不知道是不是很搞笑?